Ⓢ
φ

Ext
1st. Op.
VG (mild reader soil
on cafe au lait
cover - not nr -

399
461825973.
25-1

The Political Economy of East - West Trade

Connie M. Friesen

The Praeger Special Studies program—utilizing the most modern and efficient book production techniques and a selective worldwide distribution network—makes available to the academic, government, and business communities significant, timely research in U.S. and international economic, social, and political development.

The Political Economy of East - West Trade

PRAEGER SPECIAL STUDIES IN INTERNATIONAL BUSINESS, FINANCE, AND TRADE

Praeger Publishers   New York   Washington   London

Library of Congress Cataloging in Publication Data

Friesen, Connie M
   The political economy of East-West trade.

   (Praeger special studies in international business,
finance, and trade)
   Bibliography: p.
   Includes index.
   1. East-West trade (1945-   ) 2. United States—
Commerce—Russia.   3. Russia—Commerce—United States.
I. Title.
HF499.F74   382'.09171'301717   76-14395
ISBN 0-275-56920-9

PRAEGER PUBLISHERS
111 Fourth Avenue, New York, N.Y. 10003, U.S.A.

Published in the United States of America in 1976
by Praeger Publishers, Inc.

Printed in the United States of America

It is a pleasure to acknowledge the many people who have helped in the completion of this book. The Carnegie Endowment for International Peace made possible extensive interviewing in Western and Eastern Europe during the summers of 1974 and 1975, and provided the major support for the entire project. Grants from the American Council of Learned Societies, the Center for International Affairs at Harvard, and the University of Massachusetts, Amherst, also supported the research.

I was fortunate in having stimulating colleagues at the University of Massachusetts, especially Ferenc Vali and Peter Fliess, who provided much encouragement. Professor Joseph Nye of the Center for International Affairs at Harvard provided many helpful suggestions. Foreign trade officials in Romania and Hungary were willing to talk at length about many of the complexities of their banking and trade systems. Representatives of banks and corporations far too numerous to mention in both Western Europe and the United States listened to my questions and gave generously of their time. The librarians at the Royal Institute of International Affairs in London were efficient and helpful. Steven Fraser of Praeger has been a most patient and competent editor.

My parents, Raymond and Alice Farden, have been a marvelous inspiration and source of encouragement. The greatest debt is to my wonderful husband George who has shared many discussions and has endured both me and the book throughout the long process of research and writing.

Of course, any errors that remain are solely my responsibility.

CONTENTS

The Political Economy of East - West Trade

CHAPTER 1

DETENTE

It is one of the ironies of conceptualizing about foreign affairs that less than a year after Senator Edward Kennedy speculated in *Foreign Policy* about the shape of Soviet-U.S. policies in the "era beyond detente," Michael Kaser was explaining the shift of Soviet trade attention from the United States to Europe. This new attention to Western Europe presumably meant a reversal of earlier lofty hopes for Soviet-U.S. relations.[1] In fact, initial American hopes for detente were not realistic, and present disillusionment in the United States should lead to a more honest and productive restructuring of Soviet-U.S. relations. One major problem is that Americans have paid too little attention to Soviet conceptions of detente, ideas which have consistently been more modest than those of Americans.

As a broad statement of U.S. foreign policy objectives vis-a-vis the USSR, detente remains a viable alternative to the tense crisis decision-making patterns of the Cold War as well as to the structured but visionary Kantian world of international peace. It is a policy modest in goals and means, and it is both attainable and desirable. It is not, however, the first step on the road to convergence of Soviet and U.S. societies. It does not even imply a comprehensive program of joint Soviet-U.S. efforts, a caution that was nicely expressed a year ago by Senator Frank Church:

> In classical usage "detente" refers to a lowering of tension, an abatement of hostility; it does not mean amity or partnership, or even reconciliation. In long-term perspective, a detente may carry promise, or at least the hope of future friendship, but in the present fact, it

1

represents no more than the imposition of restraint on an otherwise
costly and dangerous policy.[2]

Similarly, the setbacks to Soviet-U.S. trade relations and disappointment over
the apparent failure to achieve cooperation from the Soviets in the Middle
East should not be equated with the failure of detente.

The outlines of new, more modest hopes for detente were developed in a
series of hearings conducted by the Senate Committee on Foreign Relations in
1974. Conceptions of detente suggested at the hearings ranged from the "limited
adversary relationship" envisioned by Marshall Shulman to the "search for a
more constructive relationship with the Soviet Union" advocated by Secretary
of State Henry Kissinger.[3] From these more limited U.S. perspectives, detente
implies the development of a communications network in which both the
Soviet Union and the United States will be able to perceive and act upon the
intentions of the other side more accurately. Still, it should be noted that the
standard American usage of "detente" implies a relationship of competition,
restraints, and cooperation, with the cooperative elements of the relationship
emphasized to the disadvantage of those of competition. Moreover, the relationship is assumed to be one of relative equality in participation and rewards
between the United States and the USSR.

The Soviet view is not so sanguine. Especially since the Politburo's January
1975 rejection of the terms of the Trade Act, the Soviet view of detente has
routinely been more pessimistic about the framework of relations with the
United States and more optimistic about the triumphant outcome of Soviet
foreign policy. In counterpoint to the U.S. version, the burden of detente is
placed on Soviet policy makers, and the United States is seen as a less than equal
colleague in pursuit of detente. The Soviets nearly always equate detente with
"peaceful coexistence," a term they interpret to mean a form of continuing
struggle between different social systems without resort to war. Like the U.S.
view of detente, the "peaceful coexistence" version stresses competition, restraint,
and cooperation, but the Soviet emphasis is clearly on competition.

Current Soviet work on detente argues that the imminent victory of socialism and collapse of capitalism make detente possible. According to one recent
statement in *International Affairs* (Moscow), "if one were to identify the most
important factor that has gone to determine the possibility for the switch . . . to
detente . . . it would be above all the objective factor of the general change in
the relationship of forces in the world arena in favor of the forces of peace and
progress."[4] Another statement emphasized that detente represented the "forced
adaptation" of capitalism to the "changing balance of strength in the world."[5]
In an article in *New Times* (Moscow), Dmitri Kostyukhin provided an especially
gloomy and complete enumeration of the tribulations of capitalism: slowdown
in growth rates, decline in industrial production, growing unemployment, social
tensions, and inflation.[6]

Other Soviet commentators have contended (in contrast to what most American analysts have said) that detente is not merely an accommodation between the Soviet Union and the United States. Rather it is said to represent the normalization of relations among all states stemming from the principles of coexistence.[7] Many recent Soviet journal articles have suggested that detente will occur first in Soviet and East European relations with Western Europe and only subsequently and secondarily in relations with the United States. This is in line with the Soviet view that capitalism everywhere is finally on the last approach to its long-awaited demise and that it is to be extinguished first in Western Europe. It is also correlated with the Soviet view that unsuccessful capitalist attempts to overthrow socialism in Cuba, Korea, and Vietnam prove the growing ascendancy of socialism.[8] In the Soviet view, the "correlation of forces" favors the Eastern bloc of socialist nations, and detente is simply a theoretical nicety that explains the growing Communist worldwide supremacy.

American generalizations about the policy of detente have blurred some important distinctions the Soviets make between different aspects of detente: its military, ideological, economic, and political components. Americans refer to the components, but too frequently confuse them with the whole of detente. Militarily, U.S. hopes for detente are usually equated with progress in the SALT talks and the hope that the United States and the Soviet Union acting together can prevent needless proliferation of the acquisition of nuclear arms by currently non-nuclear smaller powers. Ideologically, the United States likes to associate detente with a growing mutual understanding and rapproachement of the needs and aspirations of Soviet and U.S. societies. Politically, hopes for detente are often accompanied by a belief that the United States and the USSR can jointly achieve lasting peace settlements in the Middle East and other areas. Americans naively hoped that political detente would mean that the USSR would help the United States to extricate itself from Vietnam and that the Soviet Union would involve itself in a lasting Egyptian-Israeli peace settlement. Economically, detente is frequently associated with higher levels of mutually advantageous trade between the United States and the Soviet Union. Once any of these components acquires a lifelike stance, we tend to impute its contribution to "detente."

Senator J. William Fulbright's equation of military detente with the whole of detente ("the heart and core of the policy of detente—and the central purpose of our current policy—is the lessening of the danger of nuclear war") is representative of the confusion that often exists between the whole and its parts and of the tendency to interlock all aspects of detente into a rigid whole. Unfortunately, it is seldom recognized that from the Soviet point of view each of the four variations on the theme of detente can be orchestrated singly as well as jointly. Ideologist G. Arbatov, for example, has often stressed the necessity of an unending war of ideas to accompany ever higher levels of Soviet-U.S. trade. United States policy makers are just now coming to an official recognition of the fact that the separate aspects of detente do not necessarily constitute an inseparable whole. The ideological, military, economic, and political components of detente cannot be forced to work together and may never occur simultaneously. This does not mean that the components have no effect on one another. It simply means that the Soviets are willing to entertain some advances in cooperation only as distant by-products of their immediate goals for economic or military cooperation.

Americans would do well to recognize the merits of limited goals and of separate pursuit of the various components of detente. Secretary of State Kissinger has already provided some reasonable guidelines. He suggests a network of relationships that will involve the USSR in a continuing process of interaction through various channels with the United States. As he puts it, "By acquiring a stake in this network of relationships with the West, the Soviet Union may become more conscious of what it would lose by a return to confrontation."[9]

In other words, detente could be viewed as a policy adapted to the newly emerging interdependence of Soviet, U.S., and West European political and economic systems. Detente could become a means to facilitate the smooth entry of the Soviet Union into a new global structure of mutually profitable, businesslike transactions. If we define detente as the policy appropriate to interdependence, we must explore the characteristics of interdependence and the suitability of a policy of detente for them.

INTERDEPENDENCE

Interdependence, like detente, is a term with a multiplicity of would-be definitions. Kenneth Waltz has suggested that interdependence entails a relationship between states that would be difficult to break.[10] Oran Young suggests that it can refer to "the extent to which events occurring in any given part or within any given component unit of a world system affect . . . events taking place in each of the other parts or component units of the system."[11] Stanley Hoffmann, in criticizing Young's definition, points to a weakness of both conceptions: They fail to do more than delineate the outer parameters of an international system inside which events in component parts affect one another. Hoffmann also wisely points to another common weakness of these and other definitions of interdependence. Young, Waltz, and others fail to distinguish between mixed-sum interactions of interdependent international players and zero-sum interactions. Hoffmann contends that the zero-sum interactions typify the system-delineated "state of war" among nations and suggests that only the mixed-sum strategies need be equated with interdependence: "What you do affects me beneficially or adversely, but I can neither fully exploit my advantage against you, nor fully react in order to erase my disadvantage and/or inflict one on you in turn, without hurting both you and me in the process."[12] For this reason, Hoffmann sees both competition and solidarity in the process. This analysis will suggest that at a very basic level, interdependence can be viewed as a relationship among states that involves the capability of influencing policies and policy agendas across state boundaries, and the impossibility of extricating oneself from the effects of policies so influenced.

Many scholars have suggested the importance of distinguishing between political and economic interdependence, as well as between interdependence at the process level and interdependence at the structural level. It is clear that these distinctions are important in describing the interdependence of East-West trade. Economic interdependence entails a cross-boundary involvement in the production, sale, or use of goods or money. Political interdependence refers to actors' ability to arrange the structures and processes involving transfer of goods and services or welfare and security goals across boundaries.[13]

Interdependence in the arena of East-West trade can be understood only if it incorporates both economic and political aspects. As Robert Keohane and Joseph Nye suggest, East-West trade is a highly politicized area of economic activity because its pursuit so frequently involves political challenges at the structural as well as process levels in the conduct of trading relationships.[14] Others have reached similar conclusions about the need for fusing the economic and political aspects of policy. Richard Cooper has contended that the post-World War II habit of distinguishing between the low foreign policy of trade issues and the high foreign policy of security issues needs to be abandoned in favor of the tradition which acknowledges that trade issues frequently intrude into and even dominate high foreign policy disputes among states.[15] Senator Walter Mondale recently expressed a similar sentiment:

> While the major international security issues of the last quarter-century are still with us ... these are now being over-shadowed by the risk that the international economy may spin out of control. For if this happens, there will be no graver threat to international stability ... and to national security itself.[16]

It is surprising that while the intertwining of politics and economics at the "global level" has often been recongized, this recognition has not been extended to the issue area of East-West trade. Many have agreed with Cooper that international economic issues have political facets as well, but few have extended this recognition to East-West trade. Franklyn Holzman and Robert Legvold, in "The Economics and Politics of East-West Relations," are a significant exception. They acknowledge the potential intrusion of economic issues into the realm of security issues at three levels: at the level of the nation, because economic policy can be used to avoid security risks; at the level of alliances, because economic assistance can be used to enhance security; and in dealing with an enemy nation, because economic policies may dictate that he be denied goods potentially necessary for his military strength.[17] Other significant exceptions are C. Fred

Bergsten and John Mathieson, who argue that East-West trade is the most politicized area of international economic relations.[18]

Even more surprising than the failure of scholars to understand the security aspects of East-West trade policy is their failure to acknowledge East-West trade relations as a part of the otherwise widely acclaimed "global interdependence." A few examples should suffice: Hollis Chenery, noting that "the world is currently in a state of disequilibrium of a magnitude not seen since the aftermath of World War II," suggests that relations between three groups of countries will be the determining influences in restructuring the world economy: the members of the Organization for Economic Cooperation and Development (OECD), the oil-producing countries, and the developing countries. He concludes with the caveat that "only passing attention is given to the fourth major group—the Socialist countries—which has a limited impact on the problems considered here."[19] Mondale has argued that for the present the Soviet Union remains relatively insulated from the economic tides sweeping the rest of the world.[20] Cooper contends that issues of economic interdependence (which he defines as the "sensitivity of economic transactions between two or more nations to economic developments within those nations") are increasingly problematic in relations among advanced non-Communist countries.[21] Bergsten and Mathieson are much closer to the truth when they assert that "the Communist countries are just now beginning to enter the world economy and their inclusion raises a whole set of new issues."[22] In fact, it is on the basis of a recognition of the emerging interdependence of Soviet, East European, West European, and American economic and political structures that we can begin to fashion a more realistic policy of detente.

Some superficial indicators seem to support those who are skeptical about East-West interdependence. The most obvious measures of economic interdependence between East and West are trade figures. These suggest that interdependence is still at a very low level. Josef Wilczynski notes that East-West trade as a percentage of world trade fell from 6.4 percent in 1938 to 2.6 percent in 1948 to 1.3 percent in 1953.[23] In the years between 1970 and 1975, it has averaged about 3 percent of world trade. Trade between the United States and the USSR represented about 1 to 2 percent of world trade in the 1970 to 1975 period. There is even some evidence suggesting that the direction of Soviet foreign trade is changing very slightly in favor of East European countries. In 1974, Council for Mutual Economic Assistance (COMECON) members accounted for 54 percent of the USSR's foreign trade turnover, whereas in 1970 the share of COMECON members (including Cuba and Mongolia) was 50 percent.[24]

Trade figures, however, are only one indicator of the new interdependence that is slowly emerging between East and West. Far more important are the structural contacts, technological exchanges, and overall "influence factors" involved in that trade. There is a whole new series of actors on the playing field of East-West interdependence. In East-West relations as well as in the whole of international politics, we can see the emergence of what Seyom Brown calls the global "polyarchy" in which national states, subnational groups, and transnational special interests and communities are active. [25]

East-West interdependence is characterized by new institutional arrangements as well as by new issues. First, there is a new pluralism of actors. Stephen Rosenfeld refers to competing domestic forces which mean that foreign policy derives less and less from a "professed and coherent world view."[26] While this pluralism of actors in the West has long been recognized by students of U.S. and West European foreign policy, it has been formally acknowledged and studied only recently in the cases of Soviet and East European politics. H. Gordon Skilling speaks of five categories of groups capable of articulating their interests in the Soviet context: leadership groups, bureaucratic groups, intellectual groups, broad social groups, and opinion groups.[27]

In his discussion of economic interdependence, Hoffmann notes that the growing multiplicity of issues inevitably leads to a diversification of "chessboards," which in turn forces a distinction between the "formal" powers of government and the "substantive" powers of private actors that can challenge the formal powers.[28] These subunits determining foreign policy can be either divisions of government carrying out their own fairly distinct foreign policies or private actors like multinational corporations. Even in the somewhat circumscribed arena of East-West trade, it is clear that multinational corporations can pursue any or all of the three roles outlined by Nye: the "direct role" of formulating private foreign policy, the "unintended direct role" of serving as instruments of influence, or the "indirect role" of setting foreign policy agendas.[29]

New issues have accompanied the broader spectrum of actors. Interdependence means that pursuit of national economic objectives has become sensitized to international disturbances which disrupt a nation's balance of payments or otherwise affect its trade position. National authorities have been forced to consider the international barriers and incentives to fulfillment of their domestic objectives. National governments have found themselves trying to cope with new actors claiming rights and prerogatives formerly reserved to official government agencies and personalities. Even the ingredients of national power have become more slippery. Apparent advantages have been more temporary than permanent, and all too often there is little correlation between what Hoffmann has called the "ingredients" and "outcomes" of power. Complicating this elusiveness of power has been an increased sensitivity of East and West to domestic transitions and to linkages between social, economic, and political issues. Moreover, interdependence between East and West means asymmetry in access to the rewards and challenges of capitalist and socialist domestic and political systems. This asymmetry of access has been carefully noted by Raymond Vernon, who reminds us that "the capacity of U.S. interests to make contacts within the Soviet economy is still brutally circumscribed."[30]

OUTLINES FOR A POLICY OF DETENTE
IN EAST-WEST TRADE

The outlines of a policy of detente have already been suggested by observers sensitive to the challenges of East-West interdependence. Most have emphasized that our goals must be limited. Men like Isaac Deutscher, who long ago advanced the theory of convergence and predicted the transformation of both Soviet and U.S. domestic structures into patterns of democratic socialism, have been superseded by those who believe that our goals must be far more modest. For Raymond Vernon and Marshall Goldman, the hope is simply that despite its dramatic differences from U.S. society Soviet society is more likely to experience minor steps toward liberalization under detente than under conditions of rigid bipolar confrontation.[31]

Among those who advocate detente there is also a growing recognition of the needs of the Soviet regime. These needs will surely prevent detente from advancing beyond its currently modest aspirations. Holzman and Legvold have recognized the Soviet fear that "too much involvement with the advanced capitalist nations will lead to a serious erosion of empire."[32] Other advocates speak of the Soviet desire to keep economics and politics as separate as possible. They suggest that the Soviets wish to use detente simply as a way to expand trade and investment in order to augment supplies of capital and technological resources.[33]

From this perspective, there remains the hope that detente can exploit the "influence effect" long ago noted by Albert Hirschman. This is the belief that the United States and its partners in Western Europe can use their economic influence to political advantage to shape the structure of power relationships between East and West.[34] It has been restated by Kissinger, who notes that while the actual flow of trade and credits between East and West will probably remain very small, it will allow the United States to exercise some influence through U.S. ability to control the scope of trade relationships.[35] At an even more basic level, the feasibility of U.S. policy of detente has been suggested by Fulbright: "We are not at liberty to give up on detente . . . for the simple reason that . . . there is no rational alternative."[36]

It is possible to outline the elements of a workable and modest policy of detente in the area of East-West trade:

1. The goal of U.S. policy must be order first and systemic change only secondarily. A structure for an enduring relationship between East and West is all that can be hoped for now. The United States can hope to alter the old capriciousness of business and political transaction channels, but cannot hope for direct, broad leverage in social issues within the Soviet Union or in the East European countries.

2. The direction of U.S. policy must be to engage Western Europe and Japan in a common effort to involve the USSR and Eastern Europe in a truly

global economy. The objective here is to lessen competition between the United States and Western Europe and to involve the East in the global issues of energy, technological change, and economic development.

3. The United States must attempt to foster the public and private institutional building blocks that will be needed to structure detente. The United States must heed the advice of Miriam Camps in *The Management of Interdependence* that institutions are the building blocks of the new order and that institutions must include "not only organizations, but agreed rules, codes of conduct, and procedures."[37]

4. The United States must provide room for disengagement as well as entanglement. While recognizing the probable intrusion of process-level economic transactions into the structural level that governs their operations (and all the resultant politicization of mundane issues this implies), the United States must endeavor to demote ordinary transactions betweeen East and West to levels not requiring immediate political decisions at the structural level. If the USSR and Eastern Europe are to be integrated more completely into the global economy, they must find it possible to conduct ordinary business in ordinary ways.

5. The United States should try to construct a new fabric of East-West institutional arrangements out of the existing stuff of joint ventures, intergovernmental commissions, and cooperation agreements. These arrangements are not as "neat" as one might hope, but they have the distinct advantage of engaging a broad spectrum of decision makers.

6. The United States must be prepared to accept a detente that corresponds to the asymmetrical nature of East-West interdependence. The political stakes of the United States in preserving the existing outlines of global relationships are probably greater than those of the USSR, and the United States must be prepared to make some minor concessions to the USSR in the pursuit of detente.

7. The United States must be prepared to accept a detente that may falter occasionally. Accommodation and adjustment among the institutions conducting the policy of detente must be expected to result in some occasional jolts and bumps. Bargaining will be the essence of the process, and bargaining cannot hope to escape the ultimately conflicting goals of the United States and the Soviet Union.

Under these conditions, detente would become a much more modest policy. Still, while the United States needs to acknowledge that detente includes both cooperation and conflict, that does not mean that it needs to accept the injection of Suslovian outbursts of ideological antagonism into simple economic transactions. The United States must expect very modest structural gains. It must expect a continued partition of detente into economic, political, military, and ideological segments, expecting more cooperation in economic areas, and anticipating more noticeable conflict in military and ideological matters. This is in every way a policy of modesty in goals, structures, and possible outcomes. It is based on some very real elements of hesitation:

1. The United States and the Soviet Union do not share a common interest except in providing a favorable structure for the conduct of East-West transactions. They share an interest in an economic structure conducive to full exploitation of national economic potentials, but their goals are antagonistic. They have very different conceptions of ways in which supporting states in Western Europe and Eastern Europe should be incorporated into the fabric of East-West economic transactions.

2. The USSR has the delicate problem of Eastern Europe, and the United States must be more considerate of the needs and aspirations of its allies in Western Europe and Japan.

3. International politics, including East-West politics, is more and more a game of varied issues and various players. The United States must attempt to create a structure in which legitimate private actors will not find it impossible to maneuver. The legitimate foreign policy agendas of multinational corporations and international organizations must be accommodated.

4. Another element of caution is injected by the necessary recognition of similarities between domestic politics and international politics. Interest groups of various kinds are increasingly important.

5. The lessons of political development must be applied. Institutional frameworks must keep pace with the politicization of groups and interests competing in the East-West trade game.

Pursuit of a policy of detente between the United States and the Soviet Union thus involves a delicate balance between a whole series of policy-making centers. It is not merely a two-country policy, and it cannot be managed effectively by two-nation agreements. The United States and the Soviet Union must share center stage with the countries of Eastern and Western Europe. Organizations like COMECON and the European Economic Community (EEC) must be involved, as must transgovernmental actors like ministries and departments regulating exports and working in relation to the activities of similar groups in other countries. Private actors, international organizations, and transnational joint ventures must not be ignored. A structured policy of detente may well begin with two-nation agreements between the United States and the USSR, but it must be framed and regulated in such a way that all major actors can play a part. The remaining chapters in this discussion are a modest attempt to explore the nature and possibilities of this broader arena of detente.

NOTES

1. Edward M. Kennedy, "Beyond Detente," *Foreign Policy*, no. 16 (Fall 1974), pp. 3-29; Michael Kaser, "Soviet Trade Turns to Europe," *Foreign Policy*, no. 19 (Summer 1975), pp. 123-35.

2. Frank Church, *Congressional Record*, August 19, 1974, p. S15233.

3. U.S. Congress, Senate, Committee on Foreign Relations, *Hearings, Detente*, 93rd Cong., 2d Sess., August–October 1974, pp. 102, 239. Hereafter cited as *Hearings, Detente*.

4. M. Kudrin, "Objective Factors of Detente," *International Affairs (Moscow), no.* 3 (March 1975), p. 54.

5. Stefan Doernberg, "Socialist Foreign Policy and the World Situation," *International Affairs* (Moscow) no. 3 (March 1975) pp. 57-58.

6. Dmitri Kostyukhin, *New Times* (Moscow), nos. 18-19 (1974), pp. 26-27.

7. I. Grigoryev, "The Important Features of the International Detente," *International Affairs* (Moscow), no. 3 (March 1975), pp. 61-62.

8. A.I. Sobolev, "A Soviet View of Detente," *Wall Street Journal*, April 30, 1975.

9. Henry Kissinger, *Hearings, Detente*, p. 240.

10. Kenneth Waltz, "The Myth of Interdependence," in *The International Corporation,* ed. Charles P. Kindleberger (Cambridge, Mass. : MIT Press, 1970), pp. 205-07.

11. Oran R. Young, "Interdependencies in World Politics," *International Journal* 24, no. 4 (Autumn 1969): 726.

12. Stanley Hoffmann, "Notes on the Elusiveness of Modern Power," *International Journal* 30, no. 2 (Spring 1975): 191-92.

13. For an excellent discussion of the distinctions between political and economic goals and means, and between the levels of structure and process, see Robert O. Keohane and Joseph S. Nye, "World Politics and the International Economic System," *The Future of the International Economic Order: An Agenda for Research,* ed. C. Fred Bergsten (Lexington, Mass.: Lexington Books, 1973), pp. 116-17.

14. Ibid., pp. 156-57.

15. Richard N. Cooper, "Trade Policy Is Foreign Policy." *Foreign Policy, no. 9* (Winter 1972-73), pp. 18-36.

16. Walter F. Mondale, "Beyond Detente: Toward International Economic Security," *Foreign Affairs* 53, no. 1 (October 1974): 1.

17. Franklyn Holzman and Robert Legvold, "The Economics and Politics of East-West Relations," *International Organization* 29, no. 1 (Winter 1975): 303.

18. Fred Bergsten and John A. Mathieson, "Introduction," in Bergsten, ed., op. cit., p. 39.

19. Hollis B. Chenery, "Restructuring the World Economy," *Foreign Affairs* 53, no. 2 (January 1975): 242-43.

20. Mondale, op. cit., p. 18.

21. Richard N. Cooper, "Economic Interdependence and Foreign Policy in the Seventies," *World Politics* 24, no. 2 (January 1972): 159.

22. Bergsten and Mathieson, op. cit., p. 5.

23. Josef Wilczynski, *The Economics and Politics of East-West Trade* (New York: Praeger, 1969), p. 52.

24. V. Klochek, *Ekonomicheskaya gazeta,* no. 15 (April 1975), pp. 20-21.

25. Seyom Brown, *New Forces in World Politics* (Washington: Brookings Institution, 1974), p. 186.

26. Stephen S. Rosenfeld, "Pluralism and Policy," *Foreign Affairs* 52, no. 2 (January 1974): 267.

27. H. Gordon Skilling, "Group Conflict and Political Change," in *Change in Communist Systems,* ed. Chalmers Johnson (Stanford: Stanford University Press, 1970), pp. 216-17.

28. Hoffmann, op. cit., p. 192.

29. Joseph S. Nye, Jr. "Multinational Corporations in World Politics," *Foreign Affairs* 53, no. 1 (October 1974): 155-61.

30. Raymond Vernon, "Apparatchiks and Entrepreneurs: U.S.-Soviet Economic Relations," *Foreign Affairs* 52, no. 2 (January 1974): 251.

31. Raymond Vernon and Marshall Goldman, "U.S. Policies in the Sale of Technology to the USSR," mimeographed (Cambridge, Mass., September 15, 1974).

32. Holzman and Legvold, op. cit., p. 303.

33. Ibid., p. 293.

34. Albert O. Hirschman, *National Power and the Structure of Foreign Trade* (Berkeley: University of California Press, 1945).

35. Kissinger, *Hearings, Detente,* p. 253.

36. Fulbright, *Hearings, Detente,* p. 236.

37. Miriam Camps, *The Management of Interdependence* (New York: Council on Foreign Relations, 1974), p. 10.

2

CHANGING U.S. PERSPECTIVES ON TRADE WITH THE SOVIET UNION

CURRENT TRADE PROJECTIONS AND COMPETING POLICY-MAKING CENTERS

In 1971, U.S. exports to the Soviet Union were valued at about $162 million. In 1973, the estimated value of U.S. exports was over $1 billion, out-ranking the export values of the Federal Republic of Germany and of Japan, and making the United States the largest non-Communist exporter to the Soviet Union.[1] By 1974, American banks had opened correspondent offices in the USSR and a branch office in Romania, and had been working with the Export-Import Bank to provide inventment credits for massive turnkey plants and joint ventures in various Soviet and East European cities and locations.

But, also in 1974, it became obvious that earlier straight-line projections of trade growth between the United States and the Soviet Union were too optimistic. In 1974, U.S. exports to the USSR dropped to $612 million, less than half their 1973 value, and the United States fell from second to seventh among Western trading partners of the USSR. The drop in U.S. exports seemed to result almost entirely from a lack of major grain sales and from the hesitation of some American businessmen in view of the uncertain future of U.S. trade legislation. At the same time, Soviet exports to the United States in 1974 almost doubled from 1973, to $350 million.[2] The Soviets increased their exports to all capitalist countries by about 50 percent over 1973 totals. Older projections of the early 1970s that Soviet indebtedness would reach $31 billion by 1980 were forgotten as Soviet sales of oil, gas, raw materials, and gold benefited from a shift in the world price structure.[3] Still, even as Soviet exports rose dramatically, some observers were predicting that a new decline would begin in 1976 as a result of changing Soviet domestic priorities.[4] American exports increased again in 1975, owing to grain sales.

These contradictions and fluctuations in Soviet-U.S. trade patterns may be explained in part by the dependence of trade patterns on an intricate network of competing policy-making matrices. There are bureaucratic conflicts among domestic trade policy-making groups both in the United States and in the Soviet Union. There are transnational and transgovernmental linkages which sometimes threaten and sometimes reinforce the stated policies of top government officials. There are tensions between policies and attitudes which challenge the structure of relations between the United States and the USSR, and there are those which merely seek to effect some procedural innovations. There are conflicts because the economic, ideological, political, and military planes of Soviet-U.S. cooperation and conflict are sometimes hard to separate. The key is that both in the United States and in the Soviet Union, foreign policy at present seems to derive less and less from a coherent world view and more and more from competition among domestic forces.[5] If trade is to be viewed as an important element in Soviet-U.S. detente, then ways must be discovered to facilitate a continuing and structural framework for its anticipated growth as well as its occasional hesitation. Competition must be transformed into a coherent bargaining process based on realistic, pragmatic goals and methods.

The predominance of relatively unstructured competition and relationships can be seen in a number of recent incidents. Soviet activities surrounding the final passage of the Trade Reform Act in late 1974 underlined the fragility of detente and of trade patterns accompanying it. The dependence of detente on a congruence of varied foreign policy-making matrices was underscored by Moscow's angry reply to congressional approval of the trade bill. Ambassador Anatoly F. Dobrynin apparently told Kissinger that Moscow was upset by what it regarded as the failure of the United States to live up to its side of detente. An official Soviet statement complained about inadmissible meddling in Soviet domestic affairs, presumably because of the publicity about tying trade concessions to Jewish emigration. *Pravda* had earlier complained that the United States and the Soviet Union had explicitly barred such interference in 1972 by agreeing that trade between them would be conducted on a basis of complete equality.[6] On the eve of the final passage of the trade bill, TASS released a latter from Soviet Foreign Minister Andrei Gromyko to Kissinger, dated October 16, in which the USSR "resolutely declined" to accept any obligation on the part of the Soviet government regarding "departure of Soviet citizens from the USSR."[7]

Soviet hesitation in trade relations with the United States was further revealed in actions during the early months of 1975. Some articles in the Soviet press attempted to "quarantine" the trade aspects of detente by stressing that a minor setback for trade did not mean the demise of the broader policy of detente.[8] Others claimed that nothing had changed at all and suggested merely that U.S.-Soviet relations should continue on the basis of principles worked out in Moscow in 1972.[9] But Soviet officials were at the same time expressing blatant threats to American businessmen and suggesting that recent gains in Soviet trade with Western Europe could easily be expanded at the expense of the United States.[10] The Soviets also expressed bitterness at the new congressional ceiling on credits of $75 million a year over the next four years.

Earlier in the fall, another example of competing policy-making matrices had surfaced when officials of Continental Grain of New York and Cook Industries of Memphis agreed at a White House meeting to cancel contracts they had signed with Soviet foreign trade organizations (FTOs) to provide very large amounts of corn and wheat.[11] Actually, several days before the U.S. grain companies agreed to fill the Soviet corn and wheat orders that were later blocked, Department of Agriculture officials had clear signs that the Soviets wanted more grain than the American government was willing to see sold. Yet, the Department of Agriculture failed to discourage the sale and eventually precipitated the abrupt cancellation maneuvers of President Ford. In the end, according to an agreement worked out by Treasury Secretary William Simon, the Soviets were permitted to purchase 1 million tons of corn and 1.2 million tons of wheat prior to the end of 1974.[12]

In the context of the multiple policy-making centers of detente, it should not seem surprising that almost at the same time the verbal shots were fired from the Kremlin to Washington about trade problems with the United States, a meeting of the U.S.-Soviet Trade and Economic Council was held in Moscow. Seemingly oblivious to the controversies over emigration and credits, its members predicted a $9 billion total for U.S. exports to the Soviet Union in 1976-80 and simply assumed that at least $1.1 billion in Export-Import Bank credits could be obtained. That figure for Eximbank loans was about four times the level actually supported by Congress. Co-Chairman Donald Kendall of Pepsico even suggested that a $2 billion annual credit limit would be appropriate in the Soviet case.[13] One could speculate about the lack of communication between domestic groups influencing and making trade policy. Alternatively, assuming that the American and Soviet members of the Trade and Economic Council must have known about imminent congressional limitations, one could hypothesize that the Trade and Economic Council was acting as a mere propaganda forum for officials on both the American side and the Soviet side. A better answer, however, seems to lie in the view that groups with different interests and constituencies were fighting for their part of the pluralist foreign policy matrix of detente. Congress had to answer to constituents who wondered why their mortgage applications were turned down while the Soviet Union indirectly received millions in government-backed long-term credits at 7 percent interest. The U.S.-Soviet Trade and Economic Council answered to a business constituency that favored a high volume of trade because it meant higher profits for their companies.

CURRENT STAKES OF SOVIET-U.S. TRADE

Zbigniew Brzezinski has suggested that the shape of the U.S.-Soviet relationship in the near future will be determined by the interaction of three forces: the thrust of democratic developments within the two systems, the nature of the power balance between the two countries, and the patterns of autonomous global and regional development which may create pressures for involvement and withdrawal. He cautions that the United States needs to be realistic and patient in the management of its relations with Moscow and needs to remember that excessive hopes and excessive hostilities are equally misplaced.[14] Brzezinski was speaking to the broad perspective of power relations between the two countries, but his cautions can usefully be placed into the more specific framework of trade and commercial relations between the United States and the Soviet Union. The domestic constraints present both in the United States and in the Soviet Union, combined with the possibility of varied directions for the regional grouping of COMECON, create an arena where conflict and cooperation will surely intersect. It is the purpose of this analysis to isolate some of the more likely channels of conflict and cooperation in the current period of commercial relations between the United States and the Soviet Union.

A first component in this complex process can be seen in the domestic decision-making process of the Soviet Union and the United States. In both cases, competing domestic groups have alternative ideas about trade and investment policy. The pro- and antitrade groups which have surfaced to defend and attack post-1970 Soviet-U.S. commercial transactions can be seen as competing factions at the most visible levels of the Soviet-U.S. trade and investment policy-making processes. Because the scope of post-1970 transactions far exceeds that of past Soviet-U.S. deals, these groups have assumed a particularly vocal and influential position. Past experience with Soviet-U.S. trade derives mostly from 1930-32, when foreign investment in the USSR was briefly encouraged; from 1934-38, when Germany lost credibility as a trade partner; from 1942-45, when exports under the lend-lease program ran at the rate of several billion dollars a year; and from 1964, with the initial large grain sale to the Soviet Union.[15]

Projects currently underway or contemplated make these earlier phases of Soviet-U.S. business transactions seem simple and uncomplicated. From the U.S. point of view, many of the projects now planned are based on the belief that U.S. aid in exploiting the USSR's natural resources could be used to U.S. advantage. It is well known that the USSR holds first place in iron ore deposits, estimated at more than 100 billion tons (40 percent of total world reserves). The USSR also accounts for 16 percent of world copper production, 12 percent of mined zinc, 15 percent of lead output, and 20 percent of nickel production. The USSR is the world's largest coal producer. It also has enormous petroleum and natural gas reserves, and in total claims some 50 percent of world reserves of basic fuels.[16]

From the Soviet perspective, these resources provide the basis for extensive industrial cooperation with the United States. While Soviet resources are enormous, they cannot be exploited as rapidly as the Soviet leadership would like without massive technical assistance from the United States and from Western Europe. While recent surveys of Soviet energy resources have stressed that "the USSR's fuel and power resources are so great that they can supply all the needs of our developing national economy both now and in the future," they have added that the Soviet Union faces a number of problems in resource utilization. First, most of the resources are located in eastern Siberia, far from European regions of Russia, and they are expensive to transport. Most estimates place 90 percent of resources in the eastern regions, with 70 percent of consumption in the European and Ural regions. Second, the development of ferrous metallurgy in Siberia is not progressing very well. Third, the coal industry is developing slowly. Finally, the USSR lacks sufficient numbers of high-quality, long range power transmission lines.[17] For the most part, then, projects currently under consideration and debated in both the United States and the Soviet Union involve a mixture of U.S. technology and Soviet raw materials. Other projects involve the use of U.S. innovations in Soviet heavy industrial processes or transfer and sales of computers and computer technology.

The Kama River Truck Project (sometimes called KAMAZ) is perhaps the most spectacular joint project to date. It has involved large Soviet purchases of West European, Japanese, and U.S. technology. Total costs for the giant truck-building plant are estimated at $3.5 billion, and some $1 billion of U.S. equipment and technology is expected to be purchased from well over 50 U.S. companies. At full capacity, KAMAZ will produce annually 150,000 trucks and 250,000 diesel engines. Many U.S. companies have sold large amounts of component supplies for the plant. They include Swindell-Dressler, C-E Cast Equipment, Holocraft and Company, Ingersoll Rand, National Engineering, LaSalle Machine Tool, Cleveland Crane, Gleason Works, and Carborundum. Eximbank has provided $469 million in credits for the project, and the Soviet purchasing agent for Kama River has declared that "without Eximbank assistance, no more than 20% of the facility could have been built."[18]

Representative of other contemplated projects is the development of a huge chemical fertilizer plant in the USSR with U.S. investment support. In the fall of 1973, an agreement was concluded with the Occidental Petroleum Company for collaboration in the construction of a large chemical fertilizer production complex and in deliveries of ammonia and other chemicals to the United States. This particular agreement, which is to extend for 20 years, will involve a total volume of mutual exchanges estimated by Armand Hammer of Occidental Petroleum at $20 billion.[19] Credits of over $180 million for the project were granted by the Export-Import Bank. Soviet foreign trade organizations were expected to place well over $400 million of orders in the United States for equipment and materials related to the project.[20] By early summer of 1974, final negotiations for much of the project were underway. In June, the Soviet Union signed a $200 million contract with a division of the General Tire and Rubber Company for the construction of the four ammonia plants involved. If completed as planned, the ammonia complex will be the largest of its kind in the world. In addition, Occidental was hoping to design, equip, and supervise the construction of two port facilities in the USSR to handle the chemicals.[21] *Izvestia*, in a lengthy editorial statement on June 5, 1974, praised the agreement as a good example of mutual advantage.

Agreements for closely related petrochemical projects were also completed in the summer of 1974. Leonid A. Kostandov, Soviet minister of the chemicals industry, signed a tentative agreement with PPG Industries, Inc., for the construction of a plastic resin plant to be constructed near natural gas fields in Central Asia or in Orenburg. Union Carbide and E. I. du Pont de Nemours and Company were involved in other chemical plant agreements. The total value of all these in terms of orders from U.S. suppliers was equal to at least $200 million.[22]

While the Soviet Union has on occasion expressed great interest in the use of U.S. technology to improve its output of oil and natural gas, current trends indicate the existence of a rather severe internal debate about the appropriateness of pledging a portion of Soviet oil and gas resources in return for U.S. assistance in developing those resources. The debate seems far from resolved, despite the fact that an agreement on cooperative natural gas exploration has recently been signed.

Two groupings of U.S. companies have been actively investigating the possibility of developing Siberian gas resources and shipping the gas in liquefied form in tanks to the United States. Occidental, the El Paso Natural Gas Company, and the Bechtel Corporation would like to develop the Yakutsk fields of eastern Siberia to serve the American west coast. Tenneco, the Texas Eastern Transmission Corporation, and Brown and Root envisage the use of the Urengoi fields of western Siberia for supplies to the east coast.[23] In early spring and summer of 1974, these plans were at a standstill. Valentin D. Shashin, the Soviet oil minister, declared that he did not foresee any agreements with Western companies for exploration or transfer of Soviet oil and gas resources.[24] Then, in Paris, at about the time of the Vladivostok meeting between Ford and Brezhnev, the El Paso group signed an agreement for exploration of natural gas sites in eastern Siberia.[25]

Shashin's change of position seemed to extend as well to oil extraction projects. In a statement of November 1974, Shashin asserted that the Soviet oil industry was prepared to cooperate on a large scale with American oil companies that could offer needed technology. Shashin conceded that in some oil fields, Soviet techniques were capable of extracting only 10 to 15 percent of the resources, while U.S. methods could be expected to raise the extraction level to about 50 percent.[26] Shashin mentioned Union Oil Company of California and Standard Oil of Indiana as two companies interested in the Soviet proposals.

Yet, other factors point to a lessening of Soviet enthusiasm for U.S. assistance in the Soviet oil industry. Soviet economic planners have recently ordered a reversal of the nation's energy policy and a shift to a greater emphasis on coal use and coal production. This shift comes despite the fact that Soviet proven oil reserves are now put at over 68 billion tons and probable reserves, at 300 billion tons. It reflects both a concern for preservation of the oil reserves for the future and a realization that Soviet oil can be a valuable economic weapon.[27] Also, the Soviet Union seems increasingly unwilling to pledge future oil output for fixed amounts of U.S. technology.[28]

So far, indecision on joint development of oil resources does not seem to have been extended to other areas of Soviet-U.S. economic cooperation. In April 1974, the Soviet Union and a U.S. consortium signed a design agreement for a $110 million international trade center in Moscow. To support the project, the Export-Import Bank approved a $36 million credit and Chase Manhattan offered a $36 million loan. In June 1974, Boeing Aircraft signed a cooperation agreement with the USSR. The agreement provided for cooperation in the field of civil aviation, possibly including helicopter engineering.[29]

A fairly novel approach to joint Soviet-U.S. undertakings has been employed in the case of Soviet enrichment of American uranium for processing into fuel to operate power stations in third countries. While the uranium undertakings have aroused the wrath of American groups opposing all transfers of technology, and particularly military technology, to the USSR, they seem likely to encourage similar projects in the future. Edlow Instrument Company of Washington, D.C., recently received the necessary permission to export 1.4 million pounds of uranium oxide to the United Kingdom. There it will be processed into hexafluoride gas which will in turn be shipped to the USSR for processing into pellets rich in Uranium 235. The controls on projects of this kind are intricate and require a series of approvals from the Nuclear Regulatory Commission, the State Department, and Euratom.[30]

Computers are among the biggest Soviet interests at present. Recent journal articles in the Soviet Union have been emphasizing successes already achieved through the use of automated management systems and computers. As of January 1974, 1,251 automated management systems and 1,782 computer centers were operating in the Soviet Union.[31] While the USSR probably had only about 3,500 to 5,500 computers in use in nonmilitary functions in 1970, that number was expected to reach 31,500 by the end of 1975. Western sales of computer equipment to the Soviet Union are crucial to the achievement of these Soviet goals.[32]

Management techniques are another major area of Soviet interest. Since early 1973, the Soviet Union has been particularly aggressive in encouraging management and accounting firms to do business in the Soviet Union. One of the largest accounting firms in the United States has opened an office in Moscow to provide advice on auditing, international taxation, and management services.

The firm, Arthur Andersen and Company of Chicago, is the first American company to work closely with the Soviets in the field of Western business management techniques.[33] It now appears that the Soviet authorities have decided to hire Western management consultants to rationalize production in a wide range of industrial plants. The Soviets are especially interested in management consulting contracts for the reorganization of plants in the shoe, clothing, artificial leather, and machine-building industries.[34]

Another kind of agreement, much less typical than U.S. involvement in Soviet industrial, technical, and resource development undertakings, has involved Soviet sales of industrial goods in the U.S. market. For example, LaSalle Machine Tool recently purchased Soviet machine tools worth about $1 million.[35] At about the same time, an agreement was concluded between Elektronorgtekhnika and General Electric for deliveries of Soviet-made electronic components.[36] The future possibilities for such agreements are impressive within particular fields of specialization. A Rand Corporation report has suggested several areas in which the Soviet Union can be expected to accomplish technological advances which would be marketable in the United States, especially in Alaska:

1. Advances in steel technology, including the production and fabrication of heavy castings, and forging and welding techniques
2. Hydroelectric and steam turbine designs
3. Concrete technology for large structures in cold climates
4. Power transmission technologies
5. Nonferrous alloys for electrical conductors
6. Technology for protecting high-voltage lines and switching stations.[37]

Three small projects involving transfer of Soviet technology to the United States have been completed. They are an underground pneumatic rocket for punching holes in the ground for various construction projects, a cutting machine for removing scale from wires, and an evaporative cooling technique for improving the life and efficiency of blast furnaces.[38]

SOURCES OF DOMESTIC DEBATE IN THE UNITED STATES

Domestic pressures in both the United States and the Soviet Union will undoubtedly influence the future of the broad project categories mentioned above. The debate between those who would control trade and those who would promote it has been lengthily and vigorously argued in the United States. Its forerunners go all the way back to 1934 and the restrictive Johnson Debt Default Act. For this reason, examination of the current domestic debate in the United States must be preceded by a brief review of legislation dealing with trade relations between the Soviet Union and the United States. Four distinct periods in trade legislation can be distinguished:

1. The years between the passage of the Johnson Debt Default Act of 1934 and World War II
2. The post-World War II period marked especially by the Export Control Act of 1949 and the Mutual Defense Assistance Act of 1951
3. The period of more generous trade legislation beginning in 1962 and culminating in the Export Administration Act of 1969
4. The current period of deliberation and uncertainty, marked by congressional debate over agreements tentatively reached at the Nixon-Brezhnev summit of 1972.

A piece of 1934 legislation, the Johnson Debt Default Act, provided the basis for restrictive treatment of trade with the Soviet Union in the years before World War II. It attempted to control credits extended by private business or banks to foreign governments that were in default on loans made by the United States. Since the Soviet Union had defaulted on World War I debts and then later on lend-lease payments after World War II, the Johnson Act effectively barred the extension of private credits to the USSR. It did not, however, cover long-term credits guaranteed by the U.S. government.[39] Therefore, the Export-Import Bank was permitted after World War II to lend money to the Soviet Union until the subsequent passage of restrictions on the Export-Import Bank's lending. Later, the Johnson Act was modified to forbid extension of its prohibitions to members of the International Monetary Fund or the International Bank for Reconstruction and Development. Then, in 1963, hoping to spur a large wheat sale to the USSR, the Justice Department ruled that the act's provisions did not apply to short-term 90-day credits.[40] Over the years, the major purpose of the Johnson Act was to deny medium- and long-term private loans and credits to Communist countries. As Franklyn Holzman notes, the problems raised by the Johnson Act for American businessmen became particularly acute in the early 1960s, when West European and Japanese governments began permittting 15-year long-term private credits, often at low interest rates of 4 to 6 percent.[41] The Johnson Act conveyed the message that private business, in contrast to public lending authorities, could not be trusted to serve the national interest by voluntarily refusing to provide financial backing to Communist countries.

The post-World War II period, accented by the paranoia of the early Cold War years, found the United States government engaged even more seriously in the export control business. The Export Control Act of 1949 attempted to prevent the export of goods deemed important for national security. In theory, the restrictions applied to all nations; but in practice, the letter of the law was followed only with respect to Communist nations. The Mutual Defense Assistance Act of 1951, usually called the Battle Act, was largely an attempt by the

United States to enlist the cooperation of NATO countries and Japan in achieving the goals of the Export Control Act of 1949. The Consultative Group Co-ordinating Committee (COCOM), a joint body for the administration of the co-operative arrangements developed under the terms of the Battle Act, began functioning in 1951. It has no formal charter, and its decisions are not binding on member countries, but its International List has provided a modicum of mutual restraint in Western trade with the Soviet Union. During the second half of the 1950s, COCOM regulations became less significant as West European coun-tries gradually reduced the embargo list to cover only military hardware and selected items of advanced technology. The United States, in contrast, failed to revise its Commodity Control List significantly until 1966. Even today there remains the difference that while the COCOM list applies uniformly to all East European countries, American export controls distinguish among three groups of countries: Group Q (Romania), Group W (Poland), and Group Y (Albania, Bulgaria, Czechoslovakia, East Germany, Hungary, the USSR, and China).[42] It was only in the period 1972-74 that the United States began to bring its own embargo rules more closely into line with increasingly lenient COCOM rules. In September 1972, the United States maintained unilateral controls on 600 items not covered by COCOM guidelines, but by June 1974 the American list exceeded that of COCOM by only 65 items.[43]

Two additional pieces of legislation consolidated the very conservative U.S. position on trading with the Soviet Union and Eastern Europe during the early 1950s. The Mutual Security Act of 1954 authorized the president to restrict the exportation to any nation of arms, munitions, implements of war, and related technology. In practice, this act was applied primarily to Communist countries. The Agricultural Trade Development and Assistance Act of 1954 prohibited sales of agricultural commodities for local currencies or long-term dollar credits to some Communist countries.[44] The 1954 Agricultural Act was the first distinct attempt by the U.S. government to transfer the grounds of prohibition from purely military to much broader economic grounds.

In 1962, the Export Control Act of 1949 itself was amended to broaden the criteria for prohibiting exports from military to economic reasons. Congress found that "unrestricted export of materials without regard to their military and economic significance could adversely affect the national security of the United States." Thus, Congress provided for the denial of an export license for any commodity if the president made a determination that such exports could make significant military or economic contributions to those nations. The 1962 legislation provided broad possibilities for a restrictive trade policy covering all commodities of potential interest to the Soviet Union and Eastern Europe. The Export Administration Act of 1969 deleted the "economic" criterion, and only goods relating to military potential were still proscribed. The act called on the Department of Commerce to lift controls on commodities freely available to Communist countries from non-U.S. sources and on items that were only marginally of military value.

After 1969, there were some far-reaching changes and attempted changes in U.S. trade legislation. The Export Expansion Act of 1971 raised the ceiling on Eximbank loan guarantees from $3.5 billion to $10 billion and the ceiling on all financial activity from $13.5 billion to $20 billion. In 1972, the Export Administration Act of 1969 was amended by the Equal Export Opportunity Act. This act provides the legal framework for the current export control process. Administered by the Department of Commerce. it authorizes controls to the extent necessary to protect the domestic economy from the excessive drain of scarce materials and to reduce the serious inflationary potential of abnormal foreign demand; fulfill the international responsibilities of the United States; and protect the national security of the United States.[45]

Despite the broad potential restrictions of the 1972 act and the regulatory provisions of previous acts still in force, the government in practice becomes involved in the control process in only three ways. First, special products, controlled for security reasons, must be approved for export by a governmental committee from the Departments of Commerce, Defense, State, and Treasury; from the National Regulatory Commission; and from other agencies which may declare a special interest. Second, when government credits or guarantees are sought through the Export-Import Bank or the Commodity Credit Corporation, special approval of the government portion of the financing must be granted. Third, if complaints are lodged with the federal government on trade disruption or dumping, provisions for restricting imports may be brought into force.[46]

It is sometimes claimed that prior to 1972, the role of the U.S. government in trade relations with Communist countries was largely negative, whereas after 1972, the United States assumed a role in setting up ground rules designed to promote trade and to protect American businessmen against abuses at the hands of Soviet foreign trade organizations.[47] The period surrounding the Nixon-Brezhnev summit of 1972 did lead to a new round of agreements between the United States and the Soviet Union, as well as to some new pieces of trade legislation. The U.S.-Soviet Agreement on Scientific and Technical Cooperation of May 1972 opened the way to scientific joint research efforts and other cooperative projects. In July 1972, an agreement was reached to provide credit through the U.S. Commodity Credit Corporation for Soviet purchases of U.S. grain. Under the terms of a highly publicized agreement, the Soviet Union agreed to purchase at least $750 million worth of grain and the United States agreed to make available $750 million worth of credits from the Commodity Credit Corporation. By the end of 1972, more than $1 billion worth of agricultural products, mostly wheat, had been sold to the Soviet Union, and $110 million of credit had been extended by the Commodity Credit Corporation.[48]

The grain deal set the stage for the Soviet-U.S. Agreement on Trade of October 1972. The trade agreement provided for reciprocity on the extension of trade credits by the Export-Import Bank and the Foreign Trade Bank (Vneshtorgbank) of the Soviet Union. It made American business concerns eligible for extension of credits by 40 Soviet FTOs, and in return President

Nixon made a declaration of national interest for Eximbank financing of exports to the USSR.[49] The October 1972 agreement also achieved a tentative lend-lease settlement. The Soviets agreed to pay a total amount of $722 million, $48 million by mid-1975 and the remainder over a 25-year period contingent upon the official granting of most-favored-nation (MFN) status to the USSR by the United States. The provisions of the agreement had to be approved by Congress, and it was not until December 1974 that Congress finally gave approval to MFN and extended Eximbank credits. Even then it did so with the Jackson-Vanik amendment attached. The Soviet rejection of the trade agreement in January 1975 was largely unexpected, and it set the stage for a period of uncertainty about the future direction of Soviet-U.S. trade.

THE U.S. POLICY-MAKING PROCESS

Accompanying the various twists and turns of the trade legislation itself has been a broad domestic debate. The protrade lobby has included American agricultural interests, corporations hoping to sell products to the Soviet Union or to participate in Soviet development projects, and the Treasury, Commerce, and Agriculture departments. It has also included Eximbank and large private banks. An antitrade lobby has comprised labor groups, who fear that trade will mean exporting jobs, and congressional groups, including the administrative arm of Congress, the General Accounting Office (GAO).

Groups both favoring and opposing expansion of trade often claim to be the successors to policy formulations of the late 1960s and early 1970s which attempted to reformulate the international economic policies of the United States. Both are heirs to the Nixon administration's economic ideas. The domestic recession of 1969-70 and the continuing deficits in the U.S. balance of payments prompted the government to consider expanded trade with the Soviet Union as a means of increasing U.S. exports and reducing domestic unemployment. The initial foreign policy statements of the Nixon administration, despite their recognition of the need for new policies and structures to make possible an orderly transition from balanced duopoly to balanced pluralism in political arrangements, were cautious about new directions for trade.[50] Especially hesitant were the published conclusions of the Commission on International Trade and Investment Policy, which conducted a special study of foreign economic policy in the early 1970s. The commission statements urged particular caution in technology transfer and long-term credits.[51] Peter G. Peterson, assistant to the president for international economic affairs and later secretary of commerce, issued a more optimistic report which called for a new American approach to trade with the East in order to improve the balance-of-payments situation and to facilitate the entry of the Soviet Union into the world trading and financial community.[52]

While it is difficult to develop a generalized outline of the foreign trade policy-making process within the United States, Figure 1 is an attempt to present the major actors and their relationship to the process as a whole. These actors have been the sources of arguments accompanying the broad domestic debate on trade with the Soviet Union. Two broad groupings have emerged: a protrade lobby, which focuses its efforts on promoting U.S. exports and credits to the USSR; and an antitrade lobby, which demands greater attention to the potential problems of technology transfer and lenient long-term financing of exports. Within these two broad categories there are many additional points of disagreement.

Governmental Proponents of Trade

Within the protrade group, for example, there are numerous struggles to achieve administrative preeminence. The Department of Commerce, the State Department, and the Department of the Treasury all have potentially competing goals to pursue in the trade arena and are caught up as well in intradepartmental clashes concerning regulation and expansion of trade. One major attempt to reconcile actual and potential policy differences was made in the creation of the East-West Trade Policy Committee in the spring of 1973. The secretary of the treasury was designated as chairman, with the secretary of commerce as vice-chairman. Other members of the Policy Committee include the secretary of state, the executive director of the Council on International Economic Policy, and the special representative for trade negotiations. There is a working group that can be assembled more frequently and informally than the East-West Trade Policy Committee. All the member agencies have representatives on the working group, as do the Department of Defense, the Export-Import Bank, and other agencies when they declare an interest in a particular issue.[53] The East-West Trade Policy Committee has been assigned the functions of reviewing all major transfers of technology, considering all government credits in excess of $5 million, and submitting quarterly reports on East-West trade to Congress. Its activities supplement those of the Council on International Economic Policy (CIEP), which is a part of the White House staff. The CIEP views its function as harmonizing the competing interests of State, Treasury, Eximbank, and Agriculture on major questions of U.S. economic policy abroad.[54]

Council on International Economic Policy representatives almost invariably refer to the East-West Trade Policy Committee as the locus of power on issues of East-West trade. So do representatives of Commerce and State. However, they add that the East-West Trade Committee's significance is largely due to the influence of Henry Kissinger and his staffers, who have made this committee the center of their efforts to influence trade. In practice, the meetings of the East-West Policy Committee probably have intensified the potential competition over decision-making authority, particularly between the Department of State and the Department of Commerce.

FIGURE 1

The East-West Trade Decision-Making Process in the United States

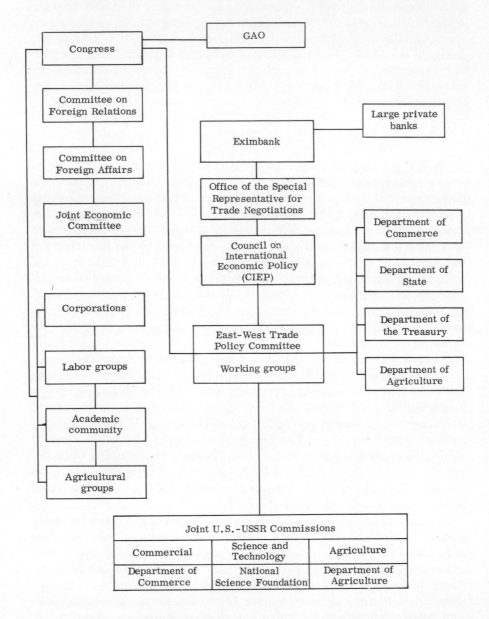

Source: Compiled by the author.

Among those who clearly view the committee as an attempt by Kissinger and Helmut Sonnenfeldt of Kissinger's staff to usurp the policy-making and policy-implementing functions of the executive departments are trade officials in the Department of Commerce's Bureau of East-West Trade (BEWT). The Bureau of East-West Trade was established late in 1972 as a separate unit within Commerce's Domestic and International Business Administration. In its own view, it was handed a mandate to pursue the major role in implementing East-West trade policy. The bureau is the major government mechanism for assisting U.S. firms interested in East-West trade, and it provides the executive secretariat for the U.S.-USSR Joint Commercial Commission, as well as for similar commissions with Poland and Romania. It administers the East-West Trade Center in Vienna, the U.S. Trade Development Center in Warsaw, and a Moscow commercial office. It publishes analytical material, including summaries of Soviet economic plans and market research reports on the USSR.[55] The emphasis of its programs is clearly on promoting trade and counteracting a quarter-century of minimal East-West trade contact, but it also has been assigned regulatory functions. BEWT oversees traditional American controls on exports of products and technologies with national security, short supply, or "other" foreign policy implications.

The Bureau of East-West Trade, directed by the deputy assistant secretary of commerce for East-West trade and a deputy director, has four main divisions, with numerous subdivisions and broad-ranging promotional and regulatory functions:

Office of Export Administration (Scientific and Electronic Equipment Division, Capital Goods and Production Materials Division, Compliance Division, Operations Division, Technical Data Division, Policy Planning Division);
Office of Joint Commission Secretariats;
Office of East-West Trade Analysis (East-West Trade Analysis Division, East-West Trade Policy Division);
Office of East-West Trade Development (Eastern European Affairs Division, Peoples' Republic of China and Other Asian Areas Division, Trade Development Assistance Division, USSR Affairs Division, Trade Promotion Division).[56]

The Department of Commerce views itself as the most competent government arm in dealing with East-West trade, while it is generally viewed as the least competent by representatives of the Department of State, the General Accounting Office, and the Export-Import Bank. The conflict in part seems to be one of difficulty in defining Commerce's appropriate functions. The Department of Commerce emphasizes that because of its broad mandate in implementing policy and in gathering information, it should provide significant inputs into the policy-making process as well. Early in 1975, after the Soviet rejection of the Trade Act, BEWT was placing priority on expanding its influence on

Capitol Hill, trying to send representatives to briefing sessions of congressional committees, and attempting to provide for the continuation of as much Soviet-U.S. trade as possible.

Policy-making prerogatives are often jealously guarded by the Department of State, CIEP, and the East-West Trade Policy Committee. These agencies grudgingly acknowledge Commerce's large and diverse staff, but they claim that the Bureau of East-West Trade is attuned only to the needs of American businessmen and that it is insensitive to the political framework so important to the day-to-day conduct of East-West trade. It is true that Commerce emphasizes its utility to the U.S. business community. Businessmen, on the other hand, tend to place greater confidence in their own corporate market research facilities and in the commercial divisions of American embassies in the USSR and Eastern Europe. The Commerce Department remains the largest source of East-West trade studies and regulatory measures, but its influence is increasingly challenged by other executive agencies and by the corporations it seeks to serve.

Three offices within the State Department play an important role in developing trade policy. They are the Office of Soviet Union Affairs, the Office of East European Affairs, and the Office of East-West Trade. The Department of State emphasizes that trade with the Soviet Union is essentially a political rather than an economic subject and suggests that this should grant the Department of State preeminence in the policy-making process. The Department of Commerce was referred to by one State Department official as "simply incompetent" in the area of East-West trade. Several State Department officials suggested that Commerce was trying to steal State's proper role by participating too actively in the policy process.

Officials in the State Department are noticeably ambivalent about the aggressive role Henry Kissinger and his staff have assumed in East-West trade. State representatives often suggest that the real decision-making power rests with the National Security Council, or with the East-West Trade Policy Committee, or even simply with Kissinger and Sonnenfeldt. The three offices concerned with East-West trade in the State Department lack staff time and resources to devote as much attention as they would like to East-West trade. Trade is not foremost among the State Department's priorities, and one frequently has the feeling that the ghost of "trade as inconsequential low politics" is still very much alive. Regulatory functions related to the administration of the Battle Act of 1951 are assigned to the Office of East-West Trade, and that office is very critical of Commerce's "usurpation" of regulatory functions.

The Office of the Special Representative for Trade Negotiations (STR), which provides staffing and background materials for trade negotiations with the USSR and Eastern Europe, shares many of the views of the State Department. In the opinion of STR, trade with the East is a political process with secondary commercial importance, and the expertise and appropriate initiative are delegated to the State Department. STR shares State Department complaints that the Department of Commerce is not always competent and that it sometimes oversteps its mandate into the making of foreign policy. Kissinger and Sonnenfeldt are again rated as key figures in the process of making trade policy.

The Export-Import Bank has institutional interest in promoting export credits for the Soviet Union. Enhanced stature for Eximbank would seem to be directly linked to higher levels of export credits. Eximbank, like the Department of State, stresses the political importance of trade, but unlike State, it emphasizes the basic economic benefits of trade with the Soviet Union for the domestic economy. Since the Export-Import Bank lost its lending authority as a result of the Soviet rejection of the provisions of the U.S. Trade Reform Act, its current concentration is on the frustration of the situation. Up to March 1975, Eximbank loans to the USSR totaled only $469 million, a figure which officials claim to be ridiculously low when compared with European government credits to the Soviet Union.

While Eximbank expresses a keen desire for more institutional authority and flexibility, it is careful not to claim adjunct status to what it views as State's rightfully dominant position. Officials of the Export-Import Bank agree with the State Department's assessment of BEWT as an agency with little credibility and of the Kissinger-Sonnenfeldt team as the pivotal decision-making center on trade matters. Eximbank claims that it does not view itself as a decision-making arm of U.S. foreign policy, but this claim is angrily disputed by the General Accounting Office. Eximbank provides the most pessimistic picture of any government agency of the Soviets' ability to pay, perhaps to lend credence to its own insistent demands for higher lending authority.

The problem of competition from official West European lending institutions is a primary Eximbank concern. Eximbank claims that a large amount of potential export business will not come to the United States from the Soviet Union because of the absence of competitive financing. The major West European countries and Japan have agreements under which over $7 billion of government-backed export credits will be available to finance sales by European and Japanese manufacturers to the Soviet Union. In late 1974 and early 1975, agreements were signed by France, Italy, and the United Kingdom, committing some $5 billion of new credits to the USSR. These new credits generally carry an interest rate of 7 to 7.5 percent and frequently support 80 to 90 percent of the price of the relevant exports. Eximbank suggests that in the absence of much greater official export financing in the United States, many American companies will carry out planned projects in the Soviet Union by purchasing the equipment in Europe and Japan in order to obtain the necessary export financing.[57]

In February 1975, William J. Casey, chairman and president of the Export-Import Bank, announced new American measures to strengthen Eximbank's support of U.S. exports. The bank was scheduled to increase the range within which it would extend direct credits to the USSR from 30 to 55 percent of the export price instead of the currently prevailing range of 30 to 45 percent. In cases where no direct credits are granted, the bank would be entitled to guarantee up to 85 percent of an export transaction's cost. Interest rates on direct credits are to range between 7 and 9 percent instead of between 7 and 8.5 percent. The hope was that these rates would make U.S. products and credits competitive with European ones.[58]

Despite its eagerness to disclaim policy-making functions, the Export-Import Bank has become a major protrade actor through its highly publicized legal battles with the General Accounting Office. In March 1974, when the General Accounting Office-Eximbank dispute was at a high point, the question was whether the president must declare each individual loan to a Communist country to be in the national interest (as the GAO wished), or whether a single "national interest" finding for all future loans to a given country would be sufficient. It was the potentially huge Soviet-U.S. deal on natural gas shipments in exchange for aid in building pipelines that caused Senator Richard Schweiker (Republican of Pennsylvania) to ask the General Accounting Office to investigate the legality of Eximbank loans. For a few weeks in the spring of 1974, Eximbank lending to the Soviet Union was halted.[59] Later in March, the Export-Import Bank announced that it would resume lending to the Soviet Union and to the countries of Eastern Europe, but the issue still seemed far from final resolution and threatened to reopen once Eximbank lending could be resumed after Soviet rejection of the Trade Act.

Public news releases from the Export-Import Bank have been exceedingly careful to provide strong protrade justification. Eximbank credits for the huge ammonia complex at Togliatti were accompanied by a publicized list of the project's advantages for the American public. The official Eximbank news releases first emphasized that the $180 million credit to aid in the construction of the ammonia plants would save U.S. natural gas supplies and would bring needed fertilizer to the United States. The fertilizer produced with Soviet natural gas would supposedly save enough American natural gas to heat a million American homes for a year. Second, the project was to represent a huge development investment in the United States. Occidental Petroleum concurrently announced that because of the deal it would invest more than $500 million in the United States to construct ships and expand production facilities to process more phosphate rock in Florida. One Eximbank news release suggested that this would generate about 2,000 to 3,000 jobs during the construction period (until 1979) and 2,900 permanent jobs thereafter. Finally, it was suggested that the project would provide balance-of-payments advantages. The United States would acquire needed fertilizer from abroad, not for cash, but in return for exporting materials in ample supply in the United States.[60]

In retaliation, General Accounting Office critics quickly argued that other kinds of fertilizer could be substituted, that Occidental Petroleum was exporting far more jobs to the Soviet Union, where many times the numbers of workers involved in Florida would be needed to construct and operate the huge ammonia complex, and that by trading elsewhere the United States might have received hard currency or products more necessary than fertilizer. Eximbank's enthusiasm for trade, expanded credits, and joint Soviet-U.S. projects in general seems directly attributable to its own desire for self-preservation and increased importance. While the Soviet and East European dealings occupy only a small portion of Eximbank's time and capital resources, these dealings have given the bank much power and prestige in the policy-making process. Some opponents of Eximbank, like the General Accounting Office, have been angered by the increased leverage acquired by this bureaucratic rival.

One of the most striking aspects of these agency positions is the predominance of tunnel vision among protrade forces. All espouse the broad foreign policy goals of economic and political detente, and their statements are compatible with those of one another and of Secretary of State Kissinger to the extent that they focus on long-range policy goals. But, for the most part, the bureaucracies are concerned with perfecting and promoting their special functions and structures. Thus, it is one of the ironies of detente that it should have almost as many specific meanings as it has separate proponents. What Commerce, Treasury, State, Eximbank, and Agriculture have in common is their desire for the enhanced power and prestige that come with being influential players in the game of detente. Where they differ is in their specific perceptions of their roles in detente and the ways to implement their special responsibilities. For Agriculture, detente means high prices for U.S. grain sold to the USSR. For Treasury, it means a chance to reverse some of the dismal figures on the balance of payments, and for Commerce it means promotion of the interests of American businessmen in the Soviet Union and Eastern Europe.

Nongovernmental Proponents of Trade

Among nongovernmental players, corporations have been particularly eager to promote trade with the USSR. Perhaps the most visible corporate representatives have been Donald Kendall of Pepsico and Armand Hammer of Occidental Petroleum, both of whom have traveled to the USSR on numerous occasions to promote their Pepsi and vodka, ammonia and phosphate deals, and to develop good business relationships with the appropriate representatives of the Soviet Ministry of Foreign Trade and of selected foreign trade organizations. Like the government agencies, corporate proponents of trade are eager to gain influence in a policy-making process that directly affects their organizational well-being. E. Douglas Kenna, president of the National Association of Manufacturers, has stressed this point on a number of occasions. He suggests that any permanent organization to promote expanded trade and business opportunities between the United States and the Soviet Union should be established in the private sector because the private industrial and financial communities are most sensitive to problems peculiar to trade with nonmarket economies.[61]

Like the executive departments, U.S. corporations are careful to build a debater's affirmative case to support their goals and institutional interests. Corporations are particularly fond of the argument that the United States has much to gain from acquiring access to the technology of the USSR. Control Data representatives contend that the United States has much more to gain than to lose in the exchange of technical information with the Soviet Union. Control Data claims that the United States is providing only standard commercial technology of little value to the Soviet military establishment. Moreover, says Control Data, the United States will gain from any technology exchanges because of the exceptionally high quality of Soviet research. The argument is that the USSR has many more scientists and engineers than does the United States and that the better ones are concentrated in the theoretical fields of chemistry, physics, and mathematics—with their mathematical sophistication being particularly important to the development of computer technology. By sharing technology with the USSR, at the very least Americans would gain equal access to new developments and avoid the risk of being left behind in some crucial investigative areas. Finally, the Control Data argument notes that since most American technology exists in other Western nations, and since these nations are already engaged in active trade with the USSR, the United States can only be the loser if it is too stubborn about technology transfer.[62] Control Data summarizes its position as follows:

> A key element of Control Data's position with respect to business in the Soviet Union is the necessity to have technology flowback. Control Data is interested in long-term cooperative ventures involving a flow of technology to the United States. Our chief interests in technology flowback are in education and medicine.[63]

The argument that trade with the Soviet Union provides incentives for expansion in American domestic markets provides another edge of the corporate protrade sword. Interviews and letters from corporate officers received in response to questions about this argument confirmed the point that better profits and more jobs are viewed as key benefits of Soviet-U.S. trade. The Caterpillar Tractor Company claimed that its recent sales of $68 million of tractors, parts, and pipes resulted in significantly increased numbers of jobs in the United States.[64] The Bechtel Corporation seemed pleased with its negotiations concerning a number of industrial projects in the USSR. The company declined to give the total dollar value of these projects, but it certainly left the impression that profits and American jobs were its primary concerns.[65] The Textron Corporation claimed to have orders for about $70 million from Soviet markets. Textron's reason for enthusiasm about East-West trade was simply that "we expect the need for capital equipment in the Soviet Union and Eastern Europe will provide a good market for U.S. industrial companies for years to come."[66]

A third protrade argument used by corporations is that increased trade will promote detente and goodwill between the two superpowers. Donald Kendall of Pepsico has been one of the most enthusiastic supporters of this particular argument and has even been interviewed in Soviet news media because of his openly prodetente views.[67] A fourth argument is that Soviet-U.S. trade will provide the American market with needed raw materials. A letter from the president of the Instrument Systems Corporation states this argument succinctly: "Our policy is to work with various companies in the Soviet Union and Eastern Europe with a view toward selling them high technology products and technology in return for raw materials that are in short supply in the United States."[68]

Testimony of various groups representing manufacturers and corporations at the hearings on the Trade Reform Act of 1973 before the Senate Committee on Finance firmly established the primacy of these four arguments—profits, jobs, raw materials, and a generalized hope for detente—in the corporate quest for trade with the Soviet Union. The National Chamber of Commerce stated its belief that two-way beneficial trade on a long-term basis would be the cornerstone of continuing detente.[69] The East-West Trade Council, a nonprofit group claiming about 100 U.S. businesses as members, contended that potential American profits were going to the Canadians, West Germans, English, and French because of U.S. restrictions on exports to Communist countries. Profits would be higher only if Congress would support MFN and a high level of export credits financed by Eximbank.[70] The National Association of Manufacturers viewed the Trade Reform Act primarily in terms of potential protection guarantees to American jobs which depend on increased exports.[71] The East-West Trade Council also suggested that the technology of the West and the natural resources of the East made them obvious and compatible trade partners.[72]

Corporations view trade legislation with their own particular structural and procedural goals in mind. As a group, they prefer the structure of detente because it facilitates free sales of their products, healthy profits, and a relatively satisfactory labor market. Individually, they have profits and market stability for their own products preeminently in focus. They seek to influence domestic policy, international economic and political structures, and Soviet and U.S. domestic economic policies to the extent that these background factors can create a suitable working environment for the particular corporation. While they happened to coincide at times in 1974 and 1975, the detente supported by American corporations is not necessarily the detente upheld by the executive departments. As one critic has wisely noted, there may be an increasing need to distinguish between private corporate gains and national benefits.[73]

Governmental Opponents of Trade

Antitrade forces have also been active in the domestic policy-making process. Some middle-rank Department of Defense officials have been especially critical of programs which seem to transfer technology to the Soviet Union. Their criticism has even aroused comment in the Soviet press. A. Tolkunov, writing in *Pravda* on January 29, 1974, accused the Pentagon of trying to prevent the American businessman from engaging in trade with the Soviet Union. The article charged that officials from the Defense Department were warning American businessmen that they endangered national security by selling technological processes to the Soviets. While the official Defense Department policy has been one of support for expanded Soviet-U.S. trade, it is true that some American military officials have been particularly concerned that a ten-year agreement between Control Data and the Soviet government to develop computer technology might be a serious mistake.[74]

The General Accounting Office has been the most severe government critic of East-West trade. Between 1973 and 1975, the GAO engaged a special trade and finance group of its personnel in an exhaustive study of East-West trade. The stated purpose was to "evaluate the whole scope and range of U.S. functions in international trade," and the group's report was expected to be highly critical of what it sees as an unjustifiably liberal policy on trade with the Soviet Union. In contrast to the executive departments, and perhaps because of its own ties to Congress, the General Accounting Office views Congress as the foremost link in the East-West trade decision-making process. The GAO locates the center of power in the Senate Foreign Relations Committee, the House International Relations Committee, and the Appropriations committees of both houses. Within the executive branch, the GAO claims that the Central Intelligence Agency, the Council on International Economic Policy, the Office of the Special Representative for Trade Negotiations, the Office of Management and Budget, and the Export-Import Bank are most important. In contrast to most other government agencies, the GAO does not concede a major policy-making force to the Department of Commerce and the Department of State. GAO's unique view of the policy-making process derives in part from its numerous public battles with the Export-Import Bank over declaration of national interest provisions in credits given to the USSR.

Congressional opposition to the expansion of East-West trade has been even more prolonged and effective than that of the General Accounting Office. Congressional opposition to trade with the Soviet Union surfaced almost immediately after the signing of the trade agreement in October 1972. Under that agreement, President Nixon sought congressional action to reduce tariffs on Soviet products to the level generally applied to products from other countries under the most-favored-nation principle. Ironically, congressional opposition to trade with the Soviet Union is in some ways based on even greater hopes than those of the protrade groupings. Those in Congress who are willing to see a slow expansion of trade have generally favored the linkage of emigration and trade issues. The basic congressional sentiment seems to be that the United States should be willing to aid the Soviet Union in return for a less conflictive ideological and military relationship.[75] In 1973, Andrei Sakharov appealed to Congress in a powerful "open letter" to link trade to emigration.[76] That letter and other speeches and letters of dissident Soviet intellectuals have been a powerful impetus to congressional caution on trade.

Senator Henry Jackson has been an outspoken advocate of the linkage between trade and changes in Soviet domestic and foreign policy. While his statements that Jewish emigration must be linked to U. S. trade concessions are most familiar, he has been equally concerned that trade agreements should be linked to cuts in Soviet military spending. On many occasions, Jackson has suggested that increased trade with the USSR without linkage simply means greater support for the Soviet military-industrial complex.[77] Senator Adlai Stevenson has been another prominent commentator on trade legislation. He was chief sponsor of some 1974 amendments to trade legislation that would have greatly strengthened congressional authority over the granting of large Export-Import Bank loans.[78]

The arguments of administration and congressional opponents of expanded trade point again to the importance of institutional interests in the pluralist arena of foreign trade policy making. Defense Department analysts had good reason to fear that transfers of technology resulting in enhanced military power for the USSR would only make their own tasks more difficult. Congressmen and senators favored a trade policy that could be sold to constituents as an idealist course of action, one that could eventually lead to a liberalization of Soviet society and perhaps even to the liberal vision of convergence. Congressional eagerness for special linkage provisions could also be traced to the raging battle between the Nixon administration and Congress for control over foreign policy initiatives. Congress wanted to use the trade agreement as a tool for regaining authority in the making of foreign policy. The General Accounting Office, eager to assume a policy-making initiative in international affairs by asserting its role as a regulatory agency, was determined to use East-West trade as a test case.

Nongovernmental Opponents of Trade

Academic critics, mostly economists and political scientists, compose an additional part of the antitrade forces in the United States. They have advanced an impressive array of antitrade arguments. A first argument questions Soviet creditworthiness. Fears about the unreliability of the Soviets as trade partners have their origins in Soviet failures to fulfill the terms of U.S.-backed credit agreements in the 1920s and 1930s.[79] Creditworthiness questions were revived recently on the basis of calculations about the Soviet foreign debt made by Michael Kaser, a prominent British economist. He projected that if Soviet demands for Western credits were met, the Soviet Union would have a foreign debt of approximately $29 billion by 1980 and that interest payments alone would absorb from 25 to 50 percent of the Soviet Union's export earnings by that time.[80]   Actually, Kaser has revised these estimates on the basis of new information about Soviet gold reserves. Kaser now points out that the Soviet balance-of-payments situation has shown dramatic improvement in the last few years. The increase in the price of gold, plus increases in Soviet prices for oil and raw materials, account for most of the improvement. As proof of the new ability to pay, Kaser points to the readiness of Soviet negotiators to provide cash for equipment purchases from West German firms for a metallurgical complex to be built at Kursk. Kaser now estimates that there will be substantial availability of gold reserves and relatively small trade deficit in the 1976-80 period.[81]

For these and other reasons, the argument about Soviet creditworthiness has shifted ground. It is generally conceded that the Soviet Union's economic capabilities have been enhanced by recent increases in the price of oil and raw materials. The Soviet Union appears to be benefiting from inflation in the West and may in fact be helping along the inflationary process. Between 1970 and 1974, the USSR exported about 40 million tons of crude oil annually to Western Europe, and the trebling and quadrupling of oil prices meant that the USSR earned between $2 and $3 billion from this trade in 1974 and 1975, as against the 1973 total earnings of $850 million.[82]

Still, according to many of those concerned with the issue, Soviet creditworthiness is not established just because of increasing raw materials prices. They point out correctly that we still have no precise information about the Soviet balance-of-payment situation or about Soviet willingness to use gold reserves to pay for Western plants and technology.[83]   It all boils down to the sticky issue of equating creditworthiness with ability to pay, when in fact it is always dependent on willingness to pay as well. It is true that the Soviet Union is primarily interested in receiving long-term loans, while its own credit transactions on Western money markets are limited to short-term lending.[84] Yet, Soviet foreign trade organizations have an excellent record for paying on time, and many Western bankers regard the Soviet Union as an underborrowed country.[85]   For the opponents of expanded trade with the Soviet Union the argument is that in the past, when political conditions seemed to warrant it, the Soviet Union refused to honor financial commitments. Trade opponents point out that no measures of gold reserves, increased earnings, and lessened debt-servicing obligation can adequately predict Soviet willingness to continue to participate in Western trade commitments. A closely related matter of concern is that before 1972 and 1973, most Western transactions with the Soviet Union were virtually devoid of exchange risks because of the extensive use of major Western currencies in such transactions and the very short-term nature of the deals. Current transactions with the Soviet Union are conducted on a very different scale, with development projects most prominent, and credits rather than cash payments providing the major financing mechanism.[86]

A second issue often raised by academic critics of trade with the Soviet Union concerns the transfer of technology. There is little agreement here except that the issue is important and that Americans need to ponder the potential uses of technology they sell or license to the Soviet Union. Brzezinski has contended that "the fact of the matter is that the economic relationship today amounts to nothing less than a fairly sizable American transfer of technology to the Soviet Union." He argues that this aid makes it possible for the Soviet Union to sustain a highly centralized and conservative economic system.[87] Others claim that economic assitance from the West will not only increase Soviet economic strength, but could also enable the Soviet government to engage in military spending on a scale that would otherwise by impossible.

There is a whole series of arguments, assumptions, and fears involved in the issue of technology transfer:

- the assumption that Soviet technology lags behind Western technology
- the assumption that U.S. technology would be useful to the Soviet economy
- the argument that any major transfer of technology would enhance Soviet military capability
- the argument that whatever the United States refuses to sell or license will be provided by the West Europeans or the Japanese
- the fear that U.S. technology will be purchased in unpredictable and changing amounts, disrupting the U.S. domestic economy yet failing to provide a stable sales market for U.S. technology
- the fear that the U.S. government lacks effective controls over sales of technology carried out by American corporations

There is a little disagreement over the validity of the first assumption, that Soviet technology lags behind U.S. technology. In Soviet industry in 1971, 45 percent of workers operated equipment manually, and in engineering industries the percentage was as high as 55 percent.[88] According to most authorities, Soviet lags in technology have resulted from Soviet isolation from international scientific work. Yet in some specific areas, Soviet technology is superior to U.S. technology. In selected steel-making procedures, in the construction of large-scale turbines, and in production of some machine tools, Soviet research and development work is very impressive. But even in these areas, the more significant the components of high technology, the less successful are the products that have resulted from Soviet research. Of course, the Soviet Union has been singularly successful in mission-oriented technology, such as military and space technology.[89] Yet, in overall terms, Soviet growth rates have lagged, expenditures for research and development are not impressive, and Soviet industrial goods are sold by necessity at lower than standard prices on the international market.

It is often assumed that U.S. technology would be very useful to the Soviet economy. Both proponents and opponents of increased trade see the Soviets gaining needed technological expertise in computers, electronics, chemicals, and truck building from the United States. Representatives of Control Data have suggested that by spending $3 million for 3 years for Control Data equipment, the Soviet Union could gain about 15 years of research and development work.[90] Representatives of Texas Instruments are equally convinced that great Soviet gains would result from technology transfer on a large scale, but in contrast to Control Data representatives, they worry about the self-defeating nature of "naked technology sales" to the USSR.[91] Others contend that only reform of internal institutions and policies will really facilitate Soviet technological process. Joseph Berliner argues that even projects which import whole manufacturing enterprises (like the Fiat plant at Togliatti and the KAMAZ project) tend to lag behind the most advanced technology still in the development stages in the West. In the case of ordinary product purchases, the problem for Soviet end-users in even more acute, for in most instances the manufacturing technology is not revealed simply through examination of the product purchased from the West. Only licenses for production processes achieve this end, and so far licensing agreements have been quite strictly controlled.[92]

Soviet management practices, frequently the targets of unkind remarks in the Soviet press, present other barriers to technological progress. A typical story appeared in 1974, when *Pravda* published "How Tons Defeated Meters." A method had been devised to make water pipes and gas pipes out of thinner than usual metal, potentially saving tons of steel and millions of rubles. The new pipes were accepted by technical inspectors. However, their use meant smaller tonnage, and plan indicators were in tons. Any manager who used the new, more efficient system was penalized.[93] The influential economic publication *Ekonomicheskaya gazeta* has repeatedly urged that industrial plan fulfillment guidelines be revised and that industrial organization by streamlined.[94] Richard Judy has written about management problems in the transfer of innovation in the computer industry. Lack of competent personnel and an incentive system that discourage taking risks encourage the production of standard rather than innovative equipment.[95] Raymond Vernon suggests that another problem may be that while the best of Soviet scientists can match the best of any country, the supply of middle-level talent is very limited.[96] These Soviet managment problems make it difficult for Soviet industry to apply new innovations purchased or licensed from the West.

A third argument in the transfer-of-technology debate is that any major transfer would have as its end result an enhanced Soviet military capacity. Holzman raises some interesting criticisms of this approach. He reminds us that "necessity is the mother of invention" and that rapid development of Soviet aluminum capacity, for example, could be traced to the post-World War II embargo policy of the United States. The embargo on natural rubber shipments to the USSR led to the rapid development of Soviet domestic production of synthetic rubber.[97] The embargo on U.S. titanium exports to the USSR produced similar results. By 1961, the Soviets were producing such large amounts of titanium themselves that they were able to export it to the United States at very low prices.[98] An industrial diamond embargo imposed by the United States had similar results. The industrial diamond embargo contributed to a research effort in which an electric arcing device was developed and used as a substitute for diamonds, and to a prospecting effort which resulted in the discovery of vast diamond resources in eastern Siberia.[99] Others argue that a sharp separation between military and civilian sectors in the USSR means that even vast computer and industrial process systems adapted to the civilian economy are unlikely to find a use in military sectors. Planning procedures which divide the two sectors are said to prevent rapid diffusion of technology across sectors.

A fourth transfer-of-technology argument is that whatever technology the Americans refuse to give the Soviet Union will be sold by the West Europeans and the Japanese. The willingness of the West Europeans and the Japanese to sell is really not a question; they have demonstrated that on many occasions already. The Soviets have also indicated their own willingness to deal much more widely with the West Europeans and the Japanese if the Americans continue to deny credits and to impose strict export controls.[100] The real question is whether the Soviets gain as much as they might from West European technology rather than U.S. technology. The answer seems to be that it depends entirely on the technology at stake. One recent study indicates that there is no longer a significant difference between the United States and the West European countries in the development of nuclear power technology. Although European nations initially depended heavily on U.S. nuclear technology gained through licensing agreements with firms such as General Electric and Westinghouse, these countries have begun to produce important innovations of their own. The United States and Western Europe are said to be equal in the field of metallurgy. In steel manufacturing, Western Europe and Japan are ahead of the United States, and in chemicals, Europe has long occupied a leading position.[101] West European industries have become very advanced in developing synthetic substitutes of all kinds. Just recently, speakers at a meeting of the National Academy of Engineering claimed that the U.S. technological challenge was now muted and that because of "passive" government attitudes and "chaotic" government regulations, the United States would continue to falter in the development of nonmilitary industrial technologies.[102] In testimony before a congressional subcommittee, former CIA director William Colby pointed to an increased reliance by the Soviet Union on West German, French, and Japanese technology and indicated that the USSR would not be significantly harmed by increased trade with Western Europe if the United

States were to become even less generous in the licensing of high-technology exports.[103]

The Europeans do face some handicaps which indicate they cannot fully replace U.S. sources of high-technology products. Raymond Vernon and Marshall Goldman isolate two key forces which have acted to limit somewhat European advances in high-technology fields. First, European government needs for sophisticated aircraft and nuclear reactors have been relatively small in comparison to demand stimulated by U.S. government needs. Second, the tendency of European national governments to buy high-technology products principally from national contractors has fractionated the market and weakened Europe's industrial base.[104]

The fifth element is the fear that purchases of U.S. technology are merely a temporary move on the part of the USSR and that purchases could be cut off at any time with potentially disruptive effects for the U.S. economy. There is much past experience on which to base this concern. The Soviet Union has periodically encouraged the import of selected forms of Western technology, only to revert suddenly to policies of industrial autarky when domestic conditions improved. In the 1920s and 1930s, the Soviets used imports from firms like DuPont, Ford, and General Electric to catch up with Western methods of producing tractors, chemicals, and radios. In the 1950s, the Soviets were especially interested in Western technology for the production of fertilizers and synthetic fibers. These interests did not prove to be sustainable over a long period of time.[105] The fickleness of Soviet interest in economic relations with the West was demonstrated again by short-term import requirements for diesel engines in the 1959-65 Seven-Year Plan. The locomotives were imported from France, but French hopes for the development of a long-term export market were not realized. Many fear that the current Soviet import demands for large-diameter pipes, chemicals, and machine-building equipment will follow the same short-term patterns.[106]

The sixth element is concern that little is being done by the U.S. government to make certain that corporate sales reflect broader national interests as well. Betsy Ancker-Johnson, assistant secretary of commerce for science and technology, argues that the corporate transfer of American technology to the Soviet Union is still largely uncontrolled and that there is no real guarantee of a correlation between business and national interests in the sale of sophisticated products to the Soviet Union.[107] Very often even corporate interests are not fully protected in sales or licensing of high-technology products to the USSR. Part of the problem stems from the USSR's failure to participate fully in international patent agreements.[108]

A third broad concern of many academic critics is the lack of corporate inspection control and the inability of participant corporations to gain complete access to U.S.-financed projects within the USSR. Some foresee a possibility that under different political conditions, U.S. investments might be nationalized. Support for these fears has been indirectly offered by statements of Valentin D. Shashin, the Soviet minister for the oil industry. They have caused some Western observers to wonder if the Soviet Union is vacillating on its invitation to Westerners to aid in the development of Soviet oil resources. Shashin sometimes complains that the price for foreign assistance in exploitation of oil reserves is depletion of Soviet resources and hard currency lost for the Soviet Union in the future. In fact, ultimate independence has always been stressed as a goal of Soviet industrial policy, and the recent Soviet moves on oil emphasize the shaky basis of all joint development ventures contemplated by the United States. Yves Laulan, director of economic affairs for NATO, has warned that there could be a major reversal of the Soviet policy inviting Western participation in exploitation of several Soviet natural resources.

A fourth major antitrade argument is that Export-Import Bank loans to the Soviet Union represent a drain on the American taxpayer, who is being asked to support the industrial development of the Soviet Union. At least until the spring of 1974, when Eximbank interest rates were raised, the difference between Eximbank's 6 percent interest rate and the commercial rates of 10 to 12 percent had to be viewed as a disadvantage to the American taxpayer.[109] Actually, since 1972, Eximbank itself has been borrowing at a minimum rate of 7.02 percent and relending the money to the Soviet Union at 6 and 7 percent, representing a net loss for the Export-Import Bank. Even in the spring of 1974, when the Eximbank lending rate had officially been raised to 7 percent, the bank was still lending at 6 percent because all of the Soviet-U.S. deals pending had been in the preliminary stages of negotiation when the 6 percent rate was still in effect.

The claim that Eximbank is providing development assistance to the Soviet Union is also easily supportable. Most credits granted to the Soviet Union have been made under a 20-year repayment plan, with initial repayment often scheduled to begin five to ten years after the signing of an agreement. If one visualizes a five-to-seven-year period as the upper limit of foreign lending rather than foreign aid, the United States is a major investor in Soviet economic development. While this policy may have its political merits, its detractors are concerned with the economic losses the United States is asked to sustain.

Finally, critics of increased trade have said there is no reason to believe, as proponents of expanded trade have often suggested, that trade and peace are causally related. For example, trade between the Soviet Union and Nazi Germany reached a high point just before Hitler's invasion of the Soviet Union.[110] Nor does increased Soviet-U.S. trade appear to have much correlation with liberalization of Soviet society. While the commercial accord signed in Moscow between the United States and the Soviet Union in July 1935 provided for major tariff concessions on the part of the U.S. government, the subsequent few years of expanded trade between the United States and the Soviet Union were years of the harshest Stalinist tyranny and mass murder. As one commentator noted, "Trade increased and the Moscow trials flourished." The suggestion that increased trade might enable the Soviets to relax their emphasis on military and heavy industrial development to focus on consumer goods seems invalidated by the fact that the trade liberalization of the 1930s only resulted in greater investment in heavy industry than had ever been possible before.[111]

As these conflicting arguments and diverse decision-making centers demonstrate, there is no coherent national policy on the issue of Soviet-U.S. trade. The policy-making process itself is ill defined, with executive departments and congressional committees, Eximbank and the GAO, all fighting interorganizational battles. There is a confusion over the proper location of policy formulation responsibilities and over the proper balance between regulation of trade with the USSR and promotion of that trade. There are two broadly defined contending groups, pro- and antitrade, but both lack cohesiveness of argument.

If one key purpose of Soviet-U.S. trade is to provide a structural basis for more regularized Soviet involvement in an increasingly complicated and interdependent world economic structure, then a more coherent U.S. trade position becomes essential. So far, the process has been chaotic rather than coherent, and one can expect U.S. attempts to deal unilaterally with the USSR on trade to be marked by failure and hesitation until a firmer national policy emerges. The danger, of course, is that the policy will lean too far in the direction of either increasing trade or inhibiting trade, but national planning on trade would at least provide a starting point for a more reasoned debate. The East-West Trade Policy Committee could assume a major role in formalizing and implementing new policy guidelines and in providing a more structured backdrop for the debates of competing domestic pro- and antitrade groups.

NOTES

1. John H. Huhs, "Developing Trade with the Soviet Union," *The Columbia Journal of World Business* 8, no. 3 (Fall 1973): 116-30.

2. New York *Times,* April 10, 1975.

3. Business International, *Eastern Europe Report*, April 18, 1975, p. 109.

4. U.S. Congress, Joint Economic Committee, *Hearings, Allocation of Resources in the Soviet Union and China,* 93rd Cong., 2d Sess., 1974, p. 24. Hereafter cited as *Hearings, Allocation of Resources.*

5. For a discussion of this problem in the making of U.S. foreign policy, see Stephen S. Rosenfeld, "Pluralism and Policy," *Foreign Affairs* 52, no. 2 (January 1974): 267. In the instance of Soviet foreign policy, see Wolfgang Leonhard, "The Domestic Politics of the New Soviet Foreign Policy," *Foreign Affairs* 52, no. 1 (October 1973): 59-74.

6. *Pravda*, January 2, 1975, December 23, 1974.

7. Radio Free Europe, *Background Report, Eastern Europe*, no. 5 (January 17, 1975), p. 2.

8. F. Stephen Larrabee, "Detente and U.S.-Soviet Relations: The View from Moscow," *Radio Liberty Research*, March 7, 1975, p. 1.

9. A. Mil'shtein, "Progress in the Main Direction," *SShA: Ekonomika, politika, ideologiya*, no. 2 (1975), pp. 3-11.

10. Business International, *Eastern Europe Report*, May 16, 1975, p. 134.

11. New York *Times*, October 8, 1974.

12. *Wall Street Journal*, October 21, 1974.

13. *Industry Week*, February 3, 1975, p. 20.

14. Zbigniew Brzezinski, "U.S.-Soviet Relations," in *The Next Phase in Foreign Policy*, ed. Henry Owen (Washington, D.C.: Brookings Institution, 1973), pp. 113-32.

15. Samuel Pisar, *Coexistence and Commerce* (New York: McGraw-Hill, 1972), pp. 75-76.

16. Business International, *Doing Business with the USSR* (Geneva: Business International, 1971), pp. 8-9.

17. M. Pervukhin, "The U.S.S.R.'s Energy Resources and Their Rational Utilization," *Planovoye khozyaistvo*, no. 7 (July 1974), pp. 14-21: V. Popkov, *Pravda*, October 9, 1974, p. 4.

18. Chase World Information Corporation, letter of March 5, 1974. See also Chase World Information Corporation, *KAMAZ: The Billion Dollar Beginning* (New York: 1974); New York *Times*, September 9, 1974.

19. *International Herald Tribune*, June 29, 1974.

20. New York *Times*, March 20, 1974, May 28, 1974.

21. *International Herald Tribune*, June 28, 1974.

22. New York *Times*, May 28, 1974.

23. Ibid., December 4, 1973.

24. Ibid., May 28, 1974.

25. Ibid., December 14, 1974.

26. Ibid., November 12, 1974.

27. Kurt Weisskopf, "Roll Out the Red Barrel," *Commerce International* 104, no. 1410 (October 1973): 47.

28. For a complete discussion of the oil situation in the USSR, see Yves Laulan, ed., *Round Table: Exploitation of Siberia's Natural Resources* (Brussels: NATO Economic Directorate, 1974).

29. New York *Times*, April 20, 1974; London *Times*, June 5, 1974, June 7, 1974.

30. *Wall Street Journal*, April 25, 1975.

31. G. Samborsky and V. Simchera, "The Way to Improve the Efficiency of Computer Technology," *Voprosy ekonomiki*, no. 7 (1974), pp. 78-89.

32. Richard W. Judy, "The Case of Computer Technology," in *East-West Trade and the Technology Gap: A Political and Economic Approach*, ed. Stanislaw Wasowski (New York: Praeger, 1970), pp. 43-72. Figures on numbers of computers come from *Technology Review* 72 (February 1970): 68-69; and John Picard Stein, "Estimating the Market for Computers in the Soviet Union and Eastern Europe," Rand Corporation, R-1406-CIEP/ ARPA, May 1974, p. 6.

33. New York *Times*, March 14, 1974.

34. Business International, *Eastern Europe Report*, October 4, 1974, pp. 305-06.

35. London *Times*, June 7, 1974.

36. Chase Manhattan, *East West Markets*, May 20, 1974, p. 6.

37. James C. DeHaven, "Technology Exchange: Import Possibilities from the USSR," Rand Corporation, R-1414-ARPA (April 1974), p. 34.

38. *Business Week*, special advertising section, May 18, 1974.

39. Josef C. Brada and Arthur E. King, "The Soviet-American Trade Agreement: Prospects for the Soviet Economy," *The Russian Review,* October 1973, pp. 346–47. See also Walter Krause and F. John Mathis, "The U.S. Policy Shift on East-West Trade." *Journal of International Affairs* 28, no. 1 (1974): 36; Pisar, op. cit., pp. 107-09.

40. Franklyn D. Holzman, *Foreign Trade Under Central Planning* (Cambridge, Mass.: Harvard University Press, 1974), pp. 204-05.

41. Ibid., p. 207. See also Josef Wilczynski, *The Economics and Politics of East-West Trade* (New York: Praeger, 1969), chap. 10.

42. Paul Marer and Egon Neuberger, "Commercial Relations Between the United States and Eastern Europe: Options and Prospects," in U.S. Congress, Joint Economic Committee, *Reorientation and Commercial Relations of the Economies of Eastern Europe*, 93rd Cong., 2d Sess., August 16, 1974, p. 559.

43. Statement of Lewis W. Bowden, deputy assistant secretary for East-West trade (acting), U.S. Department of Commerce, *Report Submitted to the Subcommittee on Europe of the House Committee on Foreign Affairs* (mimeographed), June 26, 1974.

44. John P. Hardt and George D. Holliday, *U.S.-Soviet Commercial Relations: The Interplay of Economics, Technology Transfer, and Diplomacy* (Washington, D.C.: Government Printing Office, June 10, 1973), p. 50.

45. U.S. Department of State, publication 8765, *The Battle Act Report of 1973: Mutual Defense Assistance Control Act of 1951* (Washington, D.C.: Government Printing Office, June 1974), p. 11.

46. John P. Hardt, George D. Holliday, and Young C. Kim, *Western Investment in Communist Economics* (Washington, D.C.: Government Printing Office, 1974), pp. 17-18.

47. Ibid., pp. 6-7.

48. U.S. Department of Commerce, news release, press conference by Secretary Peterson and Secretary Butz on the Soviet grain purchase (Washington, D.C., July 13, 1972).

49. Peter Parsons, "Recent Developments in East-West Trade: The U.S. Perspective," *Law and Contemporary Problems* (Summer-Autumn 1972): 551-52.

50. Richard M. Nixon, speeches of February 18, 1970 and February 9, 1972.

51. See A.L. Williams, *U.S. International Economic Policy in an Interdependent World* (Washington, D.C.: U.S. Government Printing Office, July 1971). vol. I. p. 10.

52. Peter G. Peterson, *A Foreign Economic Perspective* (Washington, D.C.: Government Printing Office, December 1971), p. 28.

53. Bonnie M. Pounds and Mona F. Levine, "Legislative, Institutional, and Negotiating Aspects of United States-East European Trade and Economic Relations." in U.S. Congress, Joint Economic Committee, op. cit., pp. 543-44.

54. Much of the information on the policy-making process was received from a series of interviews in Washington in March 1975. I spoke to representatives of the Council on International Economic Policy, the Office of the Special Representative for Trade Negotiations, the East-West Trade Policy Committee, the Bureau of East-West Trade in the Department of Commerce, the Offices of East European Affairs, Soviet Union Affairs, and East-West Trade in the Department of State, the Export-Import Bank, and the General Accounting Office.

55. Statement of Steven Lazarus, deputy assistant secretary for East-West trade, Department of Commerce, U.S. Congress, Joint Economic Committee, *Hearings, Soviet Economic Outlook,* 93rd Cong., 1st Sess., July 17, 18, 19, 1973, p. 117. Hereafter cited as *Hearings, Soviet Economic Outlook.*

56. U.S. Department of Commerce, *An Introduction to the Bureau of East-West Trade* (Washington, D.C.: Government Printing Office, 1974).

57. Export-Import Bank of the United States, *Report to the U.S. Congress on Export Credit Competition and the Export-Import Bank of the United States* (Washington, D.C.: Government Printing Office, Febuary 1975).

58. Statement of William J. Casey, chairman and president, Export-Import Bank of the United States, (mimeographed press release), February 27, 1975.

59. New York *Times*, March 12, 1974.

60. News release, Export-Import Bank, May 21, 1974.

61. E. Douglas Kenna, *Hearings, Soviet Economic Outlook*, p. 19.

62. William G. Norris, chairman of the board, Control Data Corporation, letter to the editor, New York *Times*, November 30, 1974.

63. Letter from Hugh Henig, vice president for USSR and East European relations, Control Data Corporation, Minneapolis, Minn., March 18, 1974.

64. Letter from James I. Fender, public information manager, Caterpillar Tractor Company, Peoria, Ill., March 15, 1974.

65. Letter from Arnold Khavkine, Commercial Development Department, Bechtel Corporation, San Francisco, Calif., March 19, 1974.

66. Letter from Eric W. Danneman, Investor Relations, Textron, Providence, R.I., March 1974.

67. A. Yevseyev, "Key to Success," *Izvestia*, June 7, 1974, p. 3.

68. Letter from Edward J. Garnett, president, Instrument Systems Corporation, Jericho, N.Y., March 21, 1974.

69. U.S. Congress, Senate, Committee on Finance, *Hearings on H.R. 10710, The Trade Reform Act of 1973*, III, 93rd Cong., 2d Sess., 1974, pp. 761-62.

70. Ibid., pp. 932-33.

71. Ibid., pp. 750-51.

72. Ibid. p. 933.

73. Gregory Grossman, "Prospects and Policy for U.S.-Soviet Trade," *American Economic Review* 64, no. 2 (May 1974): 292.

74. New York *Times*, January 30, 1974.

75. For a discussion of the difficulties of this position, see William R. Kintner, "The United States and the USSR: Conflicts and Cooperation," *Orbis* 17, no. 3 (Fall 1973): 691-719.

76. Andrei Sakharov, "Open Letter to the Congress of the United States," New York *Times*, September 14, 1973.

77. New York *Times*, July 15, 1974.

78. *International Herald Tribune,* June 19, 1974.

79. Marshall I. Goldman, "Who Profits Most from U.S.-Soviet Trade?" *Harvard Business Review* 51, no. 6 (November - December 1973): 86.

80. New York *Times,* October 1, 1973.

81. Michael Kaser, "The Soviet Balance of Payments." *International Currency Review* 6, no. 3 (May-June 1974): 60.

82. London *Times*, June 6, 1974.

83. Chase Manhatten, *EastWest Markets,* May 20, 1974, p. 2.

84. See editorial in *International Currency Review* 3, no. 5 (November- December 1971): 3-4.

85. Philip Hanson, "How Much Can Russia Borrow?" *The Banker* (London) 123, no. 574 (December 1973): 1479-84.

86. Gunter Dufey, "Financing East-West Business," *The Columbia Journal of World Business* 9, no. 1 (Spring 1974): 37-41.

87. New York *Times,* August 7, 1974.

88. *Voprosy edonomiki*, no. 2 (1971), p. 81.

89. Joseph S. Berliner, "Some International Aspects of Soviet Technological Progress," *South Atlantic Quarterly* 72, no. 3 (1973): 340-41; 348-49.

90. Robert Conquest et al., "Detente: An Evaluation," *Survey* 20, no. 213 (Spring-Summer 1974): 13.

91. *Research Management* 18, no. 1 (January 1975): 4.

92. Berliner, op. cit., pp. 343-44.

93. *Pravda*, August 22, 1974.

94. See especially D. Zhimerin, "Technical Progress and the Improvement of Management," *Ekonomicheskaya gazeta*, no. 27 (July 1974), p. 10.

95. Judy, op. cit., pp. 43-72.

96. Raymond Vernon, "Apparatchiks and Entrepeneurs: U.S.-Soviet Economic Relations," *Foreign Affairs* 52, no. 2 (January 1974): 254.

97. Holzman, op. cit., p. 197.

98. Raymond Vernon and Marshall Goldman, "U.S. Policies in the Sale of Technology to the USSR," mimeographed (September 15, 1974), p. 17.

99. Franklyn D. Holzman, "East-West Trade and Investment Policy Issues: Past and Future," in U.S. Congress Joint Economic Committee, *Soviet Economic Prospects for the Seventies* (Washington, D.C.: U.S. Government Printing Office, 1973) p. 664.

100. N. Patolichev, "Prospects for Trade with the U.S.A.," *SSHA–Ekonomika, politika, ideoligiya,* no. 5 (May 1974), pp. 76-79.

101. Robert C. Houser, Jr., and Steven I. Frahm, "Technology, Trade, and the Law: A Preliminary Exploration," *Law and Policy in International Business* 6, no. 1 (1974): 90.

102. New York *Times*, April 27, 1975.

103. William Colby, in *Hearings, Allocation of Resources,* pp. 22-23.

104. Vernon and Goldman, op. cit., pp. 37-38.

105. Vernon, op. cit., p. 253.

106. Hardt and Holliday, op. cit., p. 43.

107. New York *Times*, June 27, 1975.

108. *Research Management* 17, no. 1 (January 1974): 3.

109. New York *Times.* December 20, 1973.

110. Martin and Dina Spechlet, "The Human Cost of Soviet Trade," *Worldview*, November 1973, p. 39.

111. Joseph Clark, "Detente–Shadow or Substance?" *Dissent* 21, no. 3 (Summer 1974): 443-46.

3

CHANGING SOVIET
PERSPECTIVES
ON TRADE WITH
THE UNITED STATES

LAGGING GROWTH RATES AND HISTORICAL DEVELOPMENT OF TRADE TIES WITH THE UNITED STATES

The wide-ranging policy of industrial modernization implemented under Khrushchev first opened up the possibility of sustained economic relationships with the West for the Soviet Union. Under Stalin, the coal-based economy was largely self-sufficient, and production increases rather than innovations were the hallmarks of Soviet economic development. While the Stalinist guidelines permitted occasional purchases of heavy industrial equipment from abroad and utilization of Western expertise in selected factories within the USSR, it was under Khrushchev that long-term possibilities for Western industrial nations to aid in meeting the technological and industrial targets of Soviet economic planning first emerged.

The Brezhnev and Kosygin years have been marked by an even more comprehensive interest in trade with the West. It is often suggested that lagging industrial growth rates and declines in labor productivity increases are behind the current Brezhnev drive for economic detente with the United States. Infusions of U.S. technology are seen as the most expedient way for the Soviets to solve their economic problems without instituting fundamental changes in their economic planning apparatus. Soviet economic planners have long expressed concern because of significant declines in the Soviet Union's average annual economic growth rate. The official Soviet data show increases in the Soviet GNP at rates of 10.9 percent for 1950-58, 5.3 percent for 1958-67, and 3.7 percent for 1967-73.[1] Western recalculations put the figures at 6.4 percent, 5.3 percent, and 3.7 percent respectively. In addition, according to studies by Abram Bergson, there has been a steady decline in the rate of growth of factor productivity.[2] Other studies have found that despite a volume of capital investment per worker which nearly equals that of the United States, labor

47

productivity in Soviet industry is only about half the U.S. level. Farm labor is only about 10 percent as productive in the Soviet Union as it is in the United States.[3] The net result, according to some Western students, is that the USSR still lags behind the United States by 15 to 25 years in overall levels of technology and of industrial growth.[4]

Closely related to problems of lagging industrial growth and productivity rates is the problem of serious faults in the Soviet research and development process. In the Soviet Union, a long-standing tradition of separating research and development units from production enterprises has meant that research and production usually develop independently and that there are serious time lags between discoveries of innovations and their implementation in the production process. This situation was given some attention in the economic reform period of 1964-65, when special enterprise funds were designated for innovation and experimentation. The disappointing results of this change eventually led in 1973 to the grouping of enterprises into industrial associations which were to have the advantage of greater amounts of capital to finance likely-looking innovations.[5] Still, there have been problems because the results of innovative research and development work tend not to get beyond a narrow circle of organizations. In 1968, the All-Union Scientific and Technical Information Center was set up under the State Committee for Science and Technology. It gathers information on research performed in all industrial branches and disseminates it on an interbranch basis. Much coordination work remains, because under the present system individual branch information services evaluate innovations created by their enterprises and publish information for the use of the All-Union Scientific and Technical Information Center and subsequently for other branches. The process is time-consuming and often ineffective in spreading information.[6]

It is clear that Soviet economic dreams have not materialized. One Western expert claims that the gap between Soviet and Western products in areas of advanced technology is actually widening—much to the detriment of the Soviet Union. Moreover, Soviet economic performance now puts it at the bottom of the so-called middle growth league comprising nations like the United States, the Federal Republic of Germany, France, and Italy. During the 1950s, the Soviet economy had remained among the leaders of the group; in the 1960s, it fell to a middle position, and by 1974, it had fallen to last place.[7] In 1974, the Soviet Union did report some improved conditions in industrial growth in the first three quarters. The actual annual industrial growth rate of 8.2 percent was well above the planned growth rate for 1974. Labor productivity was also up an encouraging 6.7 percent.[8]

However, in a major economic statement in December 1974, Nikolai Baibakov, a deputy premier and head of the State Planning Committee of the USSR Council of Ministers (Gosplan), conceded that the 1971-75 Five-Year Plan results were not bringing long-promised gains for consumers or for high-technology industries. The plan directives issued at the Twenty-Fourth Soviet party congress in March-April 1971 had called for many advances in technology and consumer welfare. Technological change was expected to modernize the Soviet civilian economy, increase consumers' real income, and raise the efficiency of economic planning and management. By the end of 1974, there were open admissions in the Soviet media that meeting these goals had not been possible. Baibakov said the mediocre economic showing was a result of continuing problems of poor management, lagging productivity, incomplete use of industrial capacities and resources, and failure to complete new facilities in time.

The new Five-Year Plan for 1976-80 was directed to increasing overall production by 6.7 percent each year, with particular emphasis to be given to the oil and petrochemical industries and to machine building. Baibakov stressed the decision by economic planners to swing back to heavy industry. He reported that the production goal for heavy industry in 1975 would be a 7 percent increase over 1974, whereas in light industry (including the consumer sector), the goal was a more modest 6 percent increase.[9] An updated report on the 1976-80 Five-Year Plan, appearing in *Pravda* on June 11, 1975, again noted that a principal target of the new plan would be "a greater supply of fuel to the peoples' economy by means of an increase in production and all possible economies in the use of fuels."

Planning debates throughout the spring and summer of 1975 seemed crucial in determining the probable future thrust of Soviet development plans. For the first time, Soviet planners not only were concerned with the immediate five-year planning period, but were also making comprehensive projections and setting specific guidelines for the next 15 years.[10] They were establishing principles of development that were to guide the thinking of planners up to the end of the century. They were faced with fundamental decisions concerning the extent of permissible industrial cooperation with the West as opposed to increased reliance on COMECON. While the planners agreed that economic priorities should be in industrial sectors rather than in consumer and agricultural sectors, there was continuing disagreement on many specific issues. The ways in which these issues are resolved will do just as much to influence the patterns of Soviet trade with the United States as will any changes in U.S. trade legislation.

SOME UNRESOLVED PLANNING DISPUTES AND THEIR IMPACT ON SOVIET TRADE WITH THE UNITED STATES

A first planning dispute whose outcome will affect future patterns of Soviet trade with the United States is the continuing disagreement between Leonid Brezhnev and Aleksei Kosygin. Brezhnev, seeing increased trade as an essential adjunct to his policy of detente and as a way of improving the efficiency of Soviet industry without fundamental and politically dangerous economic reforms, has consistently been the most protrade of Soviet leaders. In a major speech reprinted in *Pravda* on October 16, 1974, Brezhnev spoke repeatedly of the need for greater "efficiencies of production" and suggested that Western sources would be needed for years to come in the computer and management technique areas. Brezhnev has also emphasized that the logical pattern of trade in the current world circumstances is one exchanging Soviet raw materials for Western industrial technology. Kosygin, apparently favoring a more restrained expansion of East-West trade, actually attacked Brezhnev's position on increased trade with the West in a major speech at Frunze on the fiftieth anniversary of the Kirghiz SSR. In contrast to Brezhnev's emphasis on "efficiencies of production" through technical assistance from the West, Kosygin said there was a need for greater expansion of production facilities and for changes in domestic Soviet management practices.[11]

Kosygin, who has consistently defended the economic reformers in the Soviet Union since 1965, must see increased technical assistance from the West as a way of postponing badly needed changes in planning and management in the USSR. Yet, as Franklyn Holzman and Robert Legvold note, Kosygin faces pressure as well from institutions like the powerful State Committee on Science and Technology, which is eager to secure technological information and assistance from IBM, Control Data, and Univac.[12] At the moment, Brezhnev's position is the one with more influence, but Kosygin represents a multiplicity of forces and organizations that are hesitant to substitute Western management and technological assistance for genuine economic reforms within the Soviet Union.

Another internal Soviet dispute with important implications for Soviet-U.S. trade centers around the use of computers in economic planning. Centralizers favor importing as much large-scale Western technology as possible in order to develop a complete, centrally directed, computer-based process of national planning. Decentralizers favor importing computer technology on a much smaller scale and stress the dual needs for regional flexibility in planning and for indigenous Soviet research and development work in the computer field. The current round in this dispute was initiated in September 1973, when Nikolai Lebedinski, writing in *Planovoye khozyaistvo*, claimed that the state planning system needed to be improved by the use of a national computer network in what has become known as an "automated system of planning."[13]

Advocates of the fully automated central system have contended that a complete data processing network (which they hope will be composed of IBM or Control Data computers) would be able to balance the dozens and thousands of production resources and needs against one another and would thus yield a workable long-range plan even for such a vast and complex economy as that of the Soviet Union. *Voprosy ekonomiki* presented a lengthy defense of the centralized approach in July 1974. The authors argued that a centralized time-sharing network of computer centers would save money and promote effi-ciency in several ways, especially by insuring from the start organizational, technical, and methodological unity of the management systems included in it.   Without a truly centralized computer network for economic planning, it was argued, the advantages of coordination could be only partially realized, and there would be needless duplication and waste in the use of computer technology.[14]

The so-called modern economists, led by Nikolai Federenko, director of the Central Mathematics Institute of the Academy of Sciences, maintain that the changing international situation, shifting foreign trade patterns, and the impact of technological progress cannot be properly reflected in comprehen-sive long-range centralized plans. They have proposed as an alternative "a system of optimal functioning of the economy." Abbreviated as SOFE, it would seek to relate economic planning machinery to a set of long-term development options, while retaining short-term flexibility.[15] It would be much less depend-ent on Western technology and would emphasize instead the development of domestic Soviet capabilities in computer technology.

For a time in the spring of 1974, it appeared that the pressures for flexi-bility and decentralization had been decisively overruled. In the March 1974 issue of *Planovoye khozyaistvo*, Nikolai Baibakov, head of Gosplan, stressed the need to perfect plans for complete centralization.[16] Almost simultaneously, Nikolai Smelyakov, Soviet deputy foreign trade minister, came out with impres-sive arguments for decentralization and maximum flexibility.[17] From the perspective of early 1976, it appears that the centralizers will emerge victorious. This would mean a continuing demand for large-scale imports of Western computer technology.

Both the Brezhnev-Kosygin debate and the arguments between centralizers and decentralizers in computer systems can be viewed simply as the latest rounds in the decade-old debate on economic reform and industrial reorganiza-tion in the Soviet Union. There were some modest additions to the reform process in 1973 involving the continued transfer of a part of the nation's indus-trial decision making to industrial associations.   Each industrial association was to consist of a series of multiplant complexes including either an entire national industry or all of the plants located in a particular geographic area.[18] The initial results of the reforms were very modest. Only a small percentage of the USSR's 49,000 enterprises had been formed into associations by the end of 1973. Reports claimed that these new associations were operating too much in isolation, thus hindering closer relationships with other associations and kill-ing any competitive spirit that might have emerged among industries.[19] The Soviet Council of Ministers issued a new decree on May 17, 1974, with the hope of speeding up the industrial reorganization.[20]

Reports in mid-1975 gave a somewhat more optimistic picture of the momentum of the industrial association movement. New information released by Soviet authorities indicated that by mid-1974, 1,541 associations comprising 6,084 producing enterprises had been formed. It seems likely that increased formation of industrial associations would enhance the development of Soviet-U.S. trade, though perhaps on terms potentially unacceptable to Leonid Brezhnev. Although foreign trade organizations and the Ministry of Foreign Trade would surely continue to enjoy leading positions in making decisions about foreign trade, managers and experts within enterprises and industrial associations would have increased influence on decisions concerning Western suppliers and purchasers.[21]

Other planning controversies stem from the competing demands of various industrial sectors. Ministries directing the chemical, machine-building, and petrochemical industries have all attempted to secure as much advanced Western equipment for their special industrial branches as possible. All claim that managerial and equipment problems can be solved by acquiring equipment and management assistance from the West and that their particular industries deserve priority treatment. The actions of the Ministry of Chemical and Petroleum Machine Building provide an example of ministerial lobbying. This ministry, which is the chief domestic source of equipment used in the petrochemical industry, overfulfilled its plans during 1974 but argued insistently that it could not keep up the pace without massive imports of Western equipment and technology.[22] Likewise, the Soviet pulp and paper industry claimed that machines provided by the Soviet machine-building industry were inadequate for its needs and that Western machinery would have to be secured immediately if the ambitious goals of the 1976-80 plan were to be reached.[23] Opposition within the ministries seemed minimal.

While they may compete with one another for priority in foreign trade plans, Soviet industrial ministries are united in their desire for as much Western assistance in solving industrial problems as possible. Problems revealed by the Soviet Ministry for Ferrous Metallurgy supported its arguments for Western assistance in management techniques and streamlining of industrial processes. One example cited by the ministry was a complete rolling mill which had to be scrapped because it was obsolete before it could be put into operation. The mill had been ordered in the 1950s and was finally delivered in 1967. By that time, it no longer fitted into the specifications of the ministry's re-equipment program. Similar cases are numerous even in the high-priority steel industry. A. I. Zalikov, a Soviet scientist, explained that projects are planned so slowly that they are outdated before they can be completed, and machines ordered for them become obsolete.[24]

Continuing reports of industrial inefficiency provide additional arguments for trade agreements with the West. According to reports in *Pravda* and *Izvestia* in February and March 1974, the engine-manufacturing industry was suffering from organization difficulties that were causing the overproduction of some engine types and the underproduction of others. There were also complaints about severe inefficiencies of production. Engine factories in Minsk and Rybinsk produced engines with the same numbers and sizes of cylinders which differed from each other by only five horsepower and yet did not have interchangeable parts. Planning problems create competition among ministries for priority treatment, but they also strengthen a uniform desire for more trade. Even the old intraministry debates between modernizers and traditionalists seem partially muted by the need for new equipment. Still, there remain those who suggest that industrial inefficiencies must be dealt with by the Soviet Union alone or through joint planning efforts with the COMECON countries.

BUREAUCRATIC CONFLICTS IN MAKING FOREIGN TRADE POLICY

The Soviet foreign trade policy decision-making process, like its U.S. counterpart, engages numerous organizations in the pursuit of partially shared and partially antagonistic goals. As noted earlier some Soviet policy makers see large-scale trade with the West as a way of solving Soviet economic problems with relatively little threat to the Soviet political and economic system. Others favor trade on a much more limited scale, to fill in a few gaps, while trying to build up domestic Soviet flexibility in management and capability in research and development work. Still others are in favor of minimal contact with the West and a greater emphasis on expanding mutual trade with Eastern Europe.

There are many differences between the foreign trade decision-making system of the Soviet Union and that of the United States. In the USSR, there is a greater concentration of decision-making power, a greater specificity of role function, and a much smaller effective policy-making group. As in the United States, however, there are many indications of bureaucratic struggles. The outcome of these disagreements will be important for the future direction of Soviet-U.S. trade.

Aside from Brezhnev and Kosygin, several key figures in the Soviet decision-making process can be identified: N. K. Baibakov, chairman of Gosplan; N. Inozemtsev, responsible for a key coordinating unit of Gosplan; Nikolai Patolichev, minister of foreign trade; Vladimir Alkhimov, deputy minister of foreign trade; V. A. Kirillin, chairman of the State Committee on Science and Technology; and Dzherman Gvishiani, vice-chairman of the State Committee on Science and Technology. Other key actors include appropriate members of the Ministry of Foreign Affairs, the Committee on Foreign Economic Relations of the USSR Council of Ministers, industrial ministries, foreign trade organizations, and joint U.S.-USSR commissions.[25] Figure 2 presents a brief summary of some of the key actors and channels of influence in the Soviet foreign trade process.[26]

The Ministry of Foreign Trade drafts and negotiates formal trade agreements with foreign governments, issues export and import licenses, and provides guidance for the work of the foreign trade organizations and special trade representations.[27] It is an administrative and regulatory body which does not normally undertake routine work on foreign trade transactions. In the planning process, it is subordinate to several agencies at the highest levels of the Soviet government. Gosplan enjoys final authority on matters involving general planning of Soviet foreign trade. Two other branches of the USSR Council of Ministers also have significant authority. The Committee on Foreign Economic Relations, which was founded in 1957, deals with trade matters concerning Eastern Europe and other socialist countries. The State Committee on Science and Technology is involved whenever the foreign trade issue at hand concerns the acquisition of foreign technology. Since Soviet enterprises and organizations are unable to acquire funds for scientific or technical research without approval of the State Committee on Science and Technology, its authority in the foreign trade process is greatly enhanced.[28]

The foreign trade organizations (FTOs) perform the day-to-day work of purchasing and selling goods. In practice they, rather than enterprises, buy and sell all traded products and conduct trade negotiations with foreigners. Both the president and vice-president of a foreign trade organization are ordinarily appointed directly by the minister of foreign trade. In early 1974, there were 61 Soviet foreign trade organizations.[29] They are all seperate legal entities, they can sue and be sued, they operate on principles of "economic accountability," and they each have sole authority to engage in a particular line of foreign trade transactions. Increasingly, they have acted to challenge the authority of the Ministry on Foreign Trade in the policy process. They, too, have challengers. They face pressures from the enterprises they serve. American businessmen generally prefer to deal directly with the end-user of a product, and Soviet enterprises have sometimes been successful in influencing decisions of FTOs. The State Committee on Science and Technology has emerged in the last few years as a powerful decision maker whenever purchases of foreign trade organizations include technology. Many large U.S. companies sign agreements directly with the Committee on Science and Technology. The committee also signs agreements with foreign governments. Industrial ministries can exert still another pressure on FTOs.

The Soviet foreign trade apparatus just outlined can itself act as a serious barrier to expanded trade between the United States and the Soviet Union. In contrast to the U.S. government, the Soviet government performs extensive regulatory and control functions and also serves as banker, manufacturer, and seller. American businessmen who have sold goods or licenses to the Soviet Union frequently complain that normal commercial ties are virtually impossible to establish. Because he must ordinarily deal directly with the State Committee on Science and Technology or with the appropriate FTO, the American businessman may never learn the exact needs of Soviet producers, distributors, and consumers.

FIGURE 2

The East-West Trade Decision-Making Process in the Soviet Union

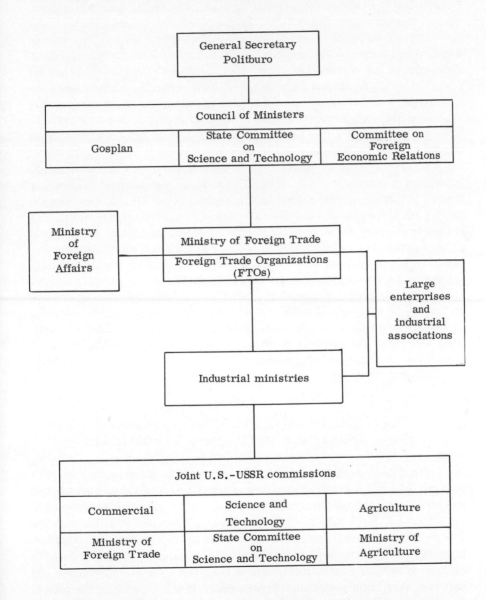

Source: Adapted from John P. Hardt, George D. Holliday, and Young C. Kim, *Western Investment in Communist Economies* (Washington, D.C.: U.S. Government Printing Office, 1974), p. 22.

Because of their own communication problems, Soviet FTOs are sometimes unable to give accurate information about the needs of potential end-users. Central planning acts as an additional complicating mechanism for the American attempting to do business in the Soviet Union. Because the Soviet foreign trade apparatus lacks some of the basics of normal international commerce, such as a convertible currency and a realistic exchange rate, American sellers often find that FTOs insist on clumsy barter transactions to provide payment.[30] The generalized barriers presented by the Soviet foreign trade system become even more formidable when one contemplates actual and potential tensions within the Soviet foreign trade apparatus. There are problems resulting from overlapping jurisdictions of FTOs, from competing claims of industrial ministries, and from high-level debates over the degree of centralization in the economy.

Yet, despite some monumental problems and hesitations, the most significant point is simply that the Soviet Union needs and wants U.S. computer technology, industrial techniques, and managerial skills. Though they disagree sharply on the extent of usefulness of imported innovations, modernists and traditionalists, centralizers and decentralizers, FTO representatives and members of the Committee on Science and Technology all agree that the Soviet economy needs to be rationalized and revitalized. However they are finally resolved, debates within the foreign trade system are likely to result in continued Soviet interest in U.S. computer technology, industrial products, and even agricultural products. The outcomes of the Soviet debates may, however, affect the nature of the Soviet institutions with which American businessmen will have to deal. They also reveal the existence of important interest groups within the Soviet Union. Even within a centrally planned economy, the potential meanings of economic detente are many.

POLITICAL ARGUMENTS FOR AND AGAINST EXPANDED TRADE WITH THE UNITED STATES

Some Soviet supporters of increased Soviet-U.S. transactions base their advocacy of trade primarily on political arguments. One of the most outspoken has been Georgi S. Schukin, chairman of the Kama River Purchasing Committee. He claims that the USSR favors development of broad economic ties with the United States because it believes that economic agreements are an essential expression of the new spirit of political detente.[31] Brezhnev has expressed similar sentiments by noting "the development of long-term economic cooperation will also have very beneficial political consequences. It will consolidate the present trend toward better Soviet-American relations generally."[32] Perhaps the beneficial political consequences that both Schukin and Brezhnev have in mind are those creating powerful vested interests in the United States. These interests would be composed of U.S. corporations anxious to preserve a lucrative market and of corporations, banks, and government agencies eager to safeguard billions of dollars in Soviet credits and investments.[33] It is clear that Brezhnev is less concerned with political cooperation than he is with this kind of economic leverage. The Soviet Union's emphasis on domestic political conformity and on military spending has increased since the onset of "detente." It may be that Brezhnev is simply using increased trade and economic cooperation to secure more subtle economic leverage gains. Schukin's statements are probably based on a simpler hope for economic gains for the Kama River Purchasing Committee.

Two quite different political and ideological trends seem to be operating simultaneously in the Soviet Union. At times, the official emphasis is on the easing of international political tensions. At other times, the ideological struggle between the Soviet Union and the United States is given more attention. The Soviet leadership does seem to have adopted a more flexible and moderate position vis-a-vis all the Western powers. Brezhnev's diplomacy abroad after 1969 and his trade agreements with West Germany, France, Italy, Great Britain, and the United States reveal a steady desire for relative internal economic and political calm. Perhaps the key to the confusing juxtaposition of hostility and friendship in Soviet statements of ideology comes from a consideration of the Soviet usage of the term "peaceful coexistence." The Soviets prefer this term over detente. As noted in an earlier chapter, "peaceful coexistence" entails a struggle between states with different social systems without resort to war. The Soviets view peaceful coexistence as a long-term foreign policy strategy which involves a mixture of competition, restraint, and cooperation.

All three elements have had ample representation in statements in the Soviet press, and competing political factions have formed to emphasize one or another of the elements. The theme of competition between the United States and the USSR remains foremost. There are conservative factions of the Soviet leadership that view the current economic and political disarray in the West as a chance to promote socialist gains in Western states. Yuri N. Ponomarev, then a candidate member of the Soviet Politburo, declared at a meeting of the European Communists in Warsaw in October 1974 that "at present the communist parties have greater possibilities and strength than ever before to exert an influence on the course of developments in Europe." Numerous journal articles have gleefully noted high rates of inflation and unemployment in the capitalist world and have suggested that they will be aids to Soviet increments in power. Mikhail Suslov, a Politburo member who is considered the Kremlin's chief ideologist, has declared that economic problems in the West have "significantly strengthened" the position of Western Communists and of the socialist world camp.[34] Another frequent theme in the Soviet press has been the steadily changing balance of power in favor of socialism.[35]

Even those who favor greatly increased trade with the United States often suggest that its spillover into the realm of better political relations with the

United States will be minimal. Ideologist G. Arbatov, writing in *Pravda* in July 1973, noted that no matter how successfully the processes of normalization and detente might develop, relations with the United States and other capitalist countries would remain relations of struggle.[36] A. Bovin expressed a similar viewpoint in an *Izvestia* article of September 1973 where he argued that the more deeply the principles of peaceful economic coexistence are implemented, the more confidently the people fighting for a radical change of sociopolitical conditions in the world can act.[37]

The Soviet press waged an unrelenting campaign of anti-American information during September and October 1974—just when the trade bill was approaching final likelihood of passage in the U.S. Congress. Soviet readers were reminded of the existence of 10 million chronic alcoholics in the United States, and they were told all about the CIA's alleged domestic spying activities. The content of the messages was not at all unusual or surprising, but the frequency and extent of such articles seemed to prove Bovin's point about the fight for radical changes in political conditions in spite of economic cooperation.[38] Even economic goodwill was stretched to a breaking point at times. Rents on hotel rooms used by U.S. businessmen in Moscow went up 150 percent in October and November 1974—raising the cost of the average hotel room from $45 or $50 a day to $115 or $120.[39]

At other times, the elements of cooperation and restraint in the process of economic and political relations between the United States and the USSR were emphasized. One important element of this type was given special attention in *Pravda* on August 6, 1974:

> Needless to say, the desire of both sides to deepen the process of detente, as well as the efforts being undertaken to this end, do not mean that there are no disagreements between them. Even in spheres where their interests coincide and they are cooperating constructively, there remain at times very important differences in the principles with which they approach the solution of a number of international problems.

There have also been a number of articles stressing the importance of cultural cooperation between the United States and the Soviet Union.[40]

NOTES

1. *Pravda*, January 26, 1974, p. 1.

2. Abram Bergson, "Toward a New Growth Model," *Problems of Communism* 22, no. 2 (March-April 1973): 3.

3. William Colby, in U.S. Congress, Joint Economic Committee, *Hearings, Allocation of Resources in the Soviet Union and China*, 93rd Cong. 2d Sess., 1974, p. 18.

4. See, for example, Michael Boretsky, "Comparative Progress in Technology, Productivity, and Economic Efficiency: USSR vs. U.S.A.," in U.S. Congress, Joint Economic

Committee, *New Directions in the Soviet Economy,* II-A, 89th Cong., 2d Sess., 1966, p. 149.

5. Raymond Vernon and Marshall Goldman, "U.S. Policy in the Sale of Technology to the USSR," mimeographed (September 15, 1974), pp. 43-44; Robert W. Campbell, "Problems of Technical Progress in the USSR," in *The Soviet Economy: A Book of Readings,* ed. Morris S. Bornstein and Daniel R. Fusfeld (Homewood, Ill.: Richard D. Irwin, 1974), pp. 348-64.

6. Artamanov and V. Malov, "Share with Your Neighbor," *Pravda,* March 18, 1975, p. 2.

7. Keith Bush, "Soviet Economic Growth: Past, Present, and Projected," *NATO Review* 22, no. 1 (1974): 22.

8. New York *Times,* October 20, 1974.

9. *Pravda,* December 18, 1974.

10. *Financial Times,* June 18, 1975.

11. Christian Deuvel, "Kosygin at Odds with Brezhnev on Economic Policy," Radio Liberty dispatch, November 6, 1974; for Kosygin's speech, see *Pravda,* November 3, 974, pp. 1-3; for Brezhnev's speech, see *Pravda,* October 16, 1974, pp. 1-2.

12. Franklyn Holzman and Robert Legvold, "The Economics and Politics of East-West Relations, *International Organization* 29, no. 1 (Winter 1975): 306-07.

13. Nikolai Lebedinsky, *Planovoye khozyaistvo,* September 1973, pp. 6-13.

14. G. Samborsky and V. Simchera, "The Way to Improve the Efficiency of Computer Technology," *Voprosy ekonomiki,* no. 7 (1974), pp. 79-89.

15. New York *Times,* October 12, 1973.

16. Nikolai Baibakov, *Planovoye khozyaistvo,* March 1974.

17. Chase Manhattan, *EastWest Markets,* March 11, 1974, pp. 5-13.

18. See Leon Smolinski, "Toward a Socialist Corporation: Soviet Industrial Reorganization of 1973," *Survey* 20, no. 1 (Winter 1974): 24-35.

19. The Economist Intelligence Unit, *Quarterly Economic Review,* no. 2 (1974). p. 4.

20. Business International, *Eastern Europe Report,* July 26, 1974, p. 229.

21. Ibid., June 13, 1975, p. 162.

22. Ibid., December 13, 1974, p. 377.

23. Ibid., September 20, 1974, p. 290.

24. Ibid., May 17, 1974, pp. 149-50.

25. For complete information about the organizations and individuals involved in the Soviet foreign trade process, the following should be consulted: V.S. Vaganov, *Vneshnyaya torgovlya sotsialisticheskikh stran* (Moscow, 1966); and Harold J. Berman and George L. Bustin, "The Soviet System of American Foreign Trade," in *Business Transactions with the USSR,* ed. American Bar Association (New York: American Bar Association, 1975), pp. 25-75.

26. John P. Hardt, George D. Holliday, and Young C. Kim, *Western Investment in Communist Economies* (Washington, D.C.: Government Printing Office, 1974), p. 22.

27. V. S. Pozdniakov, *Gosudarstvennaia monopoliia vneshnei torgovli v SSSR* (Moscow, 1974), pp. 10-17.

28. Harold J. Berman and George L. Bustin, op. cit., pp. 25-29.

29. Berman and Bustin provide a list of the 61 FTOs (Ibid., pp. 31-32, n. 24).

30. John P. Hardt and George D. Holliday, *U.S.-Soviet Commercial Relations: The Interplay of Economics, Technology Transfer, and Diplomacy* (Washington, D.C.: Government Printing Office, June 10, 1973), pp. 62-63.

31. Georgi S. Schukin, "The Soviet Position on Trade with the United States," *The Columbia Journal of World Business* 8, no. 4 (Winter 1973): 47-50.

32. *Pravda,* January 1, 1974.

33. For a similar argument, see Gregory Grossman, "Prospects and Policy for U.S.-Soviet Trade," *American Economic Review* 64 (May 1974): 289-93.

34. For example, see "Inflation in the Capitalist World," *International Affairs* (Moscow), no. 1 (January 1975), pp. 138-39; New York *Times*, October 27, 1974, October 23, 1974.

35. V. Nikitin, "Peaceful Co-existence and Soviet-U.S. Relations," *International Affairs* (Moscow), no. 6 (June 1974), pp. 3-4.

36. Georgi Arbatov, "Soviet-American Relations at a New Stage," *Pravda*, July 22, 1973, pp. 4-5.

37. A. Bovin, *Izvestia*, September 10, 1973.

38. *Pravda*, September 24, 1974; *Izvestia*, September 24, 1974.

39. Business International, *Eastern Europe Report*, November 29, 1974, p. 362.

40. See especially E. Sutina and Y. Rilov, "USSR-USA Cultural Cooperation," *International Affairs* (Moscow), no. 7 (July 1974), pp. 150-51.

4

THE INTEGRATION PROGRAM OF 1971

The Soviet and East European trade organization COMECON constitutes another important element in trade relations between the United States and the Soviet Union. Traditionally, most of the Soviet Union's external trade has been within the COMECON framework. Now, Soviet trade with the United States and with Western Europe has initiated changes in patterns of Soviet-East European relations within COMECON. The Soviet Union has been attempting to strengthen its control over COMECON members to insure that East European trade with the West will be carried out in accordance with Soviet wishes. At the same time, the Soviet Union has been seeking to develop beneficial ties with the West independently of COMECON.

It now appears that COMECON may become an economic liability of the Soviets. The Soviet Union has raised the price of oil it provides to Eastern Europe, but it is still receiving less from Eastern Europe than the average world market price. In return for oil and raw materials, the Soviet Union ordinarily receives as payment inferior manufactured goods from Eastern Europe. Both the East Europeans and the Soviets want to acquire superior Western industrial technology. Those desires conflict with the traditional patterns of Soviet dominance and East European dependence in COMECON. By encouraging independent economic linkages with the West for both the East European countries and the Soviet Union, the United States may be able to promote its own interests in restructuring relations with COMECON and between capitalist and socialist economic groupings.

Historically, patterns of economic relations between the Soviet Union and Eastern Europe have encouraged the development of an economic bloc serving the needs of the Soviet Union. Between the end of World War II and 1953,

61

when Stalin died, the transfer of economic resources from Eastern Europe to the Soviet Union was in the amount of approximately $14 billion, or the equivalent of Marshall Plan money that went from the United States to Western Europe.[1] But after the mid-1950s patterns changed, and most experts now suggest that the Soviet Union suffers from its acceptance of shipments of East European machinery and manufactured goods to pay for Soviet raw materials. Attempts by Khrushchev to impose supranational planning on COMECON and even Brezhnev's attempts to achieve integration of COMECON through a more gradual process of creating a systematic interlocking of the Soviet and East European national planning systems can be seen as additional, partially successful, attempts by the Soviet Union to reassert its once commanding economic authority and advantages in COMECON.[2]

If one assumes that the Soviet Union is eager to secure Western technology and that it is anxious as well to become a more complete partner in the world economic system of the developed nations, it becomes clear that there are both advantages and disadvantages for the Soviet Union in its current COMECON relationships. Economically, COMECON seems to be a burden. The Soviet Union has long been attempting to change the composition of its trade with Eastern Europe. In the 1950s and 1960s, more than half of all East European imports from the Soviet Union were in the categories of fuel, raw materials, and semi-manufactures. In the late 1960s, the Soviet Union was still providing more than 90 percent of total East European imports of crude oil, pig iron, and iron ore; and more than 60 percent of cotton, coal, manganese, and wheat. At the same time, the Soviet Union continued to be the major market for East European machinery, much of which was initially designed for the Soviet market and had little salability elsewhere. In the 1960s, the Soviet market was absorbing about 60 percent of Bulgarian machinery; 50 percent of Hungarian, Polish, and East German machinery; 40 percent of Czech machinery; and about 33 percent of Romanian machine exports. As raw material became more valuable on the world market, the Soviet Union became more dissatisfied with the terms of its trade with Eastern Europe. In the early 1970s, it began asking the East Europeans to purchase more Soviet machinery, to deliver more consumer goods to the USSR, and to aid in the cost of Soviet resource development.[3]

The Soviet Union now faces a dilemma in its relations with Eastern Europe through COMECON. Politically, COMECON provides a mechanism for the imposition of Soviet authority and control in Eastern Europe. Economically, COMECON inhibits Soviet dealings with the West. The real question for the Soviet Union is whether or not the political gains of the COMECON structure justify the possible economic losses.[4] Some argue that it is not really necessary for the Soviet Union to benefit economically from the COMECON system to be in favor of maintaining and even strengthening it. Even an economic loss for the Soviet Union could be offset by political gains from having the East European countries tied into a firm trading bloc and heavily dependent on the Soviet

Union for oil.[5] This view of the political importance of COMECON to the Soviet Union has been reinforced by Soviet moves to enhance bloc-wide military integration through changes in the structure of the Warsaw Pact.[6] It is also possible that declining growth rates and ever greater needs for hard currency to buy technology will convince the Soviet Union that the economic costs of COMECON are too great. Soviet sales of raw materials to the West instead of to Eastern Europe could lead to a weakening of the traditional Soviet-East European relationship. Increased Soviet sales in the West would force the East Europeans to look elsewhere for raw materials and for export markets for their manufactured goods. This would enhance East European desires to deal directly with the West. The net result would be a disintegration of the COMECON trading structure, an occurrence which could only be met with satisfaction in the United States.

The problems of COMECON and of the Soviet position within it are far from resolved, as is evident from the continuing debate over COMECON's new integration program. The program demonstrates the Soviet desire to control East European initiatives with the West and yet its concurrent desire not to be burdened by Eastern Europe's lack of industrial efficiency and lack of raw materials. An extended integration program was developed at the twenty-seventh COMECON council session in Prague in June 1973. Despite its official emphasis on national sovereignty accompanied by intergovernmental cooperation, the program has probably strengthened Soviet control over East European initiatives with the West. Yet the development of operational aspects of the integration program has also revealed the extent to which Soviet and East European interests diverge.

The integration program was first announced in July 1971 at the twenty-fifth council session of COMECON. The council adopted a comprehensive program for socialist interstate economic integration. Its official objectives were to regulate the process of the international socialist division of labor, to interlock the Soviet and East European economies, and to bring economic development in all COMECON countries up to similar levels.[7] The 1971 program was intended to represent a new level in the development of socialism by marking the end of a stage in which the socialist states were only a complex of regions and the beginning of a gradual transformation into a unified whole.[8] At the twenty-seventh session in 1973, the importance of long-term planning for integration activities was emphasized.

In April 1973 a plenary session of the Central Committee of the Communist Party of the Soviet Union (CPSU) underscored the exceptional importance attached to the integration program by the CPSU. The meeting called for the expansion of economic ties between the Soviet Union and Eastern Europe.[9] A year later, in a speech to the twenty-eighth COMECON council meeting, Kosygin was still calling for greater efforts to achieve full economic integration, which he said could be achieved by 1980.[10] Changes in the COMECON structure in 1974 and 1975 demonstrate that despite any doubts it may have, the Soviet Union is urging more uniformity and cooperation on the COMECON structure.

The June 1974 council session of COMECON in Sofia resulted in two major structural changes. The changes were publicly acknowledged only after a six-month delay, presumably because of strong opposition to the measures by several East European states. The first change provided that the principle of unanimity could be abolished in certain cases. This change was designed to prevent uninterested member countries (notably Romania) from delaying or preventing the establishment of new permanent economic commissions. A second change dictated that COMECON should become a single legal entity, a move which would make it easier for COMECON per se to deal directly with the European Economic Community (EEC) and other international organizations. The East Europeans were opposed to the second measure because it would hinder their ability to sign independent trade and cooperation agreements with Western Europe and the United States. By January 1975, only Czechoslovakia had ratified these proposed amendments.[11]

Two COMECON meetings in 1975 proposed some additional integration measures. A January meeting revised intra-COMECON pricing and initiated measures to make its collective currency, the transferable ruble, more fully convertible among COMECON countries.[12] The price changes were the most important, and they obviously were desired more by the Soviet Union than by the East European countries. It was six months before Hungary became the first East European country to publicize the new price structure. A partial list of the new Hungarian prices gives a good indication of overall changes. Prices of imports from the USSR of raw materials, including fuels, were allowed to rise 52 percent. Prices of Hungarian exports to the USSR increased according to the following patterns: machinery and equipment, 15 percent; buses, 23 percent; light-industry products, an average of 19 percent; and agricultural products, an average of 28 percent.[13]

A second 1975 meeting changed planning procedures. The council meeting in Budapest in June decided that for the 1976-80 period, all COMECON member national plans will be drawn up with particular attention to COMECON-wide projects. These include the building of steel and chemical production facilities, exploration of iron ore deposits, the construction of power grid systems, and joint construction of oil and gas pipelines. The council adopted plans to invest up to 10 billion transferable rubles in projects involving COMECON cooperation within the USSR: the huge cellulose complex at Ust-Ilimsk, the asbestos factory at Kiyembaev, ferrous metal extraction at Kursk, and the Orenburg natural gas pipeline. In contrast to earlier years, even the initial stages of planning are being marked by joint efforts. Industrial and economic ministries in all member countries are now held responsible for execution of the joint projects, and they will not be allowed to use national priorities as an excuse for failing to provide support for joint COMECON projects.[14]

Soviet statements have consistently suggested that the new institutional linkages mark an important step toward supranational planning.[15]

Many observers will undoubtedly remain skeptical about these Soviet claims. Some scholars have argued that "integration" is not a very accurate descriptive term for the activities following the introduction of the 1971 COMECON program. Jozef M. van Brabant, for example, contends that despite the integration program COMECON still acts "simply as an intergovernmental institution to set up smooth trade turnover in needed commodities." According to van Brabant, the integration program lacks measures to create economic in addition to legal and institutional frameworks for implementing integration.[16] Van Brabant argues that COMECON institutions actually form obstacles to closer cooperation among members. It is true that both Soviet and East European publications have emphasized that the COMECON program is one of interstate integration, in contrast to the misguided attempts at suprastate integration in Western Europe.[17] Soviet and East European legal experts claim that capitalist attempts at cross-national integration automatically violate the rights of smaller states. Socialism alone is said to be capable of the harmonious accommodation of national and international forces.[18] The idea that international relations of a new and distinct type could be practiced among socialist states goes back to 1960, when A. A. Gromyko's statement in the Soviet *Diplomaticheskii slovar* described the relationship between the Soviet Union and other socialist states in the following terms:

> The new type of diplomatic relations is free of antagonism and based on the principle of proletarian internationalism and brotherly cooperation in the name of common objectives, i.e. complete respect for sovereign rights and national interests of each socialist country .... [19]

CURRENT PROBLEMS OF SOVIET-EAST EUROPEAN
COOPERATION IN COMECON

Debates over the various provisions of the integration program reveal the deep problems of Soviet-East European cooperation involved. Just as domestic interests in the United States and in the Soviet Union have focused on special goals, so have the various national members of COMECON focused on the specific gains they can achieve from integration. And, to a greater degree than they would have thought possible just a few years ago, the East European members have found it feasible to advance their own interests. The result has been that the Soviet Union, though perhaps less interested now than ever in being in charge of a unified scheme of East European planning and production, finds it necessary to urge unity upon the East Europeans so that it can control East European trade with the West. The delicate nature of the Soviet-East European balance is perhaps best revealed in some points of contention that have arisen since the adoption of the integration program.

First, there have been problems in the harmonization and joint development of five-year plans. It was reported in January 1974 that Soviet and East European heads of state were busy coordinating their economic plans for 1976-80. This was felt by some to be significant because it meant that COMECON members were beginning to synchronize their plans at the initial stages, while in earlier years they had always sought to coordinate separate plans that had already been drawn up. This seemed to indicate that Hungarian economist Tibor Kiss' comment that COMECON planning methods were "featured by the presence of some autarkic tendencies" was no longer valid.[20] But by April 1974, Soviet publications were complaining that joint planning was not so common after all. One Soviet economic observer complained that "not all economic ties" between the COMECON countries were conforming to the planning principles and that joint planning was not as extensive as it needed to be.[21]

Problems in joint industrial cooperation and planning are particularly revealing of the emerging tensions both between East European countries and the Soviet Union and among the East European countries themselves. The Soviet Union favors joint planning with the East Europeans only as long as no Western cooperation deals seem imminent. Rapid joint development of the Czech computer industry was once encouraged as an aid to all of Eastern Europe and the Soviet Union. Now the Soviet Union prefers to visualize its own nationwide system of Control Data computers, and there are few indications that Czech computers will retain a significant role in intrablock planning and production activities. There are also examples of East European scrambling for advantage. In 1973 and 1974, integrated plans had been worked out for the development of the motor vehicle industry. Plans called for tractors to be manufactured in Poland and Czechoslovakia; trucks in East Germany, Czechoslovakia, and Poland; passenger cars mainly in Czechoslovakia; and buses in Czechoslovakia, Poland, and Hungary. These plans have been abandoned because each country now seeks to develop its own motor vehicle industries independently with the assistance of Italian, French, and American manufacturers.[22] Hungary, with its high level of dependence on Western trade and its relatively important economic reforms, has been especially eager for cooperation deals with American and West European industries.

There is opposing evidence pointing to the advance of joint cooperation. Direct ties between ministries and departments, research institutes and economic planning agencies have been strengthened in many ways. By mid-1974, some 860 research institutes and design offices in the COMECON countries were reported to be working on joint projects with some 700 related Soviet establishments. Over 70 ministries and departments of the USSR had arranged regular exchanges of information with 96 ministries and departments in the East European countries.[23] One could view these steps as moves toward integration, but it is equally possible that they were moves initiated by the Soviet

Union to preserve political influence and control where true economic integration was lacking.

A second basic area of contention in the implementation of the integration program comes in the expanded use of international economic associations within COMECON. The integration program has been characterized by the proliferation of new cross-national economic groupings and structures, many of which yield administrative authority directly to the Soviet Union. Among the new groups are Interatominstrument, the International Scientific and Technical Information Center, the International Institute for Economic Problems of the World Socalist System, the International Mathematics Center, and the International Society of Cybernetics. The protracted negotiations about the structure of these and other agencies during the early days of the integration program indicated conflict between the Soviet Union and its East European partners. The fact that the Soviet Union acquired the headquarters and administrative staffs of many of these new organizations indicates that Moscow often uses integration to support its administrative control over Eastern Europe.[24] There has been ample East European resistance to Soviet control of these organizations. Interatominstrument has headquarters in Warsaw and has often acted quite independently of Soviet wishes. But organizations formed after 1973 have granted many administrative concessions to the USSR. Among these organizations are Intertextilmash, Interatomenergo, and Interelektro.[25] Only Interchimvolokno, a new Bucharest-based association of East European synthetic fiber producers, provides an exception to the post-1973 pattern of Soviet dominance.

A third major part of the COMECON integration program is also open to dual interpretations. The twenty-eighth COMECON council session created the COMECON Committee on Cooperation in the Field of Material and Technical Supply. It also developed a new convention on technical norms. These two measures make possible the development of common industrial specifications throughout COMECON. The specifications are also developed with conscious reference to the practices of the International Standards Organization.[26] This should make technological innovations purchased from the West more easily adaptable to all COMECON countries. Coupled with firm administrative control by the USSR, it could provide for greater Soviet control over East European deals with the West. Of course, the East European countries would, in theory, be able to benefit equally from Soviet technical purchases from the West. However, this does not seem to be the reason for Soviet sponsorship of the new measures on technical norms.

A fourth area of the integration program concerns natual resources. Oil has been an especially delicate problem. The integration program called for the expansion of the Friendship Oil Pipeline and planned for some of the East European countries to acquire new petrochemical industries. Until recently, the completion of the Friendship project was consistently referred to in the

Soviet press as an example of "COMECON cooperation on the basis of the principle of the international socialist division of labor."[27] At the time of the initial adoption of the integration program in 1971, the Soviet Union even suggested that it would be able to meet all the oil needs of the East European countries. With the quadrupling of world oil prices, the Soviet message is quite different. The East European countries have been encouraged to secure Middle Eastern supplies of oil and were confronted with a doubling of Soviet oil prices on January 1, 1975. East European investment in the exploitation of Soviet oil and gas reserves may provide one way out of the East European fuel supply dilemma. In the 1973-75 period, there was a dramatic increase in the size and number of joint oil extraction and natural gas exploitation projects on Soviet soil. The East Europeans have been providing manpower, equipment, technical assistance, and even some hard currency, in exchange for promises of future Soviet deliveries of oil and gas.

One of the largest projects of this kind has been the construction of the 2,750 kilometer gas pipeline from Orenburg to the western border of the USSR. The pipeline is being built to make it possible to increase natural gas deliveries to the European regions of the Soviet Union and to most of the East European countries. The entire gas pipeline is divided into five sections. Polish workers will complete the section from Orenburg to Alexandrov Gai, and Czech, Hungarian, and East German workers will be responsible for the remaining sections within Soviet territory. The final section extending to the western border of the USSR will be completed by Soviet and Bulgarian specialists. The whole project is scheduled for completion in 1978.[28]

Pricing problems have also threatened the progress of the integration program. In many ways, the new Soviet oil price hikes seem justified, but they will result in severe economic hardships for the East European countries. Some estimates suggest that the new price structure will mean that the East European countries will have to pay an additional 3 billion rubles a year for raw materials. Part of this sum could be raised by increased prices chargeable for East European exports to the USSR, but most will have to come from increased transfers of East European production output to the USSR.[29]

Some East European countries have accepted the price changes with only a few protests. The Polish press has declared that the USSR had traditionally received too little for its raw material exports to Eastern Europe:

In 1973, the USSR received from Poland exactly as much for 12,000,000 tons of crude oil and oil products as it did for only 6,000,000 tons sold to the Federal Republic of Germany. Last year, the USSR was paid slightly over 1,000,000 rubles for 50,000,000 tons of oil and oil products sold to COMECON member countries, while for about 70,000,000 tons sold to other countries it received an estimated 4000 million rubles.[30]

Other East European countries have complained bitterly about the new price structure, which gives them less for products they sell to the USSR and forces them to pay more for USSR imports. During a one-day meeting with Brezhnev, Erich Honecker of the East German Communist party reportedly called upon the USSR to ease the burden of high oil prices for the East Europeans.[31] Ceausescu of Romania has also been outspoken about the need to return Soviet oil prices to their former levels.

Still another tension created by the implementation of the integration program has been the apparent increase in the percentage of East European trade conducted with the USSR. Traditionally, about two-thirds of East European trade has been conducted within the COMECON framework. While the Soviet Union has steadily advanced the percentage of its total trade volume devoted to trade with the West, the East European countries have become more trade-dependent on the USSR in the period since 1971. Since 1973, with growing numbers of joint industrial and raw material exploitation projects in the Soviet Union, East European trade dependence has increased again.[32] A study by Michael Kaser discovered very pronounced indications of greater dependence on intra-COMECON trade in the case of Romania. Romania now plans to cut its trade turnover with the industrialized West from the $920 million expected in 1975 to between $490 million and $610 million in 1980.[33] Some of the shift in Romania's emphasis can be explained by growing debt-service requirements and shortages of hard-currency reserves, but it is also strongly influenced by Soviet demands for joint participation projects in the USSR. Other East European countries are expected to show similar shifts in trade patterns. Since the East European countries share Soviet eagerness for acquisition of Western technology, such transfers of trade attention toward the COMECON grouping are not popular.

The problems revealed in the implementation of the integration program are symptoms of the broader changes that have been taking place in Soviet-East European relations. While Khrushchev sought integration through a supra-national planning authority within COMECON in 1962 and failed, Brezhnev seeks a more sophisticated kind of integration. In most ways it is unlike the integration of Western Europe. Superficially akin to the functionalist model of building integration from the bottom up, the current plans are in fact for a legal, interstate, and administrative kind of integration only. What the Soviet Union wants is political and administrative control over East European contacts with the West. East Europeans are not likely to be given more than a secondary role in that economic quest.

From the Soviet perspective, the key must be to insure East European cooperation within the framework of COMECON. In that way, the USSR can provide a juridical and political counterweight to the EEC that may prove useful if economic negotiations with the United States do not proceed satisfactorily. The USSR gains the additional advantages of East European expertise and experience in dealing with the West. But the danger is that the USSR may be unwilling to learn the painful lesson that even the peripheries of political systems can possess considerable counterweight if they feel cheated. The price of closer economic integration could well be increased social unrest in the East European countries with which the Soviet Union will have to deal in costly administrative, political, and even military ways.[34]

PATTERNS OF DOMINANCE AND DEPENDENCE IN COMECON

Going beyond the framework of the recent integration program, one can see broader symptoms of dissension between the Soviet Union and Eastern Europe. The old arguments about Soviet dominance and East European dependence still seem to be an accurate description of many facets of the Soviet-East European relationship. First, it can be demonstrated that over the years since the formation of COMECON in 1949, the Soviet Union has consistently encouraged East European industrial development to suit the needs of the Soviet Union. A case in point was Soviet support for the Czech computer industry. The Czech Research Institute of Mathematical Machines was responsible for the development of the R-20A computer. Early in 1973, the USSR sent G. D. Smirnov to check out the capabilities of the new computer. A final evaluation of excellent was achieved, and it was decided that the computer should be put into series production for use in all the COMECON countries.[35] But a short while later the Soviet Union began conducting negotiations for the purchase of some large computer systems from Control Data, and it also initiated talks with IBM and Sperry Rand. One victim of these new potential contracts was the "budding Czech computer industry," which very quickly lost its former position of primacy in Soviet plans.

The instability of Soviet interest can be devastating for East European industries once they are established. Premier Janos Kadar of Hungary decided several years ago to establish a large-scale petrochemical industry based on Soviet oil. Then, in 1973, when the Soviet Union realized it could command a far higher price for oil resources in the West, Brezhnev gave Kadar the fraternal advice to satisfy his oil needs in Iraq.[36] East Europeans fear that this may become a general trend. With the Soviet Union developing closer economic relations with non-Communist countries as quickly as possible, the Soviet market for East European goods promises to become more difficult, and the Soviet sources of raw materials supporting these industries are becoming insecure.

A second area where the problem of Soviet dominance remains acute for the East Europeans is in banking patterns. For both political and purely financial reasons, Moscow is eager to control COMECON's banking in the West. The immediate Soviet objective seems to be to handle long-term borrowing on behalf of the various COMECON countries.[37] A meeting of the Central Committee of the CPSU in April 1973 apparently considered ways of controlling COMECON partners who were looking for special credit arrangements in Brussels and for Euroloans in Frankfurt. Since that meeting, the Soviets have developed more stringent financial controls over their East European partners.[38]

A third area of dominance might be seen in Soviet encouragement of the economic projects of smaller East European groupings when it is in control of them and its attempts to prevent these projects from operating when they appear to have independent inclinations. In 1973, for example, the German Democratic Republic and the USSR established an economic association for the joint production of petrochemical products. ASSOFOTO has head-quarters in Moscow and was the first COMECON organization to engage in joint planning of an entire industrial branch on a bilateral basis.[39] The German Democratic Republic has concluded an unusually large number of bilateral industrial agreements with the USSR. At the end of 1973, official East German sources put the number of major agreements at close to 100 in areas of scien-tific-technical and economic cooperation alone.[40] The Soviet Union and Poland have developed some extensive bilateral cooperation agreements in atomic power engineering. An initial agreement, signed in February 1974, provided that the Soviet Union would help Poland build a large atomic power station on Polish soil.[41] Shortly after the announcement, Polish publications discussed the necessity for increased Polish-Soviet cooperation in other power and fuel industries.[42] The Soviet Union takes particular interest in developing bilateral agreements in areas of power production and chemicals and metal manufacturing processes. Bilateral undertakings of East European countries not involving the USSR have only rarely been given tacit approval by the Soviet Union, which regularly condemns non-Soviet bilateral projects as detrimental to the spirit of COMECON joint planning and integration.

Fourth, the Soviet Union dominates technological innovation and research undertaken by COMECON. In computer research, with the exception of the Czech R-20A project, the Soviet Union itself has been a leader in innovation. In early 1973, the Soviet Union announced the introduction of a United System of Electronic Computers, a third-generation computer family developed by the Soviet Union with the production assistance of Bulgaria, Hungary, the GDR, Poland, and Czechoslovakia.[43] In computers and in other areas of technological research, the Soviet Union has often been reluctant to share its research and development work with COMECON partners. As one observer noted, "the high technological standard which the USSR has undoubtedly attained in many areas is shared only to a very limited extent with her partners in COMECON."[44] Since the rate of indigenous technological innovation is substantially lower in Eastern Europe than in Western Europe or the USSR, the unwillingness of the Soviet Union to share the results of research and development work fully with the East European members of COMECON is especially serious.[45]

Finally, the Soviet Union has the enormous advantage of controlling resource development, especially in oil. Beginning in 1973, the East European countries confronted ever increasing difficulties in getting oil supplies from the Soviet Union. Even with the completion of joint oil and gas pipelines scheduled to be put into operation in the late 1970s and early 1980s, the Soviet supply of fuels to Eastern Europe seems open to disruption. It is always possible that by that time the Soviet Union may find it more expedient to trade oil for technology from the West European countries or from the United States. There has, of course, been much concern over the potential oil supply problem in Eastern Europe. The East European countries (except Romania) are now dependent on the USSR for about 90 percent of the crude oil they consume and about two-thirds of the raw materials they use. Their requirements are steadily growing.[46]

The Soviet Union has vacillated somewhat in its oil policy, but it is putting the interests of the Soviet domestic economy first. In January 1974, the USSR began to meet some of its East European oil commitments with shipments directly from the Middle East rather than from the Soviet Union. According to Soviet news reports, oil was being shipped from Iraq to the port of Rijecka, where it was fed into a pipeline and transmitted to Hungary and Czechoslovakia for refining and consumption. Initial plans called for a total of 10 million tons a year to be shipped in this way.[47] But as the world price of oil climbed, it became evident that this particular source of oil would require huge outlays of scarce East European reserves of hard currency.

East European concern on the oil matter is heightened by the fact that roughly half of the Soviet Union's exports of oil already go to buyers outside COMECON. This trend will almost certainly continue as the Soviet Union remains anxious for the advanced machinery and high-quality consumer goods it can buy with hard currency earned from the sale of oil. An additional problem for the East European members of COMECON is that they cannot really provide the sophisticated technology needed to develop Soviet natural resources fully.[48]

The Soviet Union also faces a dilemma of sorts. Trade with the East European countries, especially in the transfer of natural resources, can be very unprofitable for the Soviet Union. The USSR has sound economic reasons of its own for wishing to reduce its sales of oil to Eastern Europe. Projections for 1980 indicate that, even with the completion of COMECON oil and gas pipelines, the supply problem will remain serious. A Hungarian economist has calculated that by 1980, non-Soviet COMECON oil consumption (currently about 80 million tons a year) will have increased to 170 million tons, some 70 million tons of which will have to be imported from the outside because the Soviets have set a 100 million ton ceiling on annual exports to Eastern Europe. Natural gas demands of Eastern Europe will also exceed the limits of Soviet supplies by 1980. According to a Polish economist, non-Soviet COMECON could be importing up to 50 billion cubic meters of gas a year by 1985, a figure that far exceeds anticipated Soviet gas shipments.

In other fuel resources, the East Europeans may fare somewhat better. Poland possesses large quantities of good-quality coal which it is now exploiting, and East Germany is the world's largest producer of lignite. Czechoslovakia has substantial deposits of hard coal.[49] When Czechoslovakia's first nuclear power station began operating in 1973, some East Europeans noted that the successful implementation of additional nuclear power programs could diminish the need for imports of conventional fuels like oil and natural gas from the USSR.[50] But at present there are only a few nuclear power stations in the whole of Eastern Europe. Some additional ones are contemplated or under construction, but the planning operates under the handicap that the Soviet Union has the only available supplies of enriched uranium and thus has effective, if unofficial, control over the whole program. Until early 1974, Soviet journals spoke consistently of the need for joint action in the development of East European nuclear power facilities. Today, the Soviet Union seems much more reluctant to share in these East European projects.[51]

When joint fuel and raw materials development projects have been undertaken, nearly always on the territory of the Soviet Union, the Soviets have enjoyed both control of the projects and the lion's share of potential benefits. There are joint Soviet-East European projects contemplated for the production of pig iron, ferroalloys, copper, nickel, titanium dioxide, ammonia phosphate, yellow phosphorous, and isoprene rubber. All of these projects are scheduled for completion within Soviet territory. The only major resource projects scheduled for completion on East European territory are facilities in Poland for the development of zinc, copper, and coal production. In addition, the terms of investment can only be viewed as unfavorable for the East Europeans. They are ordinarily expected to provide long-term credits at 2 percent interest rates. Often the East European investor is expected to provide heavy industrial equipment in return for resource deliveries promised 10 or 12 years in the future. For example, East Germany is sending steel, electronic equipment, and consumer goods to the USSR during the 1973–78 period in anticipation of cellulose deliveries from the Soviet Union beginning in 1980.

INTRA-EAST EUROPEAN CONFLICTS IN COMECON

Soviet dominance of political and economic transaction patterns in COMECON creates serious problems, but other structural conflicts in COMECON have equally important implications for the future course of East-West trade. Like the problems between the East Europeans and the Soviets, conflicts among East European countries are primarily the result of competitive rather than complementary self-interests. Intra-East European conflicts create disarray in dealing with the Soviet challenge, differing attitudes about commercial transactions with the West, and a relentless search for solutions suiting the particular interests of individual countries rather than the general interest of Eastern Europe.

One intra-East European source of friction has been the tremendous variation in the application of economic reform programs. In contrast to the goals of reforms introduced in Hungary and in Poland, the aims of Bulgarian reforms have been primarily to improve some operational aspects of central planning. Hungary and Poland have greatly outdistanced other East European countries in reforming their planning mechanisms and in promoting economic ties with the West.[52] Romania's domestic economic reforms have been conservative, but Romania has changed its monetary policies to permit membership in the International Monetary Fund and participation in programs in the World Bank.[53] The use of some market mechanisms and the introduction of convertibility have been advocated by the Hungarians and by most Polish experts, but the East Germans have followed the opposite path of centralized, production quota planning.[54] Still another point of differentiation is that in East Germany, Poland, and Romania, the central supply allocation system has remained intact. In Bulgaria, Czechoslovakia, and Hungary, it has been much reduced in scope.[55]

It is possible to distinguish four main factions on economic integration and cooperation within Eastern Europe. They are often closely related to the nature of the internal economic reforms of the countries involved:

Romania, a conservative country on the economic reform issue, argues for doing as little as possible to further integration. Romania wants to preserve its conservative national planning system and its elaborate system of bilateral ties with the West.

Hungary, which until recently was a leader in the economic reform process, has often advocated the creation of a sort of socialist free market in COMECON. Hungary wishes to reduce economic differences among the centrally planned economies by using direct microeconomic competition and indirect macroeconomic control over each single economy through national planning institutes. Hungarians have been important advocates of joint COMECON planning, but they have also argued for national flexibility to meet particular needs.

Poland, which has followed a progressive course in economic reform, has advocated a more gradual approach to integration.

Czechoslovakia and East Germany, conservatives on the issue of economic reform, have publicly favored greater COMECON integration.[56]

The entire economic reform movement seemed to be losing ground in 1975, just as the COMECON integration program was being pushed again by the Soviet Union. It is too early to tell what effect the recentralization process now underway in several East European economies will have on ties with the West, but the current situation seems to indicate that intra-COMECON integration in trade and planning may gain slightly at the expense of innovative East-West contacts for the next year or two. This is because the forces for decentralization were in general those which also favored bilateral ties with the United States and with West European nations.

The new trends have been most pronounced in Hungary and Poland. The new Hungarian premier, Gyorgy Lazar, has denied speculation that Hungary would reverse some of the basic lines of the New Economic Mechanism. But he has also emphasized that the worsening economic situation in Eastern Europe necessitates a stricter control of all economic activities by central economic organs. [57] In Poland, in July 1975, a new pattern of provincial administrative divisions was announced, providing for 49 instead of 17 provinces. This move was expected to strengthen greatly the power of the central administrative agencies, including the economic ones.[58] But other aspects of the reorganization of the Polish economy, which began in earnest only in 1973, were being carried forward pragmatically and quietly. The Polish reform model provided for the creation of the so-called Large Economic Organization or WOG "Wielka Organizacja Gorpodarcza." Initially, WOGs encompassed 34 large enterprises which accounted for some 20 percent of Poland's industrial production. But by 1975 the total had grown to 113 large enterprises, accounting for about two-thirds of Poland's total industrial output.[59] Recentralization trends appearing in mid-1975 now make extension of the process in the 1976–80 period appear doubtful. At present, even the progressive economic reform programs of Hungary and Poland are likely to support greater cohesion within the COMECON group and fewer ties with the West. But different approaches to economic reform are certain to mean that intra-East European planning disputes will be increasingly prevalent in COMECON.

Another source of intra-East European friction comes from conflicts between more developed and less developed countries. Even Soviet commentators have acknowledged the existence of this problem, though they have attempted to mute its importance:

> One can say with complete confidence that the economic commonwealth of the countries belonging to COMECON insures the harmonious combining of national and international interests. . . . At the same time, careful account is taken of existing differences in the levels of development of the economies, cultures, and social relationships in the individual countries—differences stemming mainly from features peculiar to their previous historical development.[60]

For the less developed countries like Bulgaria and Romania, catching up with their more advanced partners is an important goal. They want economic integration within COMECON to be directed to improving their level of economic development. Countries like East Germany and Czechoslovakia, industrially advanced by East European standards, are more concerned with consolidating their lead over the other East European countries. They quite naturally tend to favor agreements assigning sophisticated projects to themselves.[61] In fact, the industrial output of COMECON is produced mainly by the Soviet Union and three East European COMECON members: East Germany, Czechoslovakia, and

Poland. Not surprisingly, differing opinions on development policy have resulted in acrimonious intra-COMECON debates.[62] The less developed members have been quick to defend their rights to acquire the whole spectrum of industrial capacities rather than to specialize in producing minerals and raw materials to be processed by the more advanced countries.[63]

Romania has been the most outspoken of the less developed countries. It has repeatedly said that it supports COMECON integration only if sufficient attention is devoted to equalizing levels of economic development among COMECON members. Romanian officials I interviewed in the summer of 1975 insisted that Romania be called a "developing country" and suggested that underdevelopment was the cause of Romania's most pressing economic problems. A major policy statement in May 1974 emphasized that since Romania is an economically underdeveloped member of COMECON, it is imperative for Romania to specialize in highly sophisticated products and to turn out as many finished industrial goods as possible.[64] Other policy statements have made similar demands. Romanian economist N. Belli acknowledges that the relative difference between the COMECON member with the highest level of per capita national income (Czechoslovakia in the 1950-60 period, East Germany in 1970) and the countries with the lowest level (Romania and Bulgaria) had diminished between 1950 and the mid-1970s. The ratio of highest to lowest levels of per capita income was 3:1 in 1950; 2:1 in 1970; and 1.6:1 in 1973. Still, Belli argued that much remained to be done to promote equalization in the development levels of East European countries.[65]

COMECON meetings have often been the settings for Romanian protests that COMECON programs have not provided adequately for the national sovereignty and equality that Romania finds essential for the promotion of the interests of the less developed states. Even the Conference on Security and Cooperation in Europe (CSCE) became the backdrop for Romanian complaints about lack of equal industrial progress in Eastern Europe.[66] At the June 1975 Budapest meeting, the Romanian prime minister, Manea Manescu, spoke out again in favor of an accelerated effort to equalize development levels. He put forward several formal proposals for narrowing these differences within the next 15 to 20 years.[67]

Romania's complaints seem well grounded. Specialized agreements are often concluded among the more developed COMECON members to the possible detriment of less developed partners. To emphasize their desire for rapid industrial development, Romania and Bulgaria have recently announced the goal of a 9 to 10 percent annual industrial growth rate between 1976 and 1980. One of the major projects will be the construction of a huge steel combine at Calarasi. Bulgarian planners also announced higher growth targets, but their projections were made only for 1975. Bulgarian planners say that in 1975 national income should increase by more than 9 percent; industrial productivity, by 8 percent; and labor productivity, by 8.1 percent.[68]

Still another intra-East European dispute stems from differing degrees of dependence on East-West trade. The relative importance of East-West trade differs markedly among the individual countries of Eastern Europe. In 1970, the share of exports going to the West varied from 23.7 percent in Bulgaria to 45.0 percent in Romania. The share of imports of East European countries coming from Western countries also varied sharply, from 26.7 percent in Bulgaria to 48.5 percent in Romania.[69] This means that some East European countries suffer more than others from the effects of unfavorable balances of trade with the West. Romania again appears to be the country most adversely affected. Romanian officials have admitted that about 25 percent of the country's total convertible currency income is spent on servicing and repaying debts to the West. In a speech made early in 1975, President Ceausescu attacked Romania's foreign trade organizations for failing to achieve export goals to hard-currency areas.[70]

Finally, there are many bilateral and trilateral agreements among the East European countries which tend to form exclusive organizations of those involved. Even where these joint programs are conducted within the confines of COMECON's integration program, they tend to work against a broad unity of all COMECON members. For example, Poland and Czechoslovakia have developed cooperation plans in the area of chemical products.[71] At the Leipzig Fair in the fall of 1973, the GDR's minister of foreign economic relations stated that cooperation between the GDR and Poland included 29 selected projects and was being intensified at two key levels: cooperation between ministerial and industrial authorities, and cooperation between enterprises.[72] Bulgaria and Hungary have their own bilateral cooperation agreement for freight transportation and for the production of agricultural machinery.[73] The Polish-Romanian Government Commission on Economic Cooperation has been active for a number of years. Early in 1975, it completed joint agreements covering the machine-tool and chemical sectors and developed specific programs to extend industrial specialization.[74] Other major bilateral and trilateral projects include the following:

There have been some agreements on joint production of motor vehicles. Three new projects have been announced that are taking place in Czechoslovakia but involve East Germany and Hungary as well.[75]

East Germany and Czechoslovakia have embarked on an ambitious integration project in petrochemicals. East Germany has completed, at a cost of 1 billion German marks, a large ethylene plant in Leipzig. The ethylene is delivered by pipeline to a Czech petrochemical complex, where it is processed into polyethylene.[76]

The new cotton-spinning mill "Przyjazn" in Zawiercie, Poland, which is owned by Poland and the GDR, is considered the first real "joint venture" between COMECON countries. Its establishment initiated some ideological discussions in COMECON about how one sovereign Marxist state could allow another to own means of production within its borders.[77]

The net result of all these bilateral and trilateral agreements has been to intensify divisions already present in Eastern Europe. Bilateral agreements tend to increase a nation's stake in specialized cooperation with countries having similar interests at the expense of broader all-COMECON cooperation. These agreements have also aroused the special concern of the Soviet Union. As noted earlier, the Soviet Union supports bilateral and trilateral agreements only when the Soviet Union can participate in them, when the projects are conducted in nonessential industries, or when the production goals are relatively modest.

U.S.-EAST EUROPEAN TRADE

Perhaps one of the best signs of tension within COMECON is the continuing attempt of individual East European states to deal with the United States and with the European Economic Community and its members on separate terms. Equally telling is the pervasive determination of the Soviet Union to control these independent contacts. Trade projections that preceded the energy crisis tend to overstate the ability of East European countries to finance Western imports, and most estimates now suggest that trade turnover between the United States and Eastern Europe will remain more or less steady at about $1 to $1.5 billion through 1978.[78] In 1974, the value of U.S. trade turnover (imports plus exports) with the East European countries was approximately as follows:[79]

Poland	$650 million
Romania	$400 million
Hungary	$110 million
Czechoslovakia	$ 90 million
East Germany	$ 30 million
Bulgaria	$ 28 million

The Joint Economic Committee estimates that with the benefits of MFN, East European exports alone to the United States could rise from 1973's $519 million to $946 million in 1976 and $1.2 billion by 1980, and that total trade volume could be much higher than some other sources predict.[80] A study by a staff member of the U.S. Tariff Commission concluded that lack of MFN has hurt Eastern Europe much more than the Soviet Union and that the industrial countries of Eastern Europe have been hurt much more than the less developed countries.[81] Yet trade gains have been quite impressive even without the impetus of MFN. Trade increases have been supported by a mutual eagerness on the part of American businessmen, U.S. government agencies, and the appropriate East

European agencies. In many cases, flexible new forms of organization have been established to deal with trade between the United States and various East European countries.

The case of Romania and the United States provides the first example. During President Ceausescu's visit to the United States in late 1973, two new joint U.S.-Romanian organizations were established. The U.S.-Romanian Economic Council was formed through an agreement by the U.S. and Romanian Chambers of Commerce. The Joint Romanian-American Economic Commission, an intergovernmental body, was announced in a "Joint Statement on Economic, Industrial, and Technological Cooperation" issued by the United States and Romania during the Ceausescu visit. The first meeting of the commission was held in April 1974. At that meeting, the Romanians announced the creation of a Department of International Cooperation in the Ministry of Foreign Trade. Headed by a deputy minister, its assigned function is to help foreign joint-venture partners experiencing difficulty in Romania.[82] Actually, the U.S.-Romanian Economic Council has been the more active of the two groups. It held a widely publicized first meeting in Bucharest in early June 1974 and has been backed enthusiastically by the energetic leaders of the Romanian Chamber of Commerce since that time.

Also in June 1974, a U.S.-Romanian seminar on the analysis and control of energy systems opened in Bucharest. It was organized jointly by the American National Science Foundation, the Romanian National Council on Scientific Research and Technology, and the Romanian Ministry of Electric Power.[83] The meetings and seminars seemed to have immediate results, for by mid-1974, the U.S. Department of Commerce was reporting a doubling of U.S. sales to Romania between 1973 and 1974.[84] Later, complete figures for 1974 indicated that U.S. exports to Romania had gone up by 138 percent in 1974 to $277 million dollars, while Romanian exports to the United States reached $130 million.[85]

In April 1975, Romania became the first East European country after the Soviet rejection of the Trade Act to sign a trade agreement with the United States. The U.S. part of the agreement was approved by President Ford and submitted to Congress in April. The agreement, based in part on claims by President Ford that the Romanian emigration procedures were liberal enough to permit him to waive the restrictive clauses of the Jackson amendment, was expected to increase greatly the flow of Romanian-U.S. trade.

Some specific agreements between U.S. companies and Romania are particularly important. Control Data was among the first companies to take advantage of Romania's joint-venture laws. The Romcontroldata factory began operations very early in 1975.[86] In September 1974, Ceausescu met with Charles B. Branch of the Dow Chemical Company to discuss the possibility of expanding economic and technological cooperation between Romanian chemical enterprises and the Dow Chemical Company.[87] By the end of 1974, some 30 American corporations or subsidiaries had registered in Romania.

The Export-Import Bank has been especially active in financing investment opportunities in Romania. Since 1971, when President Nixon made the required "determination of national interest," the Export-Import Bank has made loans and issued credits for a variety of Romanian projects, including a jet aircraft plant for making artificial leather. Private American banks have also been active supporters of Romanian projects. Manufacturers Hanover made its entry into Romania by helping to finance two aluminum rolling mills and by establishing a branch office in Bucharest. Together with Barclay's Bank of Great Britain and Romania's Bank for Foreign Trade, Manufacturers set up the London-based Anglo-Romanian Bank, Ltd. The Anglo-Romanian Bank has financed a radial tire plant as well as the sale of oil drilling equipment.[88]

The Romanians have been enthusiastic trade partners. The Romanians who work in the foreign trade apparatus are apparently uniformly eager for more trade with the United States. FTO officials I interviewed in the summer of 1975 expressed regret that Americans seemed more hesitant than West Europeans to deal in the Romanian market. One reason for the difficulty Americans have had is the relative inaccessibility of Romanian FTOs. The Romanian foreign trade system is less flexible than that of several other East European countries, for it emphasizes a "double subordination" of all FTOs to the Ministry of Foreign Trade and also to the appropriate industrial ministries. Even the Chamber of Commerce is rather rigidly obligated to the Ministry of Foreign Trade. Another problem is that FTO officials are cautious in the assertion of foreign trade initiatives. FTOs follow carefully prescribed guidelines and are unwilling to comment on general trends and possibilities not clearly related to the concerns of their particular export-import firm. Romanian enthusiasm for trade with the United States comes from several sources. The Romanians are openly displeased with many of their obligations to COMECON and to the USSR, and they view trade with the United States as one way of gaining flexibility. They obviously view the United States as the most reliable long-term source for their high-technology needs.

Trade ties between the United States and Poland were given a tremendous boost by the meeting between President Ford and Edward Gierek, the Communist party chief, in October 1974. They signed two documents expressing their determination to improve economic, industrial, and technological cooperation between the United States and Poland. They projected a volume of $2 billion in U.S.-Polish trade by 1980.[89] Actually, present greatly extended trade ties between the United States and Poland date back to Nixon's visit to Poland in 1972. One result of that visit was extension of MFN to Poland, along with access to credits from the United States' Export-Import Bank. The official declaration of national interest was made on November 8, 1972. In the 1972–74 period, Polish-U.S. trade doubled. Before the oil crisis it was expected to reach $1 billion by 1976, but now this figure has been revised downward.[90] As in the case of Romania, the United States government encouraged the development of a joint trade commission, the U.S.-PolishTrade Commission. Its accomplishments already include the expansion of Eximbank credits to Poland, adoption of procedures for the settlement of commercial disputes, and planning for a new international trade center in Warsaw, which will provide living and office space for American and other foreign businessmen.[91]

Sales and projects involving Poland and the United States are extensive partly because for 25 years, Poland has been making regular payments on a debt incurred after World War II. Payments have been made according to the original schedule, and they are also being made on credits extended to the Bank of Poland in the 1950–60 period. Typical Eximbank-supported projects have been a \$2.6 million loan to finance 45 percent of U.S. costs in the sale of furnaces for a steel plant in Poland, and a \$1.4 million loan to help finance a \$3 million sale of computer peripheral equipment to be supplied by Control Data.[92]

In contrast to general Romanian satisfaction with joint-venture agreements, the Poles have complained about the terms of some cooperative ventures. Polish foreign trade officials claim that in cooperation agreements between Polish and Western companies, Western partners reserve for themselves markets in third countries where they have previously established good sales and service networks, leaving undeveloped markets to the Polish investor. Another common complaint is that in joint-venture or cooperation agreements with Western firms, Polish partners are expected to produce the most simple and unsophisticated goods. This leads to a third Polish complaint—that American companies offer only obsolete technology to Poland.[93]

The United States has also expressed some dissatisfaction with the terms of its trade with Poland. Early in the spring of 1975, the U.S. Department of the Treasury announced its suspicion that electric golf carts from Poland were being sold in the United States at less than fair market value.[94] Poland has been the only COMECON member to enjoy MFN status, and it seems unlikely that present disturbances will outweigh a fairly long tradition of trade cooperation between the United States and Poland. Current problems seem to result in part from hesitation in the Polish economic reform process.

Cooperation between the United States and the remaining four countries of Eastern Europe has been less extensive. Most of the cooperation deals concluded between the United States and Hungary have been in agriculture. The American Corn Production Systems Corporation, of Rosemount, Illinois, has been active in Hungary as a developer of improved yields in corn production.[95] An American specialized farm equipment manufacturer, the Hesston Corporation, has concluded another series of agreements with Hungary. Under a \$3 million sales agreement with Hungary's FTO Agrotroszt, the U.S. firm will supply Hungary with harvesting equipment.[96] Recently, Hungarian-U.S. relations were placed on a broader base when the National Bank of Hungary obtained a five-year loan of \$100 million, organized by an affiliate of the First National City Bank of New York.[97]

Eventually, Hungarian-U.S. relations whould have an economic turnover approaching those of Poland and Romania. The Hungarians are handicapped by lack of MFN. Their structured trading relations with the USSR will in all likelihood prevent them from employing the independent tactics of the Romanians in the near future. Foreign trade officials in Hungary are very optimistic about the long-term future of Hungarian-U.S. relations, however. Officials in Intercooperation, a government agency charged with encouraging Western joint ventures with Hungarian firms, told me that only the lack of persistence of American businessmen made them lose out to West European competitors. Like the Romanians, the Hungarians expressed a preference for dealing with American companies because of their allegedly superior research and development capabilities. Large enterprises and FTOs have much more independent responsibility in Hungary than in most other East European countries. They are often permitted to deal directly with Western manufacturers.

The outlook for more trade between the United States and Czechoslovakia is not very bright. After 1968, relations between the United States and Czechoslovakia had been developing slowly but consistently until a conflict over the provisions of the Trade Reform Act threatened to destroy them. Possibilities for a trade accord with Czechoslovakia were complicated by an amendment to the trade bill attached by Alaska's senator, Mike Gravel. Gravel refused to accept earlier Czech concessions and promises to pay World War II debts and demanded that the Czech government do more. He wanted the Prague government to pay back about $64 million of claims by Americans whose property had been confiscated after World War II. In 1974, the Czech government had offered to pay $20.5 million of the claims, a percentage conforming to most other international claims settlements.[98] Soviet rejection of the terms of the Trade Act forced the Czech government to follow suit in any event, but Gravel's demands only added to the likelihood that U.S.-Czech trade will continue to be minuscule. Despite private assertions by Prague trade officials that they desire better economic relations with the United States, the anti-American tone of the Czech press became harsher in the summer of 1975.

Trade relations with Bulgaria and with the German Democratic Republic are even more modest. The first consular agreement between Bulgaria and the United States was signed in the spring of 1974. The new consular agreement specifically guarantees the right of U.S. consular officials to take measures for the protection of the rights and interests of U.S. nationals in Bulgaria. This has constituted a valuable step in improving the atmosphere for activity in Bulgaria by U.S. businessmen.[99] Through its Commercial Export Credit Company in London, Manufacturers Hanover Trust recently granted a $12 million credit to Bulgaria for a petrochemical plant.[100] Even after the barrier created by the Soviet Union's rejection of a commitment to freer emigration in return for more favorable trading conditions, Bulgaria has retained some eagerness to improve trade relations with the United States.[101] Pepsi-Cola has been the most eager American participant in East German business. Under the terms of an eight-year contract, Pepsi-

Cola will equip a bottling plant in Rostock to turn out 42 million bottles of Pepsi annually.[102]

While still relatively small, U.S.-East European exchanges reflect several sources of dissatisfaction within COMECON and also suggest some new possibilities for U.S. foreign policy on matters of trade. The East European countries are eager for as many contacts with the West European nations and with the United States as the constraints of their COMECON relations with each other and with the Soviet Union will allow. The United States would be wise to encourage as many independent projects with the East Europeans as seem financially possible. In this way, the United States can speed Soviet and East European entry into a pragmatic and structured set of economic relationships with the West.

NOTES

1. Paul Marer, "Soviet Economic Relations with Eastern Europe and Their Impact on East-West and U.S.-USSR Trade," Russian Research Center Seminar, Harvard University, January 16, 1975.

2. J. F. Brown, "Detente and Soviet Policy in Eastern Europe,"*Survey* 20, no. 213 (Spring-Summer 1974): 50.

3. J. T. Crawford and John Haberstoh,"Survey of Economic Policy Trends in Eastern Europe: Technology, Trade, and the Consumer," in U.S. Congress, Joint Economic Committee, *Reorientation and Commercial Relations of the Economies of Eastern Europe*, 93rd Cong., 2d Sess., August 16, 1974, pp. 41–42.

4. David Granick, "Economic Relations with the USSR," in *Resources and Planning in Eastern Europe*, ed. N. J. G. Pounds and N. Spulber (Bloomington: Indiana University Press, 1957), pp. 127–48; John P. Hardt, "East European Economic Development: Two Decades of Interrelationships and Interactions with the Soviet Union," in *Economic Development in Countries of Eastern Europe: A Compendium of Papers Submitted to the Subcommittee on Foreign Economic Policy of the Joint Economic Committee, U.S. Congress* (Washington, D.C., 1970).

5. Robert Campbell, "Siberian Energy Resources and the World Energy Market," in *Round Table: Exploitation of Siberia's Natural Resources*, ed. Yves Lanlan (Brussels: NATO, 1974), p. 80.

6. *Financial Times*, June 20, 1975.

7. Karol Szwarc, "25 Years of CMEA," *Polish Perspectives* (Warsaw) 17, no. 5 (May 1974): 5. For the complete text of the 1971 Comprehensive Integration Program, see P. A. Tokavera, ed., *Mnogostoronnes ekonomicheskie sotrudnichestvo sotsialisticheskikh gosudarstv: sborñik dokumentov* (Moscow: 1972).

8. Miroslav Nikl, "International Aspects of a New Stage in the Development of the Council of Mutual Economic Assistance," *International Relations* (Prague), no. 1 (Annual Issue, 1972), pp. 22-30.

9. N. Patolichev, "Our Trade with Other CMEA Countries," *New Times* (Moscow), no. 5 (February 1974), pp. 14-16.

10. *International Herald Tribune*, June 20, 1974.

11. Business International, *Eastern Europe Report*, January 24, 1975, pp. 26-27.

12. Michael Kaser, "Soviet Trade Turns to Europe," *Foreign Policy*, no. 19 (Summer 1975), p. 124.

13. Business International, *Eastern Europe Report*, June 27, 1975, pp. 177-78.

14. Ibid., June 13, 1975, p. 164.

15. *Financial Times*, July 8, 1975.

16. Jozef M. van Brabant, "The Program for Socialist Economic Integration," *Osteuropa Wirtschaft*, no. 4 (1972), pp. 272-74.

17. Radio Free Europe Research, *Romanian Press Survey*, June 4, 1974, pp. 10-11, cites *Era Socialista*, no. 9, May 1974.

18. George Ginsburgs, "The Implications of the 20-Year Comprehensive Programme of Economic Integration," *American Journal of International Law* 67 (November 1973): 48.

19. A. A. Gromyko, ed., *Diplomaticheskii slovar*, vol. I (Moscow, 1960), pp. 467-68, cited in Nish Jamgotch, Jr., "Alliance Management in Eastern Europe," *World Politics* 27, no. 3 (April 1975): 408.

20. Tibor Kiss, *International Division of Labor in Open Economies with Special Regard to the CMEA* (Budapest, 1971), p. 170.

21. Yu. Shiryaev, "Socialist Integration as a Process of Planned Unification of the National Economic Complexes of C.M.E.A. Countries," *Planovoye khozyaistvo*, no. 4 (April 1974), pp. 31-36.

22. The Economist Intelligence Unit, *Quarterly Economic Review, Czechoslovakia, Hungary*, no. 5 (Annual Supplement, 1974), p. 10.

23. V. Morozov, "CMEA Countries: Wide International Cooperation," *International Affairs* (Moscow), no. 4 (April 1974), p. 10.

24. Henry Schaefer, "First Year of Socialist Integration," Radio Free Europe Research, *Background Report*, (August 11, 1972). See also B. Grebennikov, "Economic Plan Coordination," *International Affairs* (Moscow), no. 2 (February 1971), pp. 72-73.

25. L. Nilolayev, "New CMEA Organizations," *International Affairs* (Moscow), no. 9 (September 1974), pp. 145-46; V. Morozov, "New Forms of Economic Ties Among Fraternal Countries," *Pravda*, June 13, 1974.

26. *Pravda*, June 22, 1974; Business International, *Eastern Europe Report*, November 29, 1974, p. 362.

27. I. Kozlov, "CMEA Countries' Cooperation in the Development of the Oil and Gas Industries," *International Affairs* (Moscow), no. 9 (September 1971), pp. 109-10.

28. V. Zakharko, "West from Orenburg," *Isvestia*, April 26, 1975, p. 1.

29. Harry Trend, "Some Effects of COMECON's Revised Price System," *Radio Free Europe Research, Background Report*, no. 27 (February 20, 1975), p. 1.

30. J. Szeliga, "The New Price Formula," *Polityka*, February 22, 1975, translated in Radio Free Europe Research, *Polish Press Survey*, no. 2472 (March 7, 1975), p. 1.

31. *Financial Times*, June 24, 1975.

32. Crawford and Haberstoh, op. cit., p. 40.

33. Kaser, op. cit., pp. 134-35.

34. Brown, op. cit., p. 50.

35. V. Grinyuk, "News in Technology: The R-20A Gets a '5'," *Pravda*, January 4, 1973, p. 5.

36. New York *Times*, May 20, 1973.

37. A. H. Hermann, "COMECON's Credit Needs: How the West Could Respond," *Banker* 122, no. 2 (February 1972): 297-302.

38. London *Times*, May 20, 1973.

39. Harry Trend, "International Economic Associations: COMECON's New Form of Joint Planning," Radio Free Europe Research, *Background Reports*, October 11, 1973.

40. Chamber of Foreign Trade of the German Democratic Republic, *Trade Partner GDR: Information on the External Economy of the German Democratic Republic* (Berlin, 1973).

41. *Ecotass*, June 5, 1974.

42. *Trybuna ludu*, no. 86, March 2

43. V. Seminikhin, "United Computer System," *Pravda*, May 8, 1973, p. 3.

44. Helmut Klocke, "COMECON Relations with the EEC," *Aussenpolitik* 22, no. 4 (1971): 431.

45. For specific information on the rate of inventions registered in Eastern Europe, see R. V. Burks, "Technology and Political Change in Eastern Europe," *Change in Communist Systems*, ed. Chalmers Johnson (Stanford: Stanford University Press, 1970), p. 272.

46. Business International, *Eastern Europe Report*, April 5, 1974, p. 101.

47. *Financial Times*, January 4, 1974.

48. Business International, *Eastern Europe Report*, April 5, 1974, pp. 101-03.

49. Ibid.

50. *Financial Times*, January 24, 1973.

51. Crawford and Haberstoh, op. cit., p. 45.

52. Edita Stojic-Imamovich, "New Elements in the Conceptions of Socialist Countries of Eastern Europe on East-West Economic Relations," *International Problems* (Belgrade) no. 1 (Annual Issue, 1972), p. 82.

53. "Report on NATO Colloquium on Money, Banking, and Credit in the Soviet Union and Eastern Europe," *Studies in Comparative Communism* 6, nos. 1-2 (Spring-Summer 1973): 202-04.

54. Stanislaw Wasowski, "Economic Integration in the COMECON," *Orbis* 16, no. 3 (Fall 1972): 771.

55. Frederic L. Pryor, "Barriers to Market Socialism in Eastern Europe in the Mid-1960's," *Studies in Comparative Communism* 3 (April 1970): 39.

56. van Brabant, op. cit., p. 283.

57. Business International, *Eastern Europe Report*, May 30, 1975, p. 146.

58. *Financial Times*, July 4, 1975.

59. Business International, *Eastern Europe Report*, April 18, 1975, p. 105.

60. M. Senin, "Socialist Integration and National Interests," *Pravda*, April 11, 1974, p. 4.

61. Wasowski, op. cit., p. 770.

62. John Michael Montias, *Economic Development in Communist Romania* (Cambridge: M.I.T. Press, 1967), chap. 4.

63. Samuel Pisar, *Coexistence and Commerce* (New York: McGraw-Hill, 1972), p. 18.

64. Radio Free Europe Research. *Romanian Press Survey* no. 976 (June 12, 1974), p. 2, cites *Era Socialista*, no. 10, May 1974; Radio Free Europe Research, *Romanian Press Survey*, no. 990 (February 14, 1975), p. 1.

65. N. Belli, "Equalizing the Economic Development Levels of the Socialist Countries," *Revista economica*, no. 13 (September 1974).

66. Karl E. Birnbaum, "The Members of the Warsaw Treaty Organization (WTO) and the Conference on Security and Cooperation in Europe (CSCE): Current Preoccupations and Expectations," *Cooperation and Conflict* 10, no. 1 (1974): 29-34.

67. *Financial Times*, July 8, 1975.

68. Business International, *Eastern Europe Report*, December 13, 1974, p. 375.

69. E. Amid-hozour and J. Somogyi, "East-West Trade," *Finance and Development* 10, no. 2 (June 1973): 32-37.

70. Business International, *Eastern Europe Report*, March 21, 1975, p. 79.

71. Radio Free Europe Research. *Polish Situation Report*, no. 38 (November 2, 1973), p. 1.

72. Kurt Weisskopf, "The Leipzig Fair in the GDR Context," *Commerce International*, December 1973, p. 43.

73. Kenneth Ames, "New Multinationals?" Chase Manhattan, *EastWest Markets*, February 11, 1974, p. 2.

74. Radio Free Europe Research, *Romanian Situation Report*, no. 5 (February 11, 1974), p. 11.

75. *Financial Times*, February 5, 1973.

76. Ibid., October 26, 1973.

77. Business International, *Eastern Europe Report*, September 6, 1974.

78. John P. Hardt, George D. Holliday, and Young C. Kim, *Western Investment in Communist Economies* (Washington, D.C.:   U.S. Government Printing Office, 1974), pp. 27-28.

79. *The Economist*, April 12, 1975, p. 100.

80. Business International, *Eastern Europe Report*, September 6, 1974.

81. A. Malish, Jr., "An Analysis of Tariff Discrimination in Soviet and East European Foreign Trade," *The ACES Bulletin*, Spring 1973, pp. 43-56.

82. *Commerce Today*, December 24, 1973, p. 13.

83. Radio Free Europe Research, *Romanian Situation Report*, no. 18, (June 5, 1974), p. 19.

84. *Commerce Today* 4, no. 21 (July 22, 1974): 26.

85. Business International, *Eastern Europe Report*, April 18, 1975, p. 107.

86. Radio Free Europe Research, *Romanian Situation Report*, no. 5 (February 5, 1975), p. 12.

87. Ibid., no. 30 (September 26, 1974), p. 5.

88. *Forbes*, February 1974, pp. 22-23.

89. New York *Times*, October 10, 1974.

90. Ibid., October 21, 1974.

91. *Commerce Today*, October 29, 1973, p. 13.

92. Export-Import Bank, News Release, May 7, 1973; Export-Import Bank, News Release, February 5, 1974.

93. Business International, *Eastern Europe Report*, February 22, 1974, pp. 50-51.

94. *Wall Street Journal*, March 14, 1975.

95. New York *Times*, April 3, 1974.

96. Chase Manhattan, *East West Markets*, May 20, 1974, p. 5.

97. Radio Free Europe Research, *Hungarian Situation Report*, no. 10 (March 11, 1975), pp. 16-17.

98. New York *Times*, February 16, 1975.

99. *Commerce Today*, April 29, 1974, pp. 5-6.

100. *Forbes*, February 1974, pp. 22-23.

101. New York *Times*, May 1, 1975.

102. Ibid., March 26, 1974.

5

WEST EUROPEAN-
EAST EUROPEAN TRADE

West European-East European trade relations provide an important counter-balance to Soviet-U.S., Soviet-East European, and East European-U.S. trading relationships. West European-East European trade ties are beset by all the problems and challenges of particularistic interests that we confronted in the other sets of relations. In addition, there is the very important limiting factor that trade with the West has always been more important to East Europeans than has trade with the East to West Europeans. Trade with Western Europe still accounts for about two-thirds of COMECON transactions with hard-currency areas, but the EEC's trade with COMECON represents only about 7 percent of all EEC foreign trade.

There is a difference between East European and Soviet patterns of trade with the EEC. Only one-quarter of the USSR's trade outside the bloc is with the European Community, while for the East Europeans the figure is much higher. The East Europeans depend particularly on the EEC's willingness and ability to absorb foodstuffs, but the USSR's main hard-currency earners are timber, crude oil, diamonds, and minerals. The Soviets depend less than do their East European allies on exports to the EEC, and their exports are less likely to encounter obstacles. The East Europeans are also much more eager to import from Western Europe than are the Soviets, who have in the past expressed a definite preference for dealing with large U.S. corporations.

It now seems that even Soviet interest is shifting to Western Europe—to the probable detriment of both Eastern Europe and the United States. An article by A. Bovin in *Izvestia* in early 1975 noted that the rejection of the U.S. Trade Act was not so serious for the Soviets because the USSR's foreign economic ties were broad enough for the Soviet Union to find partners in Western Europe who would be genuinely interested in setting up stable, mutually advantageous trade

and economic cooperation patterns.[1] In many respects, the United States is not
as complementary a trade partner to the Soviet Union as is Western Europe.
West European businessmen have a much longer tradition of dealing with the
Soviet Union and Eastern Europe than do American businessmen. There is
even a likelihood that many industrial managers in the USSR would feel more
comfortable cooperating on the grounds of West European management practices
than on American ones. As Michael Kaser notes, some Soviet managers feel that
in joint ventures, West European businessmen can be expected simply to inte-
grate Western expertise into an existing Soviet framework, while American
businessmen are intent upon changing that framework.[2] It is also possible that
the commodity composition of trade will be more acceptable in trade between
Western Europe and the USSR than in trade between the United States and the
Soviet Union.[3]

Soviet figures on the growing trade between the USSR and Western Europe
reinforce the idea that Western Europe provides a logical alternative to trade
with the United States. The Soviet minister of foreign trade, N. Patolichev,
issued the figures on the USSR's trade with the countries of Western Europe in
recent years that are shown in Table 1.

TABLE 1

The USSR's Trade with Selected Countries of Western Europe
(in millions of rubles)

Country	1970	1973	1974
Federal Republic of Germany	544	1210	2209
Finland	531	777	1540
Italy	472	614	1137
France	413	722	941
Great Britain	641	715	890
Belgium	149	354	603
Netherlands	223	356	571
Sweden	235	232	436
Austria	155	189	340
Totals	3363	5169	8667

Source: N. Patolichev, *Pravda*, April 9, 1975.

Contacts between the EEC and COMECON have become a logical extension
of Soviet and East European desires to trade with Western Europe. If they continue to develop, it is possible that Soviet and East European trade interest will
shift dramatically away from the United States in the direction of Western
Europe. For a variety of reasons, the East Europeans are even more likely

than the Soviets to desire trade with Western Europe, but as long as the Soviets continue to emphasize a unified COMECON foreign trade policy, Soviet and East European trade initiatives toward the West will move in tandem. The Soviet Union may reason that the economic costs of unified COMECON contacts with the EEC will be justified by returns in heightened political control over the East Europeans.

THE DEVELOPMENT OF RELATIONS BETWEEN
THE EEC AND COMECON

1973 was the first year in which COMECON-EEC contacts seem truly important. In June 1973, Romania became the first member of COMECON to benefit from the EEC's generalized preference system. The Romanian application for special trading concessions as a "developing nation," in abeyance since February 1972, was finally approved by the foreign ministers of the EEC. Under the generalized preference system, some 100 developing countries are able to export industrial and certain processed agricultural goods to the EEC countries at low tariff rates. The Romanian government's request came in a letter to the president of the Council of Ministers and was the first formal contact between a COMECON member and the EEC's official institutions.[4] In all, there were three "official" attempts at communication between the EEC and COMECON in 1973: the Romanian attempts, French proposals that special privileges acquired by Romania should be accorded to Bulgaria as well, and a meeting in Copenhagen between COMECON Secretary-General Nikolai Faddeev and the current chairman of the EEC Council of Ministers.

The significance of these attempts was evaluated differently by various observers. Many still took a dim view of the reality and importance of EEC-COMECON contacts. One British observer suggested that there was little that the EEC and COMECON, as institutions, could do to play a constructive part in developing flexible trade and communication links between the two trading systems. A representative of the London Chamber of Commerce's East European Division suggested it was most likely that economic integration within each of the two groupings would gain momentum in the near future and that this would mean a lack of cross-regional communication between the EEC and COMECON.[5]

Nonetheless, recent moves by COMECON do represent a real change of attitude by the Soviet Union and the East European countries toward the EEC. Up to the early 1960s, from the Soviet ideologists' point of view, an integrated Western Europe as a phenomenon of state monopoly capitalism was ipso facto ephemeral. For the COMECON nations to establish a working relationship with the EEC would be simply to prolong its existence needlessly. In 1962, however, the Soviet position on the EEC changed. *Pravda* published "32 Theses on the Common Market." These recognized that great progress had been made in implementing the Treaty of Rome and also acknowledged that the rate of economic growth in the EEC was second only to that of Japan. Khrushchev agreed that the EEC would not be ephemeral. In the 32 Theses he suggested that cooperation between the integrated organizations of Western and Eastern Europe should be considered.[6]

A year later, the French veto of British entry raised questions again. When Khrushchev fell from power in 1964, the new leaders questioned whether the EEC was a permanent reality or a passing phenomenon. After the crisis of 1965 within the EEC, Soviet assessments discounted the possibility of political unification. Placing the internal EEC crisis into the context of NATO following the French withdrawal, the Soviets began to regard the EEC as largely irrelevant to the West European situation. It may very well have been this assessment of the EEC's probable weakness that prompted Soviet tolerance of the first Polish moves to make contact with the Brussels commission in 1964-65 and of the subsequent contacts established by other East European states.

In 1966, the West European situation took a turn for the better and the USSR again spoke of official contacts and discouraged independent East European moves. Kosygin stated that "it is becoming increasingly clear that in the modern world international contacts are indispensable and that there are conditions for a broad exchange between socialist and capitalist countries."[7] The subject was reopened in 1969 with the publication of an important theoretical statement in *Ekonomicheskaya gazeta*. Mikhail Lesechko stated that the USSR would be very interested in expanding economic, scientific, and technical ties between COMECON and the EEC.[8]

In April 1972, speaking to the twenty-fourth congress of the CPSU, Kosygin again expressed a desire for Soviet economic relations with advanced capitalist and Western nations.[9] Shortly thereafter, the Soviet Union signed a trade agreement with the Benelux nations, marking the first time that the Soviet Union had entered into a contract with a regional organization of Western countries.[10] Then, as if to validate the move, a new theoretical book advocating a broadening of Soviet foreign trade relations with the EEC appeared.[11] Brezhnev addressed the COMECON-EEC question in a speech to the Soviet Trade Union Congress:

> The USSR is far from ignoring the present situation in Western Europe, including the existence of such an economic grouping as the "Common Market." Our relations with its members will depend, naturally, on the degree to which they, on their part, recognize the reality existing in socialist Europe.[12]

Some of the East European countries had expressed interest in trade with the EEC much earlier than had the Soviet Union. As early as 1948, Yugoslav officials had started to reorient their commercial relations toward the West. Romania diverged from the USSR's policy of ignoring the EEC in the very early 1960s, when Romania built steel, chemical, and petrochemical industries with Western inputs.[13] Romania always criticized the supranational tendencies it saw in West European integration, but it wanted official contacts to be possible between nations of Western and Eastern Europe. In 1965, Poland concluded "technical" negotiations with the Common Market on conditions for imports of Polish farm commodities. In 1968, Hungary held talks with the EEC on possibilities for Hungarian exports of pork to Western Europe. At the time of the first Polish agreement, Z. Nowak, a Polish expert on the EEC, had stated that "much is to be expected from the processes of European integration."[14]

Throughout most of the 1960s, the East European governments preferred to negotiate with the EEC rather than to boycott it, following the example of Moscow. Consequently, they gave public support to Soviet expressions of caution, but at the same time they tried to promote their own interests through informal contacts and arrangements with the EEC. Symbolic of this freer attitude in Eastern Europe was the establishment of full-scale diplomatic relations between Yugoslavia and the EEC in 1968. There were strong indications that on the eve of the 1968 invasion, Czechoslovakia wanted to do the same thing.[15]

After the watershed year of 1973, events seemed to move very quickly, and there was a barrage of comments from both the Soviets and the East Europeans supporting the idea of further contacts with the EEC. Brezhnev took the occasion of the fiftieth anniversary of the Soviet state to contend that business relations between the EEC and COMECON were possible. In July 1973, Kosygin, who tends to be more conservative than does Brezhnev on matters of dealing with the West, said that contacts between the EEC and COMECON might be helpful.[16] Even the East German press was calling for additional contacts between the EEC and COMECON by the end of 1973.[17]

Still, interspersed with expressions of Soviet and East European eagerness to deal with the EEC in the years between 1973 and 1975 were some harsh criticisms. Even as negotiations appeared to be under way in 1974 and 1975, East-bloc diplomats sometimes said in Western Europe that Moscow was "losing interest" in contacts with the EEC because of the EEC's political and economic disarray.[18] Soviet journals again emphasized the weakness of Western Europe's economic situation. The Soviet press gave full coverage to a January 1974 statement of the Brussels commission which sounded the alarm over the future of the EEC. Soviet statements noted that Western Europe was experiencing a period of grave economic testing and that it faced a crisis of confidence, a crisis of will, and a crisis of thinking.[19]

The Soviets have also been quick to note emerging patterns of dominance and subordination in Western Europe, perhaps to counter Western charges of that situation in COMECON. Many reports in 1974 repeated doubts first publicized in the late 1960s. In 1969, Soviet writers on the EEC had argued that West Germany, as the leading force in the EEC, wanted to impose its interests on weaker members, primarily France, and to hasten the process of integration in order to create a German-led supranational group. West Germany was also accused of trying to prevent France and other EEC countries from developing bilateral contacts with socialist countries.[20] In 1972, *Pravda* said that Britain's

Conservative government was taking the country into Europe to strengthen its position in Western Europe by turning the Common Market into a branch of NATO.[21] The Kremlin disapproved of the EEC's enlargement, and Soviet newspapers were highly critical of British entry. Before the breakdown of the first round of U.K.-Common Market negotiations, British membership in the EEC had been regarded as desirable by the USSR. It was felt that British membership in the EEC would be in opposition to Franco-German cooperation and would turn the EEC into a looser form of assembly. The USSR opposed British entry when it appeared that these consequences would not occur.

It is not surprising that the early months of 1975 proved to be a period of little progress in EEC-COMECON relations. The Soviet Union had still not quite decided what to do. On February 12, 1974, the EEC Commission in Brussels announced that it was still waiting for an official letter from COMECON's Secretary-General Faddeev, who had been invited to correspond with the commission. Then Faddeev told a press conference that he, too, was waiting. In June, commission staff members in Brussels were still convinced that not much could be expected in the line of direct EEC-COMECON ties in the near future. For one thing, both regional groupings were said to lack the ability and desire to transfer flourishing bilateral agreements from the national to the regional level.[22] In Moscow, party leaders were saying nothing, and party ideologists were still predicting the probable decline of the EEC as a regional grouping. In one article, A. Bovin concluded:

> Speaking concretely, it is obvious that the crisis in Western Europe, the general feeling of uncertainty, the sharp contradictions and mutual distrust, and the conflict of national interests and ambitions, make any stable unification of Western Europe highly doubtful.[23]

Then, quite suddenly in October, establishment of a working relationship between the EEC and COMECON appeared probable. EEC Commission President Francois-Xavier Ortoli was invited to visit COMECON headquarters for discussions, and Faddeev's written statement of invitation was widely regarded as "effective," though unofficial, recognition of the EEC by COMECON. Later in 1974, some observers began to speculate that the relationship between the EEC and COMECON might, in time, include a comprehensive agreement covering such fields as trade, general investment policy, energy, transport, technical cooperation, and the environment. Developments pointed not only to a formal recognition of the EEC by COMECON but to a close working relationship as well. The working relationship was to consist primarily of contacts between experts at the Brussels commission headquarters and specialized agencies of COMECON. But those hopes of late 1974 have not been even remotely fulfilled.

A period of pessimism about EEC-COMECON contacts emerged once more, and by February 1975, when the first official contacts did take place, reaction was considerably less optimistic. The first official contact between the European Community and COMECON occurred in Moscow on February 4-6, 1975, when an EEC delegation headed by Edmund Wellenstein, director general for external relations, met a group of COMECON officials led by Viatcheslav Moissenko, head of COMECON's external trade department. The two groups exchanged information on the respective functions of the commission within the EEC and of the secretariat within COMECON. They also spoke in very general terms about the probability of future discussions of trade problems, energy, agriculture, the environment, statistics, and planning. The commission delegation issued an invitation for COMECON officials to make a reciprocal visit to Brussels before any arrangements were made for a "summit meeting" between Ortoli and Faddeev.[24]

Few concrete results were obtained at the February meeting. Reporters noted that COMECON officials were interested only in the very narrow matter of setting dates and details of Ortoli's visit, while the EEC representatives wanted to draw up a specific agenda of concrete measures to be discussed at the high-level meeting. Actually, the February EEC delegation had hoped to see Faddeev, but upon their arrival in Moscow, they were told that he had suddenly become ill. In the end, despite the fact that the two sides engaged in nearly 30 hours of discussion, they failed to draw up a final communique because they could not even agree on the appropriate wording to describe their lapsed efforts.

A series of related issues seemed to be behind the failure of the February talks. The most urgent problem was to find a replacement for the bilateral trade agreements between individual COMECON and EEC countries which expired when the community's Common Commercial Policy took effect on January 1. One reason for the failure of the February talks was that all parties to the negotiating process were uncertain of their real interests and goals. Officially, the USSR was supporting a uniform foreign trade policy for COMECON. The East European countries seemed reasonably content to continue the old bilateral arrangements with West European countries as long as these bilateral agreements could be used to exempt them from the discriminatory effects of EEC tariff policies. The Soviet Union also appeared to be aware of the economic advantages of relatively independent dealings with the separate West European countries. In fact, the USSR's primary concern in February was more directed at upgrading COMECON's international legal status than at developing a uniform trading policy with Western Europe. Like the East European countries, the USSR was feeling the need to protect its particular economic interests in dealing with the EEC.

The hesitation of COMECON negotiators does seem a bit unrealistic in view of what the EEC draft treaty (first presented to COMECON members late last year) proposed to do for East-West trade. The EEC draft treaty for economic relations with COMECON includes several provisions. First, it stipulates that trade between EEC and COMECON countries will not be organized through a bloc-to-bloc arrangement, but rather through individual agreements negotiated by each East European government or the Soviet Union and the EEC Commission. Second, it proposes formal cooperation between the EEC and COMECON in areas like the environment and transportation. Third, it states that the EEC Council of Ministers is prepared to maintain temporarily the provisions of the bilateral trade agreements which officially were to expire at the end of 1974. (This provision amounted to an official concession by the EEC that there could not be, at least for some time to come, an official uniform trade policy toward the COMECON countries.)

The EEC draft treaty also called for a long-term nonpreferential trade policy, including the following basic guidelines: the EEC and COMECON would give each other favorable tariff consideration (equivalent of MFN) with respect to both imports and exports; the EEC would lower its Common External Tariff if these trade concessions were matched by COMECON countries; a safeguard clause would permit each party to the agreement to suspend, withdraw, or modify trade concessions whenever imports of a given product threaten to cause injury to domestic industry.[25]

Since February 1975, there have been no further EEC-COMECON contacts, owing primarily to simultaneous fears by East Europeans and West Europeans that formal relations would mean a cross-regional economic structure dictated in its Eastern half by Moscow's needs and interests and thus not reflective of the needs of the small East European countries. East European diplomats now carry on business with the commission on such topics as agricultural trade with the EEC just like the countries fully accredited to the EEC. The East Europeans and the West Europeans seemingly have no desire to see these independent contacts destroyed. The whole point of the EEC's dealings with COMECON has been to preserve as much flexibility for the East Europeans as possible. Now that it seems likely that official ties would mean Soviet dominance in an integrated COMECON structure, the West European members of the EEC no longer see official ties as particularly advantageous. The EEC has long encouraged countries like Poland and Hungary to negotiate bilateral deals with Brussels and with individual West European national governments. The recent draft treaty provisions affirm the Western desire to see those special relationships retained.

The Soviets seem content to maintain their own informal relationships with Brussels and their bilateral agreements with West European national governments for the immediate future. While the Soviets would like the greater intra-COMECON sources of control they would acquire as a result of formal bloc-to-bloc relationships, they, like the East Europeans, can see advantages in pursuing their own course in Brussels. The Soviet Union has signed many 10-year cooperation agreements with individual West European countries and has received huge credits from France and Great Britain. The Soviets would also like freedom to continue their pursuit of special trade ties with the European Free Trade Association in Geneva.

As the situation stood in late 1975, the EEC Commission was pursuing an increasingly unified West European policy directed at separate East European governments and at the Soviet Union. Bilateral arrangements were still possible for West European countries, but it was the intent of the EEC Commission to bring them under generalized control. Both trade agreements and the broader 10-year economic cooperation agreements which proliferated in the early 1970s were to be brought firmly under EEC Commission control. A declaration to this effect covering trade agreements was made on May 7, 1974, in Brussels. Another declaration stated that economic cooperation agreements were to come under EEC supervision on January 1, 1975. The EEC Commission has been refining the principles of a uniform credit policy for financing trade with Eastern Europe. The intent of EEC policy remains the furthering of a unified West European policy to meet the needs of individual East European countries and the Soviet Union.

The Romanian attempts to establish official links with the EEC are not likely to be followed by similar advances from other East European countries which are more dependent on Soviet oil and more closely tied to the USSR's economic planning structure. But the Romanian move does demonstrate that EEC-COMECON linkages are not likely to develop completely in the near future. The subject of Romania's formal link was to be discussed with French and British leaders visiting Romania in the summer and fall of 1975. The Romanians made a declaration of their intentions at the council session held in Budapest in June 1975. It was a move visibly unpopular with the Soviets. The Romanian prime minister, Manea Manescu, made a very blunt speech in which he said that dealings between the EEC and COMECON should not diminish the prerogatives of individual member states to conduct bilateral relations with the EEC.

WEST EUROPEAN ATTITUDES ABOUT FORMAL LINKAGES BETWEEN THE EEC AND COMECON

While the Soviets and East Europeans have traditionally been critical of the motives of the EEC, the West Europeans have always approached the COMECON grouping with equal hesitation. The EEC did not take COMECON seriously until about 1970 when the old hopes for COMECON integration, once raised and then abandoned by Khrushchev, were renewed by Brezhnev and Kosygin. In 1970, some very preliminary steps were taken to develop an official EEC policy with respect to COMECON. After January 1, 1970, EEC countries were not supposed to reach agreements with East-bloc countries without prior consultation with the EEC Commission. By 1973, bilateral agreements were supposed to be abandoned in favor of commission agreements. These deadlines were not met, but the EEC was beginning to develop a common policy toward COMECON.

It was in September 1973 that the EEC Council of Ministers first formally considered the official recognition of COMECON. The council proposed at that time that an unofficial reply to COMECON's request for association with the EEC should be made through the Danish ambassador in Moscow. He was to contact Nikolai Faddeev to ask for preliminary information concerning the kind of relationship that might be acceptable to COMECON members. In 1973, the ministers of the EEC expressed opposition to bloc-to-bloc talks with COMECON, fearing that the Soviets would use them as a mechanism for tightening their control in Eastern Europe. As the EEC viewed the situation then, the Soviets wanted formal relations between the EEC and COMECON, but they also wanted to preserve all the advantages they were just beginning to acquire from bilateral trade and cooperation agreements.

One can isolate several areas in which serious intra-EEC conflicts have developed on the issue of trading with COMECON. First, various EEC members have long had differing degrees of liberalization and control in their own trading arrangements with Eastern Europe. It has often been conceded that working these into an "autonomous EEC trading policy" will not be a simple task.[26] The West Europeans are no less eager than their COMECON counterparts to retain the independent status of bilateral agreements they have developed over the years. Several examples should suffice: A 10-year cooperation agreement was signed between Great Britain and the USSR in 1974. It was an obvious attempt by both parties to circumvent the implications of the EEC's Common Commercial Policy. Even though the cooperation agreement takes advantage of legal loopholes, it represents a violation of the spirit of EEC policy. A special $2 billion credit between the USSR and Great Britain was completed in the spring of 1975. Commercial relations between the USSR and France are governed by a 10-year agreement signed in 1973. The French government just recently granted the USSR somewhat over $2 billion in credits. Similar agreements on a smaller scale between West European countries and East European countries abound.

Some claim that the balance between bilateral national agreements and an emerging EEC Common Commercial Policy is changing rapidly in favor of co-ordinated EEC policy on foreign trade.[27] The long struggle to get EEC members to abandon their separate trading and economic agreements with the COMECON countries seems to indicate, however, that West European countries still place national interests in trading with COMECON members before EEC-wide interests. Initially, all trade and cooperation agreements were to come under commission control in 1973. Then 1975 was set as the target date, but it seems unlikely that the signing of bilateral trade agreements will be much curtailed in the near future. The EEC Commission challenged a French-Polish cooperation agreement in the spring of 1975 on the grounds that it constituted a violation of the EEC requirement that as of January 1, 1975, all trade agreements had to be negotiated by the EEC Commission. The commission brought the case before the EEC Council of Ministers in March, and it has not yet been resolved. A German-Soviet agreement and a British-Soviet agreement were reluctantly approved by the EEC in the late spring of 1975. West European national governments blame part of the problem on the eagerness of East European countries to secure special trade concessions, but the problem also results from a primacy of West European national interests over EEC interests.[28]

A second area of intra-EEC conflict has developed because there are strongly developed national government bureaucracies with traditionally broad authority in the area of foreign trade. These government bureaucracies are not eager to yield authority to the EEC Commission and Council of Ministers. The United Kingdom may be cited as an example. The British Department of Trade and Industry (DTI), the Export Credit Guarantee Department, and the East European Trade Council have played important roles in facilitating British trade with the East. It is through the Department of Trade and Industry that basic government policies on East-West trade are developed and that trade and co-operation agreements are negotiated. The DTI also assists and advises British merchants trading or wanting to trade with East European countries. The Export Credit Guarantee Department (ECGD) is responsible for providing credits which promote British exports. The East European Trade Council is a part of DTI which publishes information and offers advice for British businessmen on problems of East-West trade.[29] These agencies give no evidence of encouraging the commission in Brussels to play an active role in overseeing such major agreements as the British-Soviet trade agreement. Joint-venture agreements seem to be guarded with particular zeal by national governments in Western Europe. The Fiat agreement with the Soviet Union in 1966 initiated a pattern of national rather than EEC oversight of joint ventures which has yet to be challenged.[30]

A third area of intra-EEC conflict has developed in matters related to the financing of trade agreements between West European countries and their East European trading partners. Import controls, credit terms, interest rates, and barter and switch trading practices have varied widely among West European countries. They are not eager to renounce final national authority in any of these areas, even though some progress has been made in drafting all-EEC agreements.

Fourth, there has been disagreement over the treatment of East Germany. East German-West German trade continues to be treated as "internal" German trade under a special protocol of the Rome Treaty. Some of the other EEC members have criticized these arrangements now that the GDR has been recognized by all the EEC countries. East German products are given a privileged position within the German market that the other EEC countries' products do not enjoy.[31]

From the West European perspective, still another major factor in determining the outcome of the national versus EEC authority struggle in trade will be the fate of regionalism in COMECON. COMECON claims regional legal status on the basis of its integration program, and on the basis of its continuously growing industrial production, which now accounts for 35 percent of total world industrial production.[32] To many West Europeans, it seems that both claims are false. Industrial production is primarily a national undertaking and not a

COMECON one, all the claims about "joint planning" notwithstanding. The integration program has so far been described even in the East European press as an intergovernmental program. The COMECON bureaucracy is very small indeed when compared to its West European counterpart.

West Europeans are also generally unimpressed by COMECON's hope of acquiring client states, similar to the relationship between the EEC and the developing countries. It is true that Mexico, Iraq, Iran, Syria, Egypt, India, and Yemen have shown a passing interest in special arrangements with COMECON. This is in accord with the official COMECON policy that "COMECON is carrying out a consistent policy of expanding and deepening mutually advantageous economic ties with young national states."[33] However, none of these countries has actually acquired associate member status or official special treatment from COMECON. India has been dropped recently from lists of those interested in economic ties. Countries like Iran and Yemen are attractive because of their oil supplies, and while Iran has expressed some interest in investing petroleum revenues in East-bloc countries, no special relationship to COMECON's official structure has been finalized. COMECON's interest in acquiring patron-client relationships with developing countries is a part of its attempt to develop a broader geographical base to counterbalance the Generalized Preference Scheme adopted by the EEC.[34] To the West Europeans, this does not represent true "integration" or a sign of COMECON's legal and institutional maturity as a regional grouping.

TRADE RELATIONS BETWEEN INDIVIDUAL WEST EUROPEAN COUNTRIES AND THE USSR

Thus, over the years, numerous individualized East European and Soviet contacts with separate West European countries have developed. Despite all attempts at cross-regional contacts, these specific arrangements are likely to persist. Intra-EEC disputes symbolize the continuing struggle between national and regional interests in Western Europe. Differences between the USSR and Eastern Europe are too powerful to permit a unified all-COMECON policy at present. In fact, the Soviet Union has long attempted to counter contacts between individual East European members of COMECON and separate West European countries. In this struggle, it has encouraged all-COMECON contacts with the EEC when it was able to control East European inputs into intra-COMECON debates, and it has developed its own strong network of ties with the West European countries.

It is noteworthy that the original proposal for joint cooperation between COMECON and the EEC came from Khrushchev in 1962 and coincided with his plan for a supranational planning authority for COMECON.[35] Nearly all Soviet attempts to develop contacts between the EEC and COMECON have been linked

to Soviet periods of dominance in COMECON. For example, the recent confer-
ences among COMECON members concerning contacts with the West have been
initiated by Moscow in conjunction with its drive for COMECON integration.
A Moscow-sponsored symposium on East-West economic relations met in
October 1972 to discuss the need for common approaches to the EEC.[36] In
1973, soon after the twenty-seventh COMECON Council meeting in Prague
which stressed integration, the Soviets convened another conference, this time
held in Budapest, to develop a common policy for dealing with Western Europe.[37]

Many of the bilateral relationships between East and West have been established with the device of 10-year intergovernmental cooperation agreements.[38]
The initiative for the agreements usually comes from Soviet and East European
authorities, who believe that cooperation at the economic level can be successful only when carried out under government supervision. The results obtained
from intergovernmental cooperation agreements are dependent on the expertise
of permanent mixed government commissions established under the agreements
for promoting cooperation. Under these commissions, additional joint working
groups identify cooperation opportunities in a specific field or for a particular
project. Individual companies or government representatives usually staff the
working groups on the Western side. The Soviet or East European side is usually
staffed by officials from the ministry of Foreign Trade. Western corporate members often complain that they are placed in difficult situations because of the
official status of their Soviet and East European counterparts. West German
businessmen have often complained in addition that the intergovernmental
commissions are vastly unfair because not all potential West European competing
companies are represented.[39] Despite their potential disadvantages for the West,
10-year cooperation agreements today govern Soviet economic relations with
Great Britain, France, West Germany, and Italy.

British-Soviet bilateral ties may be considered first. Relations between
London and Moscow were at a low ebb for two years after September 1971,
when 105 Soviet officials in London were implicated in a spectacular spy case. It
was not until the spring of 1974 that the upward trend in Soviet-British cooperation renewed itself, and then improvement came about mostly because of fears
that EEC regulations would soon make such cooperation contracts difficult. A
10-year cooperation agreement was signed between Great Britain and the Soviet
Union in the spring of 1974. It was an obvious attempt by both parties to circumvent the implications of the Common Commercial Policy. The 10-year agreement was signed in London on May 6, 1974, by M. R. Kuzmin, the first deputy
minister of foreign trade of the USSR, and by Peter Shore, British secretary of
state for trade. The agreement provided a framework for all forms of economic,
scientific, and technological cooperation between firms and organizations of the
two countries. The agreement listed certain specific areas where profitable Anglo-
Soviet cooperation might be achieved in the future—in computers, scientific
instruments, construction materials, electric power, ferrous metallurgy, oil, coal,
mining, and transport.[40]

An even more impressive British-Soviet agreement was completed in February 1975, when British Prime Minister Harold Wilson promised the Soviets a $2.2 billion credit limit with interest rates of 7.5 percent (7.2 percent for major deals). Wilson later came under severe domestic criticism for offering such low interest rates at a time when British annual inflation was soaring well above 15 percent. He defended the credits by stating that they would help British exports. Along with the credit agreement came a whole array of documents designed to extend economic, industrial, and scientific cooperation between Britain and the Soviet Union. Good prospects were noted for large-scale contracts in the development of natural resources including oil, aviation, nuclear power, timber, chemicals, natural gas, and textiles.[41] Both British and Soviet sources seemed especially encouraged by the results of the 1975 measures. USSR Minister of Foreign Trade Patolichev suggested that the agreements had "opened a new page in Soviet-United Kingdom relations" and hinted that Britain might be able to regain its formerly more important trade position with the USSR.[42] British authorities were similarly confident that the agreement could reverse the stagnation of British trade with the Soviet Union that had occurred in recent years. Privately, officials of Barclay's Bank and Lloyds Bank have expressed concern about what they view as unnecessarily generous credit terms. Meanwhile, the British business community has been developing new contracts. Rolls Royce, Ltd., and the USSR State Committee for Science and Technology signed an agreement on the development of a gas turbine engine for civilian aviation. Another agreement was signed between the British subsidiary of Royal Dutch Shell and the State Committee for Science and Technology on technical cooperation in the production of chemicals and agricultural fertilizers.[43]

Despite progress, there have been many problems. The British have complained that the work of the Anglo-Soviet Joint Commission has resulted in inadequate trade concessions for the British.[44] Soviet sources, for their part, have complained that Britain is still plagued by "spy mania." Other difficulties in British-Soviet trade have been created by traditional British deficits in trade with the USSR (caused partly by imports of Soviet gold and diamonds for the London market).[45]

Several product types have predominated in British trade deals with the USSR. In the late 1960s, Great Britain was active in the sale of heavy-machinery technology to the USSR. In 1968, Ashmore, Benson, Pease, and Company, Ltd., a member of the Davy-Ashmore Group, announced the signing of a contract worth more than £4.7 million with the Soviet FTO Mashinoimport, for the complete supply of an iron ore pelletizing plant. The plant was to have a capacity of 4 million tons per annum and was to be located at the iron ore mining center at Krivoi Rog about 100 miles north of the Black Sea.[46] More recently, the Davy-Ashmore Group has acted as a licensee for a system of blast-furnace technology for the USSR.[47] Sales of computer technology through British subsidiaries of American companies have also gained preeminence. In 1973, Rank

Xerox staged a special promotional campaign in the COMECON area. It was apparently successful, because in early 1974 the Soviets purchased 4,000 Rank Xerox machines.[48]

Patterns in separate British-Soviet agreements reveal the intense difficulties of securing more broadly based cross-regional agreements. Within Britain, there have been severe differences over policy between those who favor fiscal responsibility in trade to the exclusion of political considerations and those who favor the use of more liberal credit policies to secure political objectives. The banking community, including Barclays, Lloyds, and Morgan Grenfell, has been quite conservative, while the Export Credits Guarantee Department has favored more liberal terms. British heavy-industrial firms have been eager to sell products, but they have been less enthusiastic about training Soviet workers and setting up joint production ventures. These policy differences are, however, subordinated to a common desire to enhance trade with Britain and the USSR. EEC-wide policies are viewed as unlikely and undesirable by corporate officials and banking leaders in Great Britain. Most refuse to take COMECON seriously and are convinced that for years to come, cross-national rather than cross-regional ties will dominate.[49]

As in the case of British-Soviet relations, there have been cyclical changes in Soviet-French trade relations. A Soviet-French Permanent Mixed Intergovernmental Commission has been in operation since the mid-1960s.[50] At present, commercial agreements between France and the Soviet Union are largely governed by a 10-year economic cooperation agreement signed in July 1973. The agreement was signed shortly after a summit meeting between Brezhnev and Pompidou which took place on June 25-27, 1973.[51] Later in 1973, French-Soviet trade relations deteriorated, a fact that was related in part to the growing momentum of Soviet-U.S. detente. Despite these fluctuations, Soviet-French relations have generally been regarded as the friendliest in the whole East-West trade spectrum. France, after all, was the first EEC country to adopt a policy of fewer quantitative restrictions on goods of Soviet origin. In Western Europe in 1964, over 90 percent of goods imported from the East were subject to quantitative restrictions. By 1966, mostly at the urging of the French, only 200 articles remained on the restricted list.[52]

In the summer of 1974, the French and the Soviets again demonstrated their special trading relationship. They pledged to double their trade by 1980. They agreed that the pattern of trade should shift from normal sales to French industrial cooperation in the Soviet Union, possibly including joint ventures in nuclear equipment. This marked a point of distinction from British policy, which favors sales rather than joint ventures. Major French-Soviet projects to be undertaken in the years before 1980 are expected to include a $600 million aluminum plant and a $100 million ammonia plant.[53] As if to emphasize the importance of continuing bilateral agreements, despite the official EEC insistence that they be ended by January 1, 1975, President Valery Giscard d'Estaing announced the signing of a new 10-year economic cooperation agreement with the Soviet Union in December 1974. He made no public reference to the new EEC rulings on joint approaches to COMECON member countries.[54] The agreement also provided that between 1975 and 1979, France would provide a $3 billion credit to finance the Soviet purchase of $3.5 billion worth of French goods. The interest rate was set at 7.5 percent, up from the average 6.05 percent interest rate granted by the French in an expiring 1970-74 agreement.[55]

French banks were active in developing these agreements. Among the banks, Credit Lyonnais, Societe Generale, and the Banque de Paris et des Pay-Bas deserve special attention. In its first year of full operations in Moscow, Credit Lyonnais granted loans to finance delivery to the USSR of French machinery worth about 320 million French francs.[56] The French are beginning to use leasing procedures to open up more trade with the Soviet Union. Credit Lyonnais, a state-controlled bank, has teamed up with the Paris-based Banque Commerciale pour l'Europe du Nord, the oldest Soviet commercial bank in the West, to form a leasing company.[57] These efforts have been so successful from the Soviet viewpoint that a Soviet economic journal has publicly praised French government agencies and government-controlled banks for their policies on long-term credits to the Soviet Union and Eastern Europe. The journal *Mirovaya ekonomika i mezhdunarodnie otnoshenie* (World Economics and International Relations) reported that in the years 1963-70, France provided the USSR and Eastern Europe with over $1 billion in long-term credits. Partly as a means of reprimanding the U.S. Export-Import Bank for its caution and hesitation in granting credits, the Soviet journal praised the active role of the French government in financing trade.

Among the more innovative Soviet-French agreements have been several in industrial coproduction and joint marketing. France's Agache-Willot and *Techmashexport* signed an agreement for the production, purchase, and marketing of Soviet textile machinery. The French firm contracted for the production and purchase of 1,300,000 rubles worth of looms and textile equipment which Agache-Willot intends to install in France and in Africa. Simultaneously, it agreed to market more Soviet textile equipment in France, other parts of Europe, and in Africa.[58] In another agreement, the Soviet Union acquired an experimental electronic telephone exchange system from France's Cie Generale d' Electricite and the ITT group in France.[59]

The French government has been enthusiastic about trade with the USSR. Sometimes this enthusiasm has been the result of French desires to remain relatively independent even within the EEC structure. French banking and corporate officials, interviewed in 1974, claimed that COMECON was "nonexistent" in the degree of control it imposed on Eastern trading partners and noted that the Brussels EEC bureaucracy was inefficient and ineffective.

By 1973, the Federal Republic of Germany had become the USSR's largest trade partner among the non-Communist countries.[60] The 1970 treaty between

West Germany and the Soviet Union had created the necessary political conditions for this expansion. By 1974, trade turnover between the USSR and the
FRG had increased more than 30 percent compared to 1970.[61] The establishment of a Joint Commercial Commission early in 1972 facilitated much of the
increase in trade.[62] West Germany has been determined to get as much mileage
as possible out of bilateral trade and cooperation agreeements. The FRG signed
a 10-year economic cooperation agreement with the Soviet Union in the fall of
1974. In contrast to the United Kingdom and France, West Germany has not
included as part of the terms of its agreement any promise to provide government subsidies of low-cost credits.

An impressive series of business deals involving joint cooperation between
West Germany and the Soviet Union has been concluded. A West German steel
consortium concluded a very large agreement with the Soviet Union for the
construction of a steel plant. The contract is one of the largest East-West industrial projects undertaken since World War II. Salzgitter AG is the largest German
investor in the project. The Soviet Union paid DM 2.5 billion in cash for the
first of the huge steel mills to be constructed in Kursk. This cash payment by
the Soviet Union represents a rare exception to the usual practice of granting
credits by Western countries delivering products to the USSR.[63] In October
1973, a complicated natural gas transmission project, involving West German
bank credits and deliveries of wide-diameter steel pipes to the USSR in exchange
for Soviet deliveries of natural gas to the FRG, was initiated. The second phase
of the project, which was to have involved Iran as well, ran into difficulty as the
result of pricing problems.[64]

Aside from the United States, the Federal Republic of Germany is probably
the most important source for the USSR of high-technology products. Agreements concluded in 1975 indicate that the USSR is determined to exploit fully
West German sources of scientific and high-technology products, especially if
the United States does not develop a more liberal trade policy.[65] A June 1975
meeting of the USSR-FRG Joint Commission pledged to further cooperation in
high-technology areas.

West German businessmen are conscious of their own special position in
trade with the USSR. Ideologically, the development of West German-Soviet
ties has been difficult for the Soviets to justify, but at the day-to-day level of
business transactions the West Germans have capitalized on their proximity to
the USSR, their long tradition of working in the Soviet market, and their ability
to conclude cash deals by providing technology the Soviets find hard to secure
from the United States. One West European banker expressed the feeling that
the Germans would continue to hold first position in trade with the USSR for
the foreseeable future because of the German businessman's ability to work
patiently and pragmatically with the Soviet FTOs and the Ministry of Foreign
Trade. The same banker suggested that American, British, and French businessmen sometimes lacked the requisite experience and patience for dealing effec-

tively in the Soviet market.[66] At any rate, bilateral ties rather than EEC ties are clearly preferred by the Federal Republic of Germany.

While Italy's precarious financial position serves to temper its enthusiasm for trade with the Soviet Union, Italy has been a consistently important West European trade partner for the USSR. Italy and the USSR increased their mutual trade turnover by 140 percent during the 1970-74 Five-Year Plan period.[67] Italy was one of the pioneers in deals with the East and sometimes suffered because of it. Fiat's problems are legendary. At times, Fiat was forced to plead with Soviet authorities for security clearance to inspect the very plants it had helped to build. Agreements involving cooperation with Olivetti, Montecatini-Edison, and other Italian firms were also concluded very early in the game of East-West trade.[68] Samuel Pisar notes that, on the whole, the Italians have been among the most persistent West Europeans in advancing their business relations with the USSR.[69] Several recent agreements point to more joint efforts in the future. An agreement has been signed between Montecatini-Edison and a Soviet foreign trade organization for the construction of seven large chemical complexes in the Soviet Union and the delivery to Italy of a number of products that those complexes will produce.[70] Ente Nazionale Idrocarburi (ENI) has negotiated a large gas pipeline deal with the USSR.[71]

The Italians have shown little enthusiasm for generalized EEC control of their contacts with the USSR. Particularly in long-term joint ventures, the Italians would appear to have little to gain from coordinated policies. They view the Common Commercial Policy in its application to the USSR and Eastern Europe as a necessary adjunct to economic union in Western Europe, but they are eager to preserve as much of their bilateral trading flexibility as possible.

COMECON-EEC cross-regional activities have been hindered not only by the bilateral nature of British, French, German, and Italian agreements with the USSR, but also by the inputs of specific intragovernmental actors. It is well to remember that while Wilson, Schmidt, Giscard d'Estaing and representatives of the Soviet Ministry for Foreign Trade sign the 10-year cooperation agreements, the companies and FTOs implementing these agreements fill in their specific content. Though they are far more strictly controlled by central planning mechanisms than are their corporate counterparts, FTOs do have sufficient authority to promote new projects or to alter orders from the government trade bureaucracy.

In practice, there is little concern for securing COMECON or EEC approval for trade agreements or individual joint ventures. While the EEC and COMECON are stressing a regional-level relaxation of tensions and cross-regional cooperative measures, it is the pluralistic substructure of COMECON and EEC countries that will ultimately determine the trend of EEC-COMECON relations. Pronouncements are relatively meaningless if they fail to result in specified behavioral changes or constraints, and so far there has been little indication that the EEC or COMECON can really control the course of inter-European trade relations. This is a greater problem for COMECON than it is for the EEC. COMECON lacks even that most fundamental of policy-making tools, a well-disciplined, efficient, and sufficiently large central bureaucracy.

TRADE RELATIONS BETWEEN INDIVIDUAL WEST EUROPEAN COUNTRIES AND EAST EUROPEAN COUNTRIES

Contacts between individual East European members of COMECON and individual West European states have also been numerous. There are, however, some general problems which suggest that the potential of these contacts may be somewhat limited. There is the growing problem of indebtedness of the various small East European countries. Poland's trade situation in particular has been steadily worsening. A leading Polish economist, Professor Tabaczynski, revealed recently that Poland has been forced to set a ceiling on credit purchases in the West. Poland's trade deficit with Western Europe and the United States widened from only $316 million in 1972 to $2.31 billion in 1974. Hungary also anticipates a growing trade deficit with the West. In both cases, annual debt-servicing costs are approaching a 25 percent level, widely regarded as too high.[72]

While acknowledging the problem, many bankers in Western Europe suggest that the uncertainty of debt-servicing requirements should simply encourage more imaginative financial relationships between Western and Eastern Europe. Joint ventures, equity investment, and greater participation in Western financial and trade organizations are seen as possible means of circumventing the problem. Long-term bilateral cooperation agreements are also a popular solution and rest on East European convictions that EEC policy will remain flexible with respect to Eastern Europe even if not with respect to the Soviet Union. Romanian officials are particularly adamant on this point. They predict that trade and cooperation agreements will soon be guided by general EEC principles, but that specific arrangements will still be worked out on a case-by-case basis. Hungarian trade officials, particularly those involved in the promotion of joint ventures, claim simply that the idea of a common West European policy applicable to specific East European deals has been dropped.[73]

Great Britain has been somewhat less active than France and Germany in developing trade agreements with East European countries. Still, in 1973, Eastern Europe's trade with Britain doubled, and the trend has been upward since that time.[74] In fact, there has been a developing tradition of trade between Great Britain and Eastern Europe since the early 1960s. As early as 1964, Great Britain decided to abolish its severe quota system on imports of East European origin in favor of a more flexible trade policy. Quantitative controls on virtually all goods of Polish, Czech, Romanian, Hungarian, and Bulgarian origin were lifted under the so-called open general license in return for assurances by the countries concerned that prices would be aligned to world levels.[75]

Great Britain's current trade ties are primarily with Poland and Romania. Poland remains Great Britain's largest East European customer. In 1974, a very large contract for British assistance in the construction of a huge tractor plant in Poland was signed. In 1975, still further expansion in all kinds of U.K.-Polish commercial ties was predicted despite British unwillingness to grant large long-term credits to the Poles. Romania, eager to develop as many bilateral ties with the West as possible, has been encouraging British companies to form joint ventures in Romania. By the end of 1975, it was expected that six British companies might start production in Romania. The joint-venture contracts looked newly attractive to British companies partly because of the lessened pressure from Romanians about price stability clauses in contracts. At the end of 1974, because of Romanian unwillingness to include inflation adjustments in contract prices, British exporters had been forced to withdraw from four or five major contracts negotiated with the Romanians in the fields of pulp and paper, metallurgy, chemicals, and petrochemicals.[76]

France has also been developing active commercial ties with individual East European countries. After 1972, French-Polish cooperation has been developing with dynamism. This can be explained by the favorable implementation of the long-term economic agreement concluded at the end of 1972.[77] A visit to Warsaw in October 1973 by then French Finance Minister Valery Giscard d'Estaing opened prospects for even closer French-Polish cooperation.[78] A new five-year economic cooperation agreement was signed when Giscard d'Estaing visited Warsaw in June 1975. That agreement provided for the granting of 5 billion French francs in long-term credits to the Poles to help finance a new coal-mining development project south of Warsaw.[79] The five-year agreement made no mention of the new EEC restrictions on trade agreements.

The Romanians have successfully extended their campaign for more West European participation in joint ventures to the French. At a meeting of the Franco-Romanian Joint Commission in September 1974 it was decided to set up a joint enterprise for the production of electronic medical equipment. The enterprise will be known as Electronica Aplicata Romana-Elaron, and it was established under an agreement between Romania's Industrial Central for Electronics and Calculating Techniques and France's L'Electronique Appliquee.

West Germany was the last of the Common Market countries to reduce the severity of its import control system. In 1966, the Federal Republic instituted a liberalization under which a long-term permit could be issued for the entry of certain East European items without limit as to quantity.[80] The slow change on the import policy issue contrasts with other aspects of West German trade policy with Eastern Europe. In many ways, West Germany has long had special trade interests in Eastern Europe, in part because of its ties to East Germany. West German trade with Eastern Europe has been developed in recent years on the foundation of bilateral long-term agreements. The first cooperation agreement was concluded with Yugoslavia in 1969, followed by Romania in 1973, Poland and Hungary in 1974, and Czechoslovakia early in 1975.[81]

There are still only a few contacts between Italy and the various East European countries. But, perhaps as a precursor of change, a seminar on technology transfer and trade was held in Milan in 1974. Typical of the nascent efforts in Italian-East European contacts is a series of projects in petrochemicals. A Rome-based joint Italian-French group called Technipetrol is building two large chemical production complexes in Romania.[82]

Finally, there have been a number of contacts between East European countries and the smaller West European members of the EEC. Some examples can be found in contacts between Belgium and a couple of East European countries. Under an agreement between a Belgian consortium, headed by the Banque de Bruxelles and the Romanian Foreign Trade Bank, medium-term financing for the purchase of Belgian industrial goods has been made possible.[83]

Several important factors distinguish intra-European contacts from Soviet-U.S. or Soviet-West European contacts. Corporate interests play a more decisive role in the East European trading activities undertaken by West European governments than they do in West European trade with the Soviet Union. This is due primarily to the smaller political stakes which governments see involved. West European companies, for their part, see the East European countries as smaller but more reliable markets and trading partners. Most companies have expressed a broad interest in simply expanding trade and investment in Eastern Europe. They seem relatively unconcerned about the political implications of their trade agreements. They lobby within national governments and even at EEC Commission Headquarters for credits and for lessening of import and export restrictions, but they are advocates of better business opportunities and of higher profits, not of political reconciliation. For them, as for U.S. companies involved in East European trade, the emphasis is on making the present political structure work to their best advantage. Detente means little outside the realm of specific corporate gains, and it is rarely emphasized within the East European context.

This set of corporate beliefs and goals is important because it appears to be so different from the aims of governments signing 10-year economic agreements and urging high-level cross-national political and economic cooperation. West European governments appear to be following the old functionalist approach to political institution building while West European companies are pursuing a strategy with much more limited aims. The irony of all this is that governments are attempting to promote the activities of corporations, with their specific and limited goals, to achieve the governmental aspirations of broad political accommodation. The companies neither think about the broad plane of political detente nor care about it very deeply. It is only when specific matters of company concern arise that governments are sought out by corporations. One result of all this in the West European-East European framework has been an intense, competitive pluralism of interests.[84]

IMPLICATIONS OF CONTINUED BILATERALISM IN
EAST-WEST TRADE

The near future is likely to encourage a victory for the forces of national self-interest and corporate self-interest over bloc-to-bloc negotiations between COMECON and the EEC. Assuming the continued existence of a relatively incomplete set of formal relationships between the EEC and COMECON, one might expect several things to happen to East-West trade. Most aspects of the pattern should work to the advantage of the United States, and probably would work to the advantage of the East European countries and the Soviet Union as well. The West European countries may find only the first aspect of the situation to their liking.

1. There could be a fairly important credit battle between the United States and Western Europe, as governments compete with each other to provide favorable rates of interest on long-term credits to the East. The result of this struggle would probably help no one in the long run, but it may give some temporary advantages to West European countries.
2. Because of the relatively greater inflation in most of the West European countries, U.S. companies would be able to retain a slight competitive advantage in dealing both with East European countries and with the Soviet Union.
3. The East European countries would have somewhat greater flexibility in choosing trading partners if COMECON does not become engaged in a series of bloc-to-bloc relationships with Western Europe, and this, too, could work to the advantage of the United States.
4. In the absence of formal bloc-to-bloc EEC-COMECON relations, the United States could probably be more successful in developing its own economic ties with the USSR.

We will first consider the possibility of a credit battle between the United States and Western Europe. There are already many signs that the USSR has embarked on a program to pressure the United States into doing something about the collapse of the trade agreement. So far, the main thrust of the USSR's campaign has been that the Soviet Union is going to buy a great deal in the West and that if the United States does not choose to facilitate its trade with the USSR through low-cost credits, purchases will be made elsewhere. In the 1974-75 period, France, Great Britain, Italy, and Japan made credits totaling $8 billion available to the USSR. The United States has supplied only about $469 million in credits since February 1973 and now has cut off government subsidies entirely.[85]

A recent Export-Import Bank report underlined the importance of this competition for the future of U.S. trade. The February 1975 report complained that Eximbank rates simply cannot compete with export credit agencies in

Europe and Japan, which continue to supply as much as 85 percent of the export prices of their own products at 6 and 7 percent, while the blended rate of Eximbank and commercial financing in the United States sometimes runs up to 11 percent and even higher. Therefore, from Eximbank's perspective, the United States cannot compete very effectively with European countries in interest rates offered or in the percentage of export prices financed by government credits.[86]

There have been some joint efforts among the United States, the EEC, and Japan to reach agreement on terms for export credits. Talks were started in the fall of 1973 and are still in progress, but a number of unresolved differences remain. In October 1974, the United States and the EEC discussed proposals that would have forced government-backed export credits of more than five years duration to carry an interest rate of at least 8 to 9 percent, but only four of the EEC countries signed the agreement.[87]

The problem of credits appears to be a serious one for the United States. A recently declassified CIA study notes that "Western medium- and long-term credits have been an important factor in the growth of Soviet imports from the West. They almost certainly will be less of a factor over the next five or six years, although the USSR will continue to draw on the large volume of Western credits already extended." The CIA report notes that with export earnings rising rapidly, Moscow will have little need to solicit Western credits in order to increase imports substantially during 1975-80. However, as long as Western governments continue to offer long-term credits at interest rates below the expected world long-term inflation rates, Moscow will certainly opt for credits. At the same time, it will probably reduce the export of goods and raw materials whose value may be expected to increase in time. Under these conditions, the large credits extended by West European governments may tend to give them a significant trade advantage over the United States in particular areas.[88]

Some effects of the lesser U.S. willingness to supply credits have already been felt. In February 1975, Armand Hammer of Occidental Petroleum announced that he had reached an accord to build a $300 million ammonia pipeline in the USSR. He said that American companies would miss out on much of the business because of the collapse of the Soviet-U.S. trade agreement and because of the greater West European willingness to provide favorable credit and financing terms. Most of the financing will come from Entrepose of France. The French partners will provide financing and equipment, valued at about $250 million, and the Americans will do the engineering, valued at about $50 million. Hammer said that U.S. companies would have secured a larger share of the pipeline project if the trade agreement had not fallen through.[89] Barring a unified EEC policy in dealing with COMECON, it seems very likely that the battles over credits among the West European countries, the United States, and Japan will continue.

A second factor may work to the ultimate advantage of the United States. Because of the relatively greater inflation in most of the West European countries,

U.S. companies should be able to retain a slight competitive advantage in dealing with the East European countries and with the USSR. The Soviet Union seems to be well aware of this particular advantage in dealing with the United States. An article in *International Affairs* (Moscow) cited the following average annual rates of decline in purchasing power of currencies, comparing 1974 with 1973. Its figures (in percent) come from calculations made by the First National City Bank of New York.[90]

United States	9.3
Federal Republic of Germany	6.4
France	11.1
Britain	12.1
Italy	12.7
Japan	18.2

This means that projected price stability for U.S. goods is greater than that of any of the West European countries except West Germany. This should enhance the attractiveness of purchasing from the United States in the absence of a unified EEC price policy, which presumably could achieve greater price stability than is currently possible.

A third factor is that in the absence of bloc-to-bloc relations, the East European countries will have somewhat greater flexibility in choosing trade partners, especially if the United States passes new trade legislation granting MFN to East European countries. Also, in the absence of formalized bloc-to-bloc relations, the United States will probably be more successful in dealing with the Soviet Union. Just as the East European countries would have greater freedom in preserving the relative independence of their ties with the United States, so the Soviet Union would be able to exploit its contacts with the United States. This assumes, of course, that some changes will be made in U.S. trade legislation.

IMPLICATIONS OF FORMAL RELATIONSHIPS BETWEEN THE EEC AND COMECON

One also needs to consider the possibilities that would arise with a greater development of formal EEC-COMECON ties. Formal relations would probably give a substantial trade advantage to the EEC group and a few advantages to the USSR. It would mean a unified West European credit policy, a more uniform legal operating code for West European corporations, and perhaps a greater West European technological unity and advantage. It would make Western Europe a bigger market and seller and would tend to reduce the advantages of size that now accrue to the United States. It would mean a unified COMECON trade policy, presumably more reflective of Soviet than of East European interests. Formal ties would reduce the flexibility the United States now has to develop ties with Eastern Europe and even with the Soviet Union. From the American point of view, it would seem more advantageous to have EEC-COMECON relations remain in their relatively fragmented state and less advantageous to encourage the emergence of unified EEC-COMECON relations.

NOTES

1. A. Bovin, "Trade and Detente," *Izvestia*, January 19, 1975, p. 2. See also Michael Kaser, "Soviet Trade Turns to Europe," *Foreign Policy*, no. 19 (Summer 1975) p. 123.

2. Kaser, op. cit., p. 132.

3. Samuel Pisar, *Coexistence and Commerce* (New York: McGraw-Hill, 1970), p. 75.

4. London *Times*, June 6, 1973.

5. Interview with Robert Anthony and other East European division members of the London Chamber of Commerce, June 7, 1974. See also Robert Anthony, "Uniting the Two Europes," in *Commerce International* (London) 105, no. 1 (January 1974): 37.

6. Charles Ransom, *The European Community and Eastern Europe* (Totawa, N. J.: Rowman and Littlefield, 1973).

7. *Pravda*, April 8, 1966, p. 1. This was Kosygin's speech to the twenty-third congress of the CPSU in 1966.

8. Mikhail Lesechko, *Ekonomicheskaya gazeta*, no. 10 (1969).

9. *Pravda*, April 7, 1972.

10. Edita Stojic-Imamovich, "New Elements in the Conceptions of Socialist Countries of Eastern Europe on East-West Economic Relations," *International Problems* (Belgrade), no. 1 (Annual Issue, 1972) p. 99.

11. Yu. N. Belyaev and L. S. Semenova, *Sotsialisticheskaya integratsiia i mirovoe khozyaistvo* (Moscow, 1972).

12. *Trud* (Moscow), March 22, 1972, p. 1.

13. John P. Hardt, George D. Holliday, and Young C. Kim, *Western Investment in Communist Economics*, (Washington, D. C.: Government Printing Office, 1974), pp. 2-3.

14. Z. Nowak, *Koncepja integracji Evropy Zachadniej* (Poznan, 1965), p. 8.

15. Jerzy Lukaszewski, *The Round Table*, January 1973, p. 45.

16. *The Guardian*, July 6, 1973.

17. *Neues Deutschland*, November 4, 1973.

18. *International Herald Tribune*, March 8, 1974.

19. Charles Aroche, "Western Europe: Crises and Prospects," *International Affairs* (Moscow), no. 1 (January 1975), p. 25.

20. D. Andreyev and M. Makov, "The Common Market After Eleven Years," *International Affairs* (Moscow), no. 1 (January 1969), pp. 43-49.

21. *Pravda*, February 20, 1972.

22. Interviews at EEC Commission headquarters in Brussels with staff members working on East-West trade in the external affairs cabinet. Interviews with Michael Vesey were especially helpful.

23. A. Bovin, "Latest Attempts," *Izvestia*, September 8, 1974, p. 4.

24. *European Community*, March 1975, p. 19.

25. Business International, *Eastern Europe Report*, November 15, 1974, p. 346.

26. Ibid., October 18, 1974, p. 327.

27. R. C. Fischer, "The European Community," in *East-West Business Transactions*, ed. Robert Starr (New York: Praeger, 1974), p. 52.

28. Business International, *Eastern Europe Report*, April 4, 1975, pp. 91-92.

29. Juliam D. M. Lew, "The United Kingdom," in Starr, ed., op. cit., pp. 97-98.

30. U. S. Congress, House, Committee on Banking and Currency, Subcommitte on International Trade, *The Fiat-Soviet Automobile Plant and Soviet Economic Reforms*, 89th Cong., 2d Sess., Washington, March 1967.

31. Anthony, op. cit., pp. 33-35.

32. A. Alekseev, "V rusle sotsialisticheskoi integratsii," *Mirovaya ekonomika i mezhdunarodnye otnosheniia*, no. 3 (March 1974), pp. 13-15.

33. O. Bogomolov and L. Zevin, "In the Name of Freedom and Progress," *Pravda*, June 8, 1974, p. 4.

34. Business International, *Eastern Europe Report*, February 22, 1974, p. 59.

35. C. F. G. Ransom, "Obstacles to the Liberalization of Relations Between the EEC and COMECON," *Studies in Comprative Communism* 2, nos. 3-4 (July-October 1969): 67.

36. Harry Trend, "COMECON Symposium on East-West Economic Cooperation," Radio Free Europe Research, *East-West Report*, no. 7 (November 9, 1972), pp. 1-3.

37. Harry Trend, "Problems and Issues of Expanded East-West Economic Relations," Radio Free Europe Research, *East-West Report*, no. 9 (August 13, 1973), pp. 1-2.

38. R. C. Fischer, "The European Community," in Starr: op. cit., pp. 64-65.

39. Business International, *Eastern Europe Report*, May 30, 1975, p. 147.

40. London Chamber of Commerce, *Eastern Europe*, May 15, 1974, pp. 2-3.

41. *London Times*, February 18, 1975.

42. *Pravda*, April 9, 1975.

43. *Izvestia*, April 26, 1975.

44. *International Herald Tribune*, January 17, 1974.

45. Chase Manhattan, *East West Markets,* May 20, 1974, p. 2.

46. Press Release, Davy Ashmore, Ltd., Sheffield, March 14, 1968.

47. Letter from T. W. Sherburn, manager for sales administration, Davy Ashmore International, Ltd., June 3, 1974.

48. *Financial Times*, February 7, 1974.

49. Interviews with representatives of Shell, Ltd., Davy Ashmore, Barclay's Bank, and Lloyd's Bank, June 1975.

50. A. Voinov, "The Socialist Countries' Economic Relations with the Capitalist States," *Planovoye khozyaistvo,* March 1973, pp. 110-120.

51. I. Ilyin, "Soviet-French Cooperation Gains Strength," *International Affairs* (Moscow), no. 8 (August 1973), p. 68.

52. Pisar, op. cit., pp. 105-06.

53. New York *Times*, July 14, 1974.

54. Ibid., December 2, 1974.

55. Business International, *Eastern Europe Report*, December 13, 1974, p. 379.

56. *Le Monde*, April 5, 1974.

57. *International Herald Tribune*, January 17, 1974.

58. Chase Manhattan, *EastWest Markets*, March 11, 1974, p. 4.

59. Ibid, p. 2.

60. G. Sokolnikov, "Potentialities and Problems of Soviet-West German Relations," *Mirovaya ekonomika i mezhdunarodnie otnosheniia,* no. 10 (1973), pp. 17-25.

61. N. Patolichev, "The Present Stage of the Soviet Union's Trade and Economic Relations with Western Countries," *Pravda*, April 9, 1975, pp. 4-5.

62. Y. Balod, V. Nikitin, *Vneshnyaya torgovlya*, March 1973, pp. 8-10.

63. New York *Times*, March 20, 1974; see also Chase Manhattan, *EastWest Markets*, February 11, 1974, p. 3; Business International, *Eastern Europe Report*, April 5, 1974, p. 100.

64. New York *Times*, October 1, 1973; *International Herald Tribune*, July 3, 1974.

65. V. Pshenkin, "Favorable Prospects," *Izvestia*, June 13, 1975, p. 3.

66. Interviews in London, June 1975.

67. N. Patolichev, "The Present Stage of the Soviet Union's Trade and Economic Relations with Western Countries," *Pravda*, April 9, 1975, pp. 4-5.

68. V. Ardatovsky, "Gas Pipeline Strides Across the Alps," *Izvestia*, June 11, 1974, p. 4.

69. Pisar, op. cit., pp. 60, 106.

70. *Pravda*, December 27, 1973; *Izvestia*, June 8, 1974.

71. *Izvestia*, June 11, 1974.

72. Business International, *Eastern Europe Report*, November 29, 1974, p. 363.

73. Interviews with officials of the Romanian Ministry of Foreign Trade in Bucharest, May 1975, and with officials of the Hungarian agency, Intercooperation, Ltd., in Budapest, June 1975.

74. *Financial Times*, February 6, 1974.

75. Pisar, op. cit., p. 105.

76. *Financial Times*, December 20, 1974; *The Guardian*, July 4, 1974.

77. *Trybuna ludu*, no. 43 (February 12, 1974), p. 1.

78. Chase Manhattan, *EastWest Markets*, May 20, 1974.

79. *Financial Times*, June 18, 1975.

80. Pisar, op. cit., p. 106.

81. Business International, *Eastern Europe Report*, May 30, 1975, p. 147.

82. Chase Manhattan, *EastWest Markets*, May 20, 1974, p. 2.

83. Business International, *Eastern Europe Report*, November 15, 1974, p. 353.

84. Comments based largely on letters from and interviews with representatives of the following companies in May and June 1974: Shell International Petroleum, Ltd; Cassella Farbwerke Mainkur AG (Frankfurt); Imperial Chemical Industries, Ltd.; International Computers, Ltd.; Linde AG (Wiesbaden); British Petroleum; Compagnie Bruxelles Lambert (Brussels); British Leyland International, Ltd.; Gutehoffnungshutte (GHH) (Oberhausen); Mannesmann AG (Dusseldorf). Interviews with representatives of the following banks revealed similarly specific concerns: Internationale Handel-und-Treuhand GmbH (Vienna); Banque Populaire Suisse (Berne); Societe Generale de Banque (Brussels); Credit Suisse (Zurich); Lloyds Bank Ltd.; Barclay's Bank, Ltd.; Banque de Bruxelles, S.A.; Deutsche Bank AG.

85. Business International, *Eastern Europe Report*, March 21, 1975, p. 78.

86. Export-Import Bank of the United States, "Report to the U.S. Congress on Export Credit Competition and the Export-Import Bank of the United States," Washington, D.C., February 1975.

87. Business International, *Eastern Europe Report*, March 8, 1975, pp. 67-68.

88. New York *Times*, April 8, 1975.

89. *Wall Street Journal*, April 8, 1975.

90. *International Affairs* (Moscow), no. 1 (January 1975), pp. 138-39.

6

THE INFRASTRUCTURE OF
EAST-WEST TRADE

Especially important in the whole complex network of East-West trade are several categories of intermediary actors other than nation-states and their domestic bureaucracies and regional groupings. They include transnational actors and activities, international organizations, and transgovernmental actors and activities. These are the actors responsible for implementing or blocking broad policies on East-West trade, and their potential power is enormous. They often perform at the process level of ordinary transactions, but they have the power to threaten and sometimes to change the broad structure of East-West trade.

They are best visualized as actors who limit, extend, and fulfill the obligations incurred by nation-states or regions in East-West trade. They must be taken seriously in any proposals for change in U.S. policy on East-West trade. As actors resembling and including the multinational corporations studied by Joseph Nye, they can perform direct roles, indirect roles, and agenda-setting roles.[1] They can act directly by making or implementing decisions on East-West trade policy. They can perform indirect roles by speeding up or blocking policy decisions of nations or regions. They can set agendas for policy decisions by creating issues which must be resolved by national governments or regions.

The intermediaries demonstrate the interlocking of the issues of economics and politics in East-West trade and the interrelationship of levels of structure and process. These actors are intended to facilitate economic policies following from high-level political decisions. Their functions are specific, but very often they serve indirectly to make or change broad policies. They compose the material for the beginnings of a new framework for the conduct of East-West trade. But, like their regional, national, and bureaucratic counterparts, they need to be managed and structured more effectively.

114

A list of the major intermediary actors is presented below:

Transnational actors and activities: banks; corporate licensing agreements; joint
ventures; insurance activities; barter and switch groups; corporations and
individual experts.

International organizations: International Monetary Fund; General Agreement
on Tariffs and Trade; Economic Commission for Europe.

Transgovernmental actors and activities: International Investment Bank; International Bank for Economic Cooperation; foreign trade organizations; trade
fairs; intergovernmental commissions and joint chambers of commerce; arbitration commissions.

TRANSNATIONAL ACTORS AND ACTIVITIES

Banks

Banks have played a particularly visible and important role in the development of East-West trade. They have been the vehicles for implementing and expanding credit policies of governments. The following categories of banking
activity can be isolated for the purpose of analysis: U.S. banks, West European
banks, Western banks operating in the Soviet Union and Eastern Europe, Soviet
and East European banks operating in Western Europe, and East-West banking
ventures.

Private banks in the United States became active once Eximbank's ability
to support credits was undermined by lack of congressional support. For example, the Bank of America planned to offer a $500 million short-term revolving
line of credit for the Soviet purchase of U.S. goods after it became evident that
the Export-Import Bank would be unable to support those credits in the near
future. The Bank of America also considered the possibility of forming a syndi-
cate to increase the value of funds it could offer to the Soviets on a short-term
basis. Chase Manhattan and First National City Bank were viewed as the likely
partners in the consortium, and several other U.S. banks expressed interest.[2]

West European banks compose a second source of funds for Soviet and East
European trade projects. In 1975, European banks joined American banks in
developing special arrangements to provide $250 million in credits to the USSR.
One consortium included Lazard Freres and Company, Morgan Guaranty Trust,
Banque Nationale de Paris, and several other West European and North American
banks. The five-and-one-half-year loan granted by the banks carried an initial
interest rate that was only about 1 percent above the prevailing London international rate. Earlier in 1975, the National Westminister Bank of Britain provided a $100 million loan to the USSR.[3] Other West European banks that have
been exceptionally active in East-West trade include Dresdner, Credit Lyonnais,
Morgan Grenfell, Bolsa, Kleinwort, BCI, and Lavoro (Italy).[4]

Western banks have often found it advantageous to develop branch or representative offices in Eastern Europe and the USSR. About 20 Western banks now have representative offices in Moscow. In 1974, the First National Bank of Chicago opened an office in Warsaw, where it was followed by the Banque Nationale de Paris, Credit Industriel et Commercial, and Banca Commerciale Italiana (BCI). Manufacturers Hanover Trust, with the opening of its branch office in Bucharest in 1974, became the first Western bank to develop a full-fledged branch office in any East European country. With a staff of two Americans and about ten Romanians, it is permitted by Romanian law to extend credits and raise funds in all currencies except the Romanian lei. First National City Bank opened a representative office in Budapest in 1975. Even in the GDR, where authorities have been most hesitant to admit Western banking authorities, Credit Lyonnais and Societe Generale, as well as BCI, have received permission to set up representative offices in East Berlin.[5]

Some socialist banks have assumed active roles in East-West trade. In the first instance, there are foreign trade banks, through which payments for foreign trade are often channeled. Perhaps the best known of the socialist banks are the West European-based banks controlled by various East European countries and the USSR. The Moscow Narodny Bank was established in London in 1919. Other Soviet-owned banks operating in the West include the Banque Commerciale pour l'Europe du Nord in Paris, the Wozchod Handelsbank in Zurich, the Ost-West Handelsbank in Frankfurt, and the Banque Unie Est-Ouest S.A. in Luxembourg.[6] The Czech Zivnostenska Banka has had an office in London since World War II. The Bulgarian and Romanian foreign trade banks have established representative offices in London. The Polish Bank Handlowie has a representative office in London, and the National Bank of Hungary opened an office in London in 1968.[7]

Socialist banking operations in the West have been particularly influential in two sets of circumstances: First, they are very active in the area of cash settlements. Here, the London-based Moscow Narodny Bank and the Paris-based Banque Commerciale pour l'Europe du Nord play major roles. Second, they are important in working out problems of currency convertibility.[8] In addition, East-West banking operations are becoming increasingly visible in contracting loans for socialist countries in the West. Borrowing by the socialist countries directly on the Western market is something that would have been unthinkable only ten years ago but is now becoming quite important.

Hungary placed two bond issues in the West between 1971 and 1973, and Poland arranged for a $20 million Eurocurrency loan.[9] The Hungarian move in May 1971 to raise a loan via the Eurobond market was especially important in setting precedents for the future. Hungary also proved to be a pioneer in transactions on the Eurodollar market. In 1968, the London office of the National Bank of Hungary was instrumental in raising a four-year Eurodollar credit. This was the first medium-term borrowing by an East European country from this source. These medium-term bank credits have shown a startling increase in recent years, with the total market growing by about $20 billion between 1971 and 1975.[10] Prior to 1970, 2 years was the normal term of credit, but now there are cases of up to 12 or more years, with repayment often linked to exports from the country where the credit is organized.[11]

The control of Soviet foreign-based banks is enjoyed largely by official Soviet government agencies. This dictates the pattern for control of East European banking operations by the appropriate official government agencies as well. Shareholders of Soviet West European-based banks like Moscow Narodny include the State Bank of the USSR (Gosbank) the Capital Investment Bank of the USSR (Stroibank), the Foreign Trade Bank of the USSR (Vneshtorgbank), and some Soviet foreign trade organizations. The Soviet foreign-based banks are chartered under the laws of the host countries, but they remain in consultation with Soviet government agencies through a USSR-based Supervisory Council composed of economists and planners drawn primarily for the ranks of Gosbank, Stroibank, Vneshtorgbank, and the FTOs. The Supervisory Council is supposed to encourage two-way flow of information between Soviet international banking representatives and Communist party and government officials. In practice, it serves to make certain that bank policies are implemented according to the wishes of party leaders.[12]

East-West joint banking ventures provide a final category of banking facilities and activities. Since 1971, a number of mixed banks have emerged. The Banque Franco-Roumaine (Paris, 1971) has a 51 percent participation held by the Romanian Foreign Trade Bank. The Anglo-Romanian Bank in London has a 50 percent participation held by the Romanian Foreign Trade Bank, and 30 percent held by Barclay's Bank International. The Mitteleuropische Bank AG in Frankfurt has shareholding by the Trade Bank of Warsaw. These banks serve many of the same purposes as do the foreign-based banks, but they are less tightly controlled by government authorities of their home countries.

One of the most important results of these banking operations has been to lessen the secrecy once so pervasive in financial dealings with the East. A lessening of secrecy has led, in turn, to the beginnings of a fuller integration of the socialist financial system into the money markets of the Western industrialized nations. There were some particularly encouraging signs in 1975 when a group of Western banks, led by a London-based affiliate of Chase Manhattan, was able to gain detailed technological and financial information to back up a $240 million loan to the Bank Handlowie of Poland to help develop Polish copper reserves.

In past years, socialist-bloc countries had been able to secure large loans without complete documentation—because of their protests about the sensitive and private nature of such information and because of their excellent record of repayment of international debts. But, in 1975, Western banks were generally tightening their requirements because of the rapidly growing indebtedness of East-bloc countries. In the Polish loan case, representatives of Chase Manhattan said that Chase's outside consultants were able not only to check out copper deposits but also to analyze financial aspects of the copper project.

In other cases, a growing desire for partial integration into the Western financial world has been revealed by the creation of special government agencies in the East bloc to deal with trade-related banking and financial problems. One example is the Department for International Cooperation in the National Bank of Hungary. Established in 1972, the Department of International Cooperation is a section of the bank's Division of Foreign Trade and has been assigned some specific functions in coordinating Hungary's foreign trade activities.

First, it is assigned the task of working with COMECON's International Investment Bank as this agency gradually widens its authority to promote financial integration among socialist countries. Second, it is supposed to help facilitate cooperation between Hungarian and Western firms, and it maintains an advisory service for Hungarians and foreigners seeking partners for cooperation. Third, it cooperates with the credit and foreign trade divisions of the National Bank of Hungary in maintaining contacts with all factories and foreign trade organizations in the country.[13] While other East European countries have not adopted this particular Hungarian innovation, it seems likely that they may do so in the future. This kind of structure could provide a bridge between the separate interests of socialist banking institutions, enterprises, central planning agencies, and Western businessmen and banks. So far, its activities are overshadowed by those of foreign-based banks and jointly owned East-West banks engaged in financing trade.

All these East-West banking agencies have been important because they build up important links with the Western banking process which are difficult to terminate once initiated and because they facilitate understanding of Western and Eastern banking processes by the banks and personnel involved in various transactions. Still, like so many other institutions involved in East-West trade, each banking agency tends to promote its particular goals and concerns. State-controlled banks are designed to carry out financial policies of governments. Privately controlled banks are profit-oriented institutions with more specific policy goals. Both types of banks can sometimes develop their own policies to facilitate East-West trade, and these may or may not coincide with the wishes of national or regional actors trying to restructure trade between East and West.

Corporate Licensing Agreements

Corporate licensing agreements are a second major transnational component in East-West trade. Licensing agreements have often been used in the Soviet Union, where Ministry of Foreign Trade and State Committee for Science and Technology officials view them as a quick and relatively inexpensive means of securing desired Western technology. Several hundred licensing agreements have been concluded, with the United States and West Germany forming the most usual Western partners.[14] Within the Soviet Union, though, there has been some debate over the appropriateness of these licenses. Soviet research institutes are often opposed to the purchase of licenses because they are viewed as a threat and insult to domestic research activities. Large Soviet enterprises and many heads of industrial ministries view licenses as cheap and practical ways to improve Soviet industrial efficiency. It takes between four and eight years, on the average, before Soviet inventions can be applied in industry, but it takes only one or two years to put Western licensed technology to practical use.[15]

The East European countries have also been eager to acquire Western licenses. In Eastern Europe, there has been little of the domestic debate that has been so prevalent in the USSR. East European research institutes are smaller and less powerful than their Soviet counterparts, and they view licensing arrangements as a way to ease their research burden rather than as a mechanism for challenging it. They see licensing agreements as one way of becoming less dependent on the USSR.[16]

Poland has been the most active East European country in the procurement of licenses. Western firms sold 200 licenses to Polish firms in the period between 1971 and 1973, doubling the number sold during the 1966–70 period. In 1974, the upward trend continued, and Poland purchased licenses in such industries as electronic data processing, chemicals and petrochemicals, marine engines, machine tools, automotive products, and textiles. Despite Polish eagerness to extend sales of its licenses abroad, purchases of Western licenses have so far vastly outnumbered Polish sales of licenses to Western firms.[17]

In Hungary, the HUNICOOP Foreign Trade Organization for Cooperation in the Engineering Industry is the major agency involved in securing licenses from the West. It has an impressive series of deals to its credit. One recent agreement providing for licenses in machine-tool building was signed between the National Engineering Laboratory in Great Britain and Technoimpex, the Hungarian machine-tool FTO.[18]

Czechoslovakia and Bulgaria have been the most cautious of the East European countries in pursuing licensing agreements. Czechoslovakia is expected to buy at least 25 Western licenses to produce consumer durables during the next few years. In contrast to other East European countries, the ministerial level rather than the FTO apparatus is most active in securing licensing agreements in Czechoslovakia. The Czech Ministry of Technical and Investment Development is responsible for securing licenses from Western countries.[19] Even Bulgaria now anticipates stepped-up acquisitions of Western licenses for the electronic and electrical equipment industries and is engaged in a program to encourage better coordination among Bulgarian industrial ministries that will be purchasing licenses.[20] As in Czechoslovakia, the ministries in Bulgaria control licensing agreements.

In the cases of Poland and Hungary, licensing agreements with the West seem to strengthen potentially competitive forces. A Polish or Hungarian foreign trade organization concerned with acquiring a license for a particular machine-tool product and a Western firm wishing to sell a license have on occasion collided with ministerial efforts at joint planning with the USSR, with domestic research efforts, and even with the efforts of other FTOs to develop joint ventures rather than to purchase licenses. Officials are reluctant to talk about these cross-pressures but do admit their presence. In Bulgaria and Czechoslovakia, the competition is between ministries rather than foreign trade organizations, but the end result is often the same: emphasis on particular short-term goals.

Joint Ventures

Joint ventures are contractual arrangements between Eastern and Western enterprises that establish a separate organizational entity. Foreign investment in the conventional sense of equity investment is a minor part of joint-venture agreements except in Yugoslavia, Romania, and Hungary, where foreign participation in management and profits is permitted. In the East-West context, joint ventures are perhaps best identified by two universal characteristics. First, they involve contracts extending over a number of years between partners belonging to different economic systems. These contracts extend beyond the simple sale or purchase of goods into complementary or matching operations in production, developments of technology, and so on. Second, they are specifically set up as joint ventures in bilateral or multilateral agreements.[21]

Beyond sharing these two universal characteristics, joint-venture agreements can exist in several forms:

Subcontracting agreements. The Western firm subcontracts the production of an item to an Eastern country. The agreement is usually for a short period of time and involves little transfer of technology.

Coproduction agreements. These involve dividing the production of a particular product, with the Western firm supplying some technology to the Eastern partner and continuing to manufacture the more sophisticated component itself.

Specialization agreements. Here, the aim is for each partner to manufacture part of a product line. Typically, the Western firm will continue to produce the technologically more advanced items, and the Eastern enterprise will specialize in labor-intensive products.

Joint marketing. Partners will usually establish a joint venture in the West to sell the Eastern output of a licensed product.

Project agreements. The Western firm, usually a consortium, is responsible for the development of massive industrial facilities in the East.

Joint construction of industrial plants in the developing world.

Cooperative research and development of products or processes.

To date, the development of true joint ventures along any of these patterns has been a very slow process. Romania passed legislation permitting joint ventures in 1971 but has established only five so far: U.S. Control Data (Romcontrol-data); West Germany's Renk (Resita-Renk); Italy's Romalfa (Rifal); Japan's Dainippon (Roniprot); and France's L'Electronique Appliquee (Elaron). Hungary passed a law permitting joint ventures in 1972, but only two have been established: Sweden's Volvo (Volcom), and West Germany's Siemens (Sicontract). Poland had also announced its intentions to establish joint ventures early in the 1970s but so far has delayed these plans indefinitely.[22]

The slow progress has been caused mostly by the stringent requirements and limitations of East European joint ventures, especially the 49 percent limit on Western ownership. Slow progress is also attributed by some observers to the fact that Eastern partners want to receive more than they are willing to contribute. It is true that East European partners have been far more enthusiastic about joint ventures than have their potential Western partners. Hungary and Romania have presented several optimistic projections about the future development of joint ventures, and the Romanians now claim to be carrying on serious negotiations on possible joint ventures with some 25 Western firms.[23]

Romania and Hungary, along with Yugoslavia, are the only East European countries which have fully developed implementing legislation for joint ventures. The joint-venture concept is a tricky one for all the East European countries because technically it involves the non-Marxist concept of Western ownership of a share of socialist property. Hungary, Romania, and Yugoslavia have sidestepped this issue by permitting equity participation only up to 49 percent and by setting up new institutional arrangements to guarantee the accountability of joint-venture projects to the domestic industrial planning apparatus.[24]

Romanian joint-venture legislation permits foreign investment in agriculture, transportation, construction, and tourism. At present, however, Romanian interest is concentrated on joint ventures in industry, principally in the machine-building and chemical sectors.[25] Hungary's new foreign trade law has been even more encouraging than that of Romania for the development of joint ventures.[26]

Early in 1973, the Polish government launched a campaign to attract Western attention to possible joint ventures in Poland. Later it seemed to lose interest, and Poland has yet to develop enabling legislation of the Hungarian or Romanian variety. Polish trade authorities have explained their new lack of interest in terms of the lengthy procedures involved in setting up joint ventures and in view of their feeling that they could not secure the kind of Western technology they want. The Poles have typically been interested in joint ventures only with major Western companies possessing the most advanced technology in their field, plentiful financial resources, the desire to share research and development information with the Polish partner, and the wish to enter into a long-term arrangement.

Prime Minister Piotr Jaroszewicz has emphasized that Poland has no objection in principle to joint-venture agreements. However, Deputy Foreign Minister Dlugosz has maintained that while Poland would not necessarily reject joint-venture agreements in the future, Polish preference would probably be for less structured cooperation or licensing agreements.[27] It seems likely that joint-venture development in Poland will be hampered by the Polish desire to use the mechanism to secure research and development information and by Polish unwillingness to permit joint ventures on terms as generous as those of Hungary and Romania. The ideological aversion to foreign control of socialist property has also been more clearly expressed in Poland than in Hungary or Romania.

Most joint-venture agreements are based squarely on the Soviet and East European hope that in this way they will get access to advanced Western technology. Perhaps this is also why less structured interfirm arrangements, more properly called industrial cooperation agreements than joint ventures, have become so popular. The industrial cooperation agreements do not involve heavy Western investment in a particular socialist enterprise, nor do they present as many problems of ideology. Hungary and Romania have been the leaders in cooperation agreements. Hungary claimed to be participating in more than 200 such agreements by the summer of 1974.[28] Early in 1973, there were over 1,000 of these agreements between East-bloc enterprises and Western firms, and the number may have approached 2,000 in 1975.[29]

In addition to their exceptional value as a source of technical information, individual cooperation agreements are viewed by Eastern and Western observers alike as ways of solving economic problems in East European countries with minimal political disruption. However, while industrial cooperation agreements may start out as simple ways of conducting business, they may end up as significant factors in altering an East European country's economic and political structure. Often viewed as minor components of the East-West trade process, industrial cooperation agreements can have significant political effects.

This has been true even in the USSR, where industrial cooperation arrangements have been greatly preferred over the more innovative and risky joint ventures. Cooperation agreements are typically signed between major Western firms and the USSR State Committee for Science and Technology, which supervises and coordinates research and development in the USSR. The agreements usually provide for joint research programs, exchanges of information and of personnel, and purchases of Western equipment and technology. Firms in the United States, including General Electric, American Can, and Occidental Petroleum, have concluded cooperation agreements with FTOs in the USSR through the supervision of the State Committee on Science and Technology.[30] Industrial cooperation agreements between the USSR and Western firms enable the USSR to gain many of the benefits of more formalized joint ventures without suffering the accompanying ideological and political problems. As one observer noted, "Industrial cooperation is a strategy designed to limit some of the financial and political effects of increased trade with the West."[31] Industrial cooperation presents fewer pressures than do joint ventures to several important political groupings in the USSR. For party bureaucrats who oppose internal economic reforms, industrial cooperation provides a means of modernizing the economy without imposing stability-threatening systemic modifications. Industrial cooperation also seems to be a satisfactory solution to the demands of technocrats and managerial groups concerned with industrial efficiency.

Insurance Activities

Insurance activities compose a fourth facet of transnational involvement in East-West trade patterns. Special insurance arrangements have become necessary to facilitate joint ventures, industrial cooperation agreements, and even simple sales arrangements. Soviet agencies with government connections but without official government control have been preeminent in the insurance field. The Garant Versicherungs AG, a Soviet-owned insurance company operating from Vienna, has so far been the most important nongovernmental insurer of the East West trade. The focus of its activities has been in four areas: nonpayment by importing Soviet companies, failure of Soviet FTOs to keep contract dates, risks of assembly in the Soviet Union, and transportation risks involving suppliers. Garant Versicherungs AG operates as a subsidiary of Ingosstrakh, a Soviet foreign trade organization. So do the other two Soviet-dominated companies, Black Sea and Baltic, Ltd. (London), and Schwarzmeer und Ostsee AG (Hamburg).[32] Garant has also started to offer insurance covering the performance guarantee usually made by Western suppliers to Soviet and East European foreign trade organizations. This insurance covers the Western supplier in cases where problems within the Soviet or East European industrial structure make it impossible for a Western product to perform as specified in a contract.[33] While less important than joint ventures, licensing arrangements, and banking facilities, insurance activities have been important in providing a climate of trust without which East-West trade could not function.

Barter and Switch Groups

Barter and switch houses constitute one of the most complex and potentially influential instruments of East-West trade. They have a certain basic importance simply because more than a third of all East-West trade is still conducted within the barter and switch format.[34] Western barter houses expect a large increase in counterpurchase transactions between East European and Soviet foreign trade organizations and Western companies in the 1975-77 period. In the first five months of 1975, the three leading barter houses in Vienna had recorded more counterpurchase deals than in all of 1974. The forecast of a continued increase is based on past experience of Eastern behavior during economic slowdowns or recessions in the West. At such times, the Soviet Union and the East European countries find it more difficult to earn hard currencies through

exports to the West and they exert greater pressure on Western suppliers to accept barter goods.[35] Among the most important barter and switch houses dealing with East-West trade are the following:

Vienna: Allgemeine Waren-Treuhand AG, Bank Winter and Company
Paris: Louis Dreyfus et Cie, J. A. Goldschmidt S.A.
Zurich: Bank Hoffmann AG, Bank fur Handel und Effekten
London: M. Golodetz
Brussels: Eurintrade
Frankfurt: Wolff Finanzberatung AG

The most important centers are those in London and Vienna.[36] Switch
trading, which involves complicated transfers of East European and other inconvertible currencies into convertible ones, composes a greater proportion of business in some agencies than it does in others. Waren-Treuhand AG and Bank
Winter and Company, Golodetz, and Eurintrade are the leaders. Of these, Eurintrade alone has the distinction of an office in Moscow.[37]

Barter is popular in East-West trade primarily because of the difficulties of
open currency exchange between soft-currency and hard-currency areas and because of the time-consuming nature of switch trade. Three forms of barter are
commonly used and they are of differing value to the Western partner. First, the
Western seller may be offered a product being sold by the particular FTO with
which it is negotiating. Second, a somewhat broader list of items may be offered
the Western seller. This is the most frequent option, and it is also a better option
because the products involved are not limited to the foreign trade organization's
line. Third, a counterpurchase obligation is the most flexible arrangement and
simply involves the purchase of products produced in the Eastern country within
a specified period of time.

Generally, there are differing degrees of willingness to use barter among the
COMECON countries. The USSR is usually more generous in the terms of barter
arrangements it offers than are the East European countries. Both the East Europeans and the Soviets have the disconcerting habit of increasing the number of
items on a barter list in times of economic recession in the West and decreasing
the number of items when times seem to be getting better.

Switch trading is the transaction involved in clearing inconvertible currency
balances in bilateral trading accounts. The means of payment underlying these
transactions are the clearing currencies in bilateral payment agreements, currencies which are not freely convertible. Switch transactions make it possible to
mobilize these otherwise useless funds.[38] Some large Western companies with
high volumes of switch transactions with Eastern Europe have divisions within
their own enterprises to handle the switch trading. These include such companies
as Fiat, Renault, and some German petrochemicals companies. Smaller companies most often use the services of the barter and switch houses already mentioned. Various COMECON members have developed differing degrees of

flexibility in switch trading. The German Democratic Republic is generally re- garded as the most effective switcher, but it also seems to be the most restrictive. Hungary and Czechoslovakia are regarded as the most flexible switch trade part- ners, while barter remains dominant in Romania, Bulgaria, and Poland.[39] In con- trast to barter arrangements, the number of switch clearing agreements between East European and West European countries continues to shrink.[40]

Barter and switch trading constitutes part of the day-to-day routine of East- West trade. The houses that handle these transactions are rarely singled out for their important policy-making or policy-implementing roles. Yet in many ways they are the groups that establish the parameters of the whole trade process. If foreign trade organizations in the East and barter and switch houses in the West develop stable working relationships, the whole climate for East-West trade is vastly improved. Without the assistance of barter and switch houses, trade would be limited to strict bilateral balancing, and cross-regional trade and investments would be greatly curtailed.

One of the most notable aspects of the barter and switch process is the fact that it shows little relationship to policy decisions and declarations by national foreign trade bureaucracies or by regional groupings. Barter and switch houses continue their operations despite the ups and downs of 10-year cooperation agreements and despite shifts in EEC-COMECON contacts. They operate on the basis of profit, and unless their actions are declared illegal or restrained by trade control bureaucracies in any given country, their work tends to continue. In fact, barter and switch houses could be expected to sustain a relatively high level of East-West transactions even if the political climate were to deteriorate. They op- erated successfully during the darkest days of the Cold War, and there seems to be no reason to expect a sudden slowdown in their activities now.

Corporations and Individual Experts

Not to be ignored in the study of transnational networks in East-West trade are some individual Western experts who have been exceedingly influential and active. Donald Kendall of Pepsico and Armand Hammer of Occidental Petroleum have directed corporate strategies that have greatly expanded Soviet-U.S. trade. In Western Europe, Ara Oztemel of Satra, Sir Rudi Sternberg in London, Samuel Pisar in Paris, and Peter Trummer of Brussels have been leaders.[41] Simon Mos- kovics of Bank Winter and Company and Wilhelm Henrichs of Allgemeine Waren- Treuhand have been exceptionally important in the switch trading area.[42] Many of these individuals have directly inspired the eagerness of Western corporations to conduct business in the Soviet Union and in Eastern Europe.

In the United States, Control Data, Occidental Petroleum, the El Paso Natural Gas Company, IBM, and LaSalle Machine Tool were among the first corporations to deal actively in East-bloc markets and to become promoters of that trade in the public policy-making process. In Western Europe, leaders have included International Computers, Ltd. (London), Cassella Farbwerke Mainkur AG (Frankfurt), Imperial Chemical Industries, Ltd. (London), Linde AG (Wiesbaden), British Petroleum (London), British Leyland International, and Compagnie Bruxelles Lambert. Perhaps the most striking fact about the comments of representatives of these companies when they were interviewed in June 1974 was their total focus on specific company plans and concerns, with very little reference to national government or EEC trade expansion preferences or purposes.

INTERNATIONAL ORGANIZATIONS

International Monetary Fund

The International Monetary Fund (IMF) has been the most important international organization operating in East-West trade. This is true despite the fact that only Yugoslavia, as associate member of COMECON, and Romania have been very active in the IMF. Yugoslavia has been in the vanguard of East-bloc countries seeking IMF support for balance-of-payments difficulties.[43] Romania joined the IMF in December 1972, and Romanian representatives played a prominent part in an IMF meeting held in Washington in September and October 1974.[44] The Romanians are concerned about the lack of convertibility of their currency, and they view membership in the IMF as a major step toward the eventual convertibility of the Romanian lei.

There seem to be definite advantages for the East Europeans in IMF membership: IMF credits, eligibility for World Bank loans, and the right to a share of new issues of Special Drawing Rights. As Holzman and Legvold note, these advantages are particularly important to nations with serious hard-currency balance-of-payments problems.[45] Romania has already secured some important loans from the World Bank. In 1974, the Romanian steel industry received a $70 million credit from the World Bank to help finance the planned $200 million expansion of the Tirgoviste specialized steel complex north of Bucharest. Romania also received a $60 million loan to construct a fertilizer plant.[46]

General Agreement on Tariffs and Trade

Association with the General Agreement on Tariffs and Trade (GATT) has been another indirect avenue of approach between East and West. Czechoslovakia, Poland, Romania, and Yugoslavia are already full members of GATT. Czechoslovakia's membership dates back to before the Communist takeover, and Poland became a member in 1967. To gain membership in 1967, Poland had to promise that it would increase imports from GATT partner countries by 7 percent a year. Romania applied for membership in GATT in the late 1960s but was unsuccessful until 1971 because it declined to accept the required amounts of imports from other GATT countries.[47] Hungary has just recently completed steps preliminary to becoming a full GATT member.

In practice, the requirements concerning imports from GATT countries have been partially overlooked for the East European countries. This is because of the simultaneous desire of Western countries to retain practical quotas on goods from the East.[48] Of all the East European signatories to GATT, Romania has attached greatest significance to membership. Romania has supported GATT sponsorship of concrete measures to facilitate the economic growth and industrial diversification of developing countries. Romania numbers itself among the developing countries of the world and hopes to benefit from these provisions of the GATT.[49]

United Nations Economic Commission for Europe

The United Nations Economic Commission for Europe (ECE) has been another source of East-West communication.[50] The ECE was established shortly after World War II. The proposal to establish the ECE, made by a subcommittee of the Economic and Social Council of the United Nations in 1946, was at first rejected by the Soviets but accepted by them later that same year. The first session of the ECE in May 1947 was attended by a large group of Soviet representatives. With the exception of the early 1950s, the Soviet Union and all the East European countries except East Germany have been active participants in ECE undertakings. The ECE has conducted cross-regional economic research, prepared statistics, and acted as a forum for the exchange of economic proposals between Eastern and Western Europe.

The ECE was probably the best forum for East-West economic dialogue during the Cold War years, and it still plays a distinctive role in economic coordination and cross-regional planning. The ECE's first real success came in 1961, when it helped to develop a European Convention on International Commercial Arbitration. This convention was designed to provide for the arbitration of disputes relating to East-West trade. In 1966, efforts to improve the 1961 convention led to a new set of arbitration rules, this time drafted directly by ECE experts. The arbitration rules achieved real practical importance in the 1970s for the first time. The 1972 trade agreement between the United States and the USSR called for possible arbitration under ECE rules. Today, many East-West trade agreements call for ECE arbitration.[51]

From the perspective of 1975, the ECE has yet to realize its potential for influencing East-West trade. In recent years, it has assumed a few new roles. It has conducted continuous surveys of joint ventures. Also, the ECE has attempted to equalize participation of developed and underdeveloped West and East European economic regions in joint-venture projects.[52]

TRANSGOVERNMENTAL ACTORS AND ACTIVITIES

International Investment Bank

Transgovernmental actors, defined here as agencies that are parts of national or regional bureaucracies which operate with relative independence in cross-national situations, have also been important in the development of East-West trade. Among these actors, specific attention should be given to the International Investment Bank (IIB), the International Bank for Economic Cooperation (IBEC), foreign trade organizations, trade fairs, and intergovernmental commissions.

The International Investment Bank is the long-term investment banking arm of COMECON. It was created in 1971 to finance long-term investment projects within the COMECON area. It provides medium-term credits for up to 5 years and long-term credits for up to 15 years. The International Investment Bank has been successful in attracting Western loans, and about 40 to 50 percent of total credits granted by the IIB to COMECON members are in the form of convertible currencies.[53] The IIB received a seven-year $50 million Eurocurrency loan in 1973.[54]

East European sources consistently rate the financial capacities of the IIB very highly, partly because it does provide access to much-needed hard currency. In early 1974, the official capital reserves of IIB amounted to 1.052 billion rubles, of which transferable rubles accounted for 70 percent and gold and convertible currencies the remaining 30 percent.[55] As early as 1972, after one full year of operation, the IIB had provided credits of 17 million transferable rubles for projects. By the end of 1973, 53 IIB-financed projects were underway in Romania; 9 in Poland; and 4 in Bulgaria.[56] The Romanians have been the most favored recipients of funds and have been the only East Europeans to receive credits exceeding dues to the IIB.[57]

International Bank for Economic Cooperation

Until recently, COMECON's International Bank for Economic Cooperation was less important than the International Investment Bank. IBEC was established in 1964 as a sort of European payments union for socialist states. It was intended to put East-bloc trade on a multilateral basis through the use of the transferable ruble.[58] Reforms in 1970 and 1971 enabled IBEC to retain its basic role as a clearing institution while giving it the additional function of a short-term credit bank. By late 1973, IBEC had obtained three medium-term credits in the West, totaling about $140 million. Few details are available about IBEC's dealings with nonmember Western banks, but IBEC is believed to have entered into correspondent relations and business transactions with more than 300 banks from all over the world.[59]

The flow of Arab petrodollars into the world economic system signals some important possible changes for IBEC and IIB and may increase their importance in the conduct of commercial relations between East and West. Michael Kaser has discussed the possibility that the OPEC countries might deposit large amounts of their earnings in Eastern Europe. He suggests that one indicator of such potential interest has been the $100 million credit for ten years granted by the Kuwait Foreign Trading Contract and Investment Company. Kaser expects that over the long term, Middle Eastern credits and investments in the East bloc would most likely find their way into the deposits of the IIB and IBEC since these banks appear to provide greater flexibility and somewhat freer political selection than do the national banks of the Soviet Union or individual East European countries.[60] If the petrodollar transfer were to take place, it would increase the authority of the IIB and IBEC and would give a boost to COMECON integration as well. Strengthened COMECON banking institutions could be a threat to the activities of the foreign trade banks of the small East European countries.

Foreign Trade Organizations

Soviet and East European foreign trade organizations compose another part of transgovernmental activity. FTOs are subordinate to foreign trade ministries in making decisions about foreign trade policies, but they have considerable independent scope as well. The role of FTOs in the USSR provides a case in point. The economic reforms of 1965 and 1973 did very little to alter the dominance of FTOs over individual enterprises in the Soviet Union but increased the power of the FTOs slightly at the expense of the Ministry of Foreign Trade. The Soviet Ministry of Foreign Trade still has much more power than the FTOs. East European economic reform programs have provided greater powers for FTOs in relation to foreign trade ministries and for individual enterprises in relation to FTOs. A number of East European firms now have the right to handle their own importing and exporting, but the Soviet enterprises do not have similar privileges.[61]

In Hungary, with many trading powers granted to enterprises rather than to FTOs, the functions of FTOs are somewhat circumscribed. Foreign trade activities are carried out by large production enterprises themselves if these functions were assigned to them by the Minister of Foreign Trade at the time of their creation. While some enterprises carry on foreign trade activity through their own foreign trade divisions, other enterprises utilize FTOs as agents. In these cases, the FTO acting as agent performs sales and purchase functions within the terms of its mandate. The FTO receives a commission for services performed. In still other cases, the Hungarian enterprise and the FTO enter into joint-venture agreements.

At the end of 1973, there were 39 specialized Hungarian FTOs and 133 commercial enterprises vested with direct foreign trade privileges.[62] Thus, most decisions about Hungarian exports and imports are made by producing enterprises and FTOs carrying out their activities in accordance with the wishes of enterprises. Officially, the relationship is supposed to be like the relationship between the production and marketing divisions of large enterprises in the West. In practice, the FTOs frequently have the skills and the personnel to be more influential than enterprises in developing trade agreements with Western corporations.

In Czechoslovakia, organization is more centralized, and most foreign trade decisions are made at the ministerial level. Western firms find that they must do business with the 11 FTOs specifically set up for this purpose under the direction of the Association of Firms for Foreign Agencies (USOZ) located in Prague. Recently, Western firms seeking representation by several of the 11 agencies have been turned down because new Western firms can be accepted only if others drop out. The 11 Czech agencies represent more than 600 Western firms.[63]

Romanian FTOs present still another variation. There are about 50 Romanian FTOs, which are responsible under the principle of "double subordination" to both the Ministry of Foreign Trade and the relevant industrial ministries or industrial centrals. Romanian officials emphasize that there are rarely differences of opinion between FTOs and industrial ministries or between FTOs and the Ministry of Foreign Trade. However, when disputes do occur, the FTO must yield to the wishes of the ministry.[64]

Trade Fairs

Trade Fairs are another important transgovernmental unit in the East-West trade process. The Leipzig Fair is generally recognized by COMECON countries as their leading trade fair.[65] The Leipzig Fair is important in the diffusion of technological information between East and West. It serves as a place where formal and informal contacts between Western businessmen and Eastern foreign trade organizations can be initiated. The Leipzig Fair is divided into spring and autumn sections. The spring fair provides for the display of heavy engineering and electrical engineering equipment, as well as for display of electronics equipment including automation technology.

The USSR has often used the Leipzig Fair as a means of promoting its own interests and its preeminence in COMECON. The 1975 Leipzig spring Fair was planned as a demonstration by the East-bloc countries of their uninterrupted economic growth and collaboration within the COMECON framework. The Soviet Union exhibited some 4,000 items, many of them resulting from "socialist cooperation." These included the electric motors it had developed with the support of Czechoslovakia and the GDR.[66] The autumn trade fair at Leipzig typically emphasizes somewhat more specialized industrial branches, including plastics engineering, medical technology, and data-processing equipment.[67]

The Hungarian fair Hungexpo also has spring and fall divisions, but in the Hungarian case the spring fair is largely technical, while the autumn fair concentrates on consumer goods. Spring fair exhibits typically include such products as precision engineering tools, telecommunications machines, and transport machines.[68] Strong Hungarian interest in automated systems from the United States resulted in exhibits sponsored by the U.S. Department of Commerce's Bureau of East-West Trade in 1975.[69]

The Bucharest International Fair is a biennial technical fair which focuses on the exhibition of products delivered by the fundamental branches of the machine-building industry: machine tools, electromechanical products, and electronics goods.[70] The Brno Trade Fair and Exhibition displays technical products in Czechoslovakia. Less well established than the Leipzig or Hungexpo fairs, Brno is nonetheless attracting increasing numbers of West European and American exhibitors. Among the major exhibitors at Brno in the fall of 1974 was Rank Xerox, Ltd., which hoped to improve its already impressive sales record in Czechoslovakia. General Motors and the Philips Company also presented major exhibits. The September 1974 Brno Fair was attended by 1,800 firms from 30 countries.[71]

Typically, U.S. and West European corporations who exhibit at any of these trade fairs provide a unique contact between officially controlled FTOs and socialist enterprises, and Western corporations. Even the trade fairs are viewed as official agencies in the East bloc. They are generally responsible directly to the ministry of foreign trade or to a special division of a national chamber of commerce which in turn reports to a ministry of foreign trade.

Intergovernmental Commissions and Joint Chambers of Commerce

Intergovernmental commissions are now active between nearly all countries involved in East-West trade. The U.S.-USSR Joint Commercial Commission is a representative example. It was set up originally to negotiate specific aspects of trade relations between the United States and the Soviet Union which had been discussed at the 1972 Nixon-Brezhnev summit. It was charged with responsibility to negotiate: an overall trade agreement including reciprocal MFN treatment, arrangements for the reciprocal availability of government credits, provisions for the reciprocal establishment of business facilities to promote trade, and an agreement establishing an arbitration mechanism for settling commercial disputes. The commission consists on each side of the principal, three deputies, and a staff. The U.S. secretary of commerce and the Soviet minister for foreign trade serve as principals. The U.S. staff for the commission is supplied through the Bureau for East-West Trade in the Department of Commerce.[72]

The work of the U.S.-USSR Joint Commercial Commission has been important in providing a means to continue Soviet-U.S. economic ties despite Soviet rejection of the terms of the Trade Act. At a meeting in Moscow on April 11,

1975, the commission agreed to work on a five-year program for the development of Soviet-U.S. trade. The official communique of the meeting stressed that normalization of the terms of reciprocal trade, including its financing, would be the most important prerequisites for continued progress in Soviet-U.S. economic relations.[73] The Joint Commercial Commission remains the most important official mechanism for commercial dialogue between the United States and the USSR. Its enthusiasm for greater trade often exceeds the hopes of executive departments in the United States and ministries in the USSR.

The U.S.-USSR Trade and Economic Council provides contacts of a different nature. It is billed as a binational grouping which aims to strengthen ties and economic relations between American businessmen and Soviet officials. It was first established at a meeting in Washington in July 1973. Its first full meeting took place in Washington in February 1974, when it arranged to open offices in Moscow and New York and decided to reconvene in Moscow in May 1975. The Soviet delegation was headed by Minister of Foreign Trade N. Patolichev and by Deputy Minister Vladimir S. Alkhimov. It included officials of the Soviet Foreign Trade Ministry, leaders of Soviet FTOs, the chairman of the Soviet Bank for Foreign Trade, some Gosplan officials, and a few Soviet industrial plant managers. In contrast to the purely "official" composition of the Soviet delegation, U.S. membership was drawn entirely from the private sector. In fact, the council's 52-member board has 26 members from U.S. private industry and 26 representatives from official Soviet government agencies. For the American contingent, the leader is Harold B. Scott, a businessman from New York who formerly served as assistant secretary of commerce for domestic and international business. The chairman of Pepsico, Donald M. Kendall, serves as deputy chairman of the U.S. group.[74]

Among joint chambers of commerce, which are increasingly popular, the Franco-Soviet chamber is probably the most dynamic. It has two permanent offices, one in Paris and one in Moscow, each staffed by both Soviet and French personnel. About 30 Soviet FTOs have representatives in the Franco-Soviet Chamber of Commerce, and there are representatives from an even larger number of French industrial and commercial firms, banking institutions, and professional groups. All of the East European countries and the Soviet Union maintain national chambers of commerce. All have joined into an extensive array of joint chambers with West European countries and with the United States. There are variations from country to country, but most function in the manner of Western chambers of commerce.[75]

Arbitration Commissions

Arbitration is a voluntary agreement by parties to a contract that any controversies or claims arising out of the contract will be settled by one or more arbitrators, rather than by litigation in the courts.[76] Arbitration clauses are of critical importance in commercial agreements between Western firms and their East European counterparts. In the early 1930s, the Soviet Union created a Foreign Trade Arbitration Commission under the aegis of the Soviet All-Union Chamber of Commerce. The Soviet example was later followed in the East European countries. The national foreign trade arbitration commissions in Eastern Europe have been quite successful in resolving commercial disputes between foreign trade organizations in various socialist countries.

In their contract negotiations with Western firms, East European foreign trade organizations often seek permission to submit any disputes to their own national foreign trade arbitration commissions. Although a Western firm is free to accept or reject such a proposal, the bargaining situation is such that many Western firms acquiesce rather than press for arbitration through some other organization. Most knowledgeable observers would give the East European arbitration commissions high marks for their overall record of accomplishment in resolving East-West trade disputes submitted for their opinion.

There are some alternatives to this form of arbitration. Soviet and East European foreign trade organizations have sometimes agreed to so-called home and home arrangements, whereby arbitration takes place in the country of the defendant. However, the home and home system does not insure impartiality. It can lead to complicated maneuvering by the parties to secure designation as defendant. Sometimes neutrally sponsored arbitration in a third country is used as a substitute. The chambers of commerce in Berne, Zurich, and Vienna have sometimes been called upon to settle disputes about contents of foreign trade agreements or compliance with their terms.[77]

The transnational actors, international organizations, and transgovernmental actors that conduct the day-to-day transactions of East-West trade are vitally important and at the same time relatively isolated from the structural level of trade dominated by national and regional policies. At times, national governments may find that changes in policy are difficult to enforce at the process level. Actors like FTOs, banks, and joint chambers of commerce often pursue their own narrowly defined goals with minimal reference to national policy objectives of "detente" or regional policy objectives of "international cooperation."

It is largely due to the consistent and narrowly defined goals of most of these actors that the process of East-West trade has revealed a great deal of continuity despite some broad national policy shifts. While continuity and caution have been the hallmarks to date of the transactions of these actors, there remains the real possibility of future chaos and disruption if their activities were to become even more highly politicized. At the process level, as at the structural level of East-West trade, there remains a serious need for a reordering of relationships into a stable and predictable international framework.

NOTES

1. Joseph S. Nye, Jr., "Multinational Corporation in World Politics," *Foreign Affairs* 53, no. 1 (October 1974): 155-61.

2. Business International, *Eastern Europe Report*, March 21, 1975, p. 88.

3. New York *Times*, April 12, 1975.

4. Andrew Knight and Chris Cviic, "The Scent of Honey: A Survey of East-West Trade," *The Economist* 246, no. 6750 (January 6, 1973): 28.

5. Business International, *Eastern Europe Report*, May 16, 1975, pp. 135-36.

6. Ivan Meznerics, *Law of Banking in East-West Trade* (Dobbs Ferry, N. Y.: Oceana, 1973).

7. Leopold de Rothschild, "East-West Banking," *Commerce International* 104, no. 2 (February 1973): 41.

8. R. J. Familton, "East-West Trade and Payments Relations," *International Monetary Fund Staff Papers* 18, no. 1 (March 1970): 184-85.

9. Thomas A. Wolf, "New Frontiers in East-West Trade," *European Business*, no. 39 (Autumn 1973), p. 27.

10. Estimates of Moscow Narodny Bank and the London branch of the National Bank of Hungary, interviews, June 1974.

11. Rothschild, op. cit., p. 43.

12. John W. Harrison, "The Unkown Competitor—Soviet International Banking," *The Bankers Magazine* 158, no. 3 (Summer 1975): 83-85.

13. Erzsebet Birman, "A New Department of the National Bank of Hungary for International Cooperation," *Marketing in Hungary*, no. 4 (1974), pp. 25-26.

14. U. S. Licensing Executive Society, *U. S.-USSR: Sale and License Prospects for Technology and Patents* (Pittsburgh: LES Publications, 1974). This exhaustive study is the result of a series of meetings in July 1973 between American patent and licensing experts and 175 Soviet specialists.

15. Business International, *Eastern Europe Report*, May 2, 1975, p. 124.

16. Interviews with 11 separate foreign trade organizations in Romania and Hungary in May and June 1975 consistently elicited this argument about the desirability of licensing agreements.

17. Business International, *Eastern Europe Report*, September 20, 1974, p. 296.

18. Karoly Hoffmann, "Hunicoop Promoting Engineering Cooperation," *Marketing in Hungary*, no. 1 (1974), pp. 18-19.

19. Business International, *Eastern Europe Report*, November 1, 1974, p. 336.

20. Ibid., April 19, 1974, p. 101.

21. Economic Commission for Europe, *Analytical Report on Industrial Cooperation Among ECE Countries* (Geneva: United Nations, 1973), p. 2.

22. Business International, *Eastern Europe Report*, June 13, 1975, p. 165.

23. *Ibid*.

24. Carl H. McMillan and D. P. St. Charles, *Joint Ventures in Eastern Europe: A Three Country Comparison* (Montreal: C. D. Howe Research Institute, 1974), p. 1.

25. Business International, *Eastern Europe Report*, November 15, 1974, p. 349.

26. Radio Free Europe Research, *Hungarian Situation Report*, no. 43 (November 5, 1974), p. 6.

27. Business International, *Eastern Europe Report*, October 18, 1974.

28. *Christian Science Monitor*, February 8, 1974.

29. Knight and Cviic, op. cit., p. 28.

30. Kenneth Yalowitz, "USSR-Western Industrial Cooperation," in U. S. Congress, Joint Economic Committee, *Soviet Economic Prospects for the Seventies* 93rd Cong., 1st Sess., June 27, 1973, pp. 712-18.

31. Ibid., p. 716.

32. Chase Manhattan, *EastWest Markets*, May 6, 1974, p. 3.

33. Business International, *Eastern Europe Report*, July 25, 1975, p. 208.

34. James P. Roscow, "East-West Trade: New Route," *Financial World*, November 21, 1973, p. 6; E. E. Bridges and Mirjana Samardzija, "The Role of Switch and Barter in Financing East-West Trade," mimeographed, Vienna, 1974. Bridges and Samardzija put the estimate at 20 percent of East-West Trade.

35. Business International, *Eastern Europe Report*, July 11, 1975, pp. 193-94.

36. For an analysis of London-based barter houses, see Anne Smith, "Barter Trade—A Necessary Evil?" *Commerce International* 104, no. 1411 (November 1973): 11-15.

37. Knight and Cviic, op. cit., p. 15. An interview with representatives of Eurintrade (June 1974) confirmed the impression of company strength but elicited little information about the company's office in Moscow.

38. B. Narpati, *The Monetary System: Its Components and Some Trade Issues* (Rotterdam: Rotterdam University Press, 1973), p. 114.

39. Bridges and Samardzija, op. cit., pp. 1-15.

40. Business International, *Eastern Europe Report*, July 26, 1974, p. 232.

41. Knight and Cviic, op. cit., p. 28.

42. Roscow, op. cit., p. 6.

43. Thomas A. Wolf, "New Frontiers in East-West Trade," *European Business*, no. 39 (Autumn 1973), p. 27.

44. Radio Free Europe Research, *Romanian Situation Report*, no. 34 (October 24, 1974), p. 11.

45. Franklin Holzman and Robert Legvold, "The Economics and Politics of East-West Relations," *International Organization* 29, no. 1 (Winter 1975): 318.

46. Radio Free Europe Research, *Romanian Situation Report*, no. 34 (October 24, 1974), p. 11.

47. Helmut Klocke, "COMECON Relations with the EEC," *Aussenpolitik* 22, no. 4 (1971): 444-45.

48. Wolf, op. cit., p. 27.

49. Romanian Chamber of Commerce and Industry, *Economic Guide to Romania* (Bucharest: 1974), p. 65.

50. See Jean Touscouz, "Les diverses formes de la cooperation est-oest en Europe," *Etudes Internationales* 4, no. 9 (September 1973): 249; A. F. Butov, "Legal and Institutional Forms of East-West Contacts," *Acta Oeconomica* 9, nos. 3-4 (1972): 233-41.

51. Robert Starr, "Settlement of East-West Trade Disputes," *Commerce International* 104, no. 7 (July 1973): 51, 53.

52. For a further discussion of these activities, see Gerda Zellentin, "Institutions for Detente and Cooperation," *The World Today*, no. 1 (January 1973), pp. 12-13.

53. T. M. Padolski, "Socialist International Banking under the Microscope," *The Banker* (London) 123, no. 574 (December 1973): 1465-70.

54. Wolf, op. cit., p. 27.

55. *Trybuna ludu*, no. 41, February 10, 1974.

56. *Ekonomicheskaya gazeta*, no. 18 (1973), p. 20.

57. J. T. Crawford and John Haberstoh, "Survey of Economic Policy Trends in Eastern Europe: Technology, Trade, and the Consumer," in U. S. Congress, Joint Economic Committee, *Reorientation and Commercial Relations of the Economics of Eastern Europe*, 93rd Cong., 2nd Sess., August 16, 1974, p. 43.

58. Holzman and Legvold, op. cit., p. 319.

59. Padolski, op. cit., pp. 1467-68.

60. Michael Kaser, "Oil and the Broader International Participation of IBEC," *International Currency Review* 6, no. 4 (July-August 1974): 25-26.

61. *Foreign Trade* (Moscow), no. 1 (January 1972), pp. 59-60.

62. Hungarian Chamber of Commerce, *Business Guide: Hungary* (Budapest, 1973).

63. Business International, *Eastern Europe Report*, November 29, 1974, p. 360.

64. Interview with officials of the Romanian Ministry of Foreign Trade, Bucharest, May 1975.

65. Kurt Weisskopf, "The Leipzig Fair in the GDR Context," *Commerce International* 104, no. 12 (December 1973): 43.

66. Leipziger Messe, Deutsche Demokratische Republik, Presse-Information, Spring 1975, p. 1.

67. Chamber of Foreign Trade of the German Democratic Republic, *Trade Partner GDR: Information on the External Economy of the German Democratic Republic* (Berlin, 1973).

68. HUNGEXPO, "The Budapest International Spring Fair" (information bulletin) (Budapest, 1975).

69. *Industry Week*, September 23, 1974, p. 56.

70. *Catalog Tirgul International Bucuresti, Romania, 1974* (Bucharest, 1974); Business International, *Eastern Europe Report*, November 1, 1974.

71. Information Bulletin of the Brno Trade Fairs and Exhibitions (Brno, September 1974).

72. John P. Hardt, George D. Holliday, and Young C. Kim, *Western Investment in Communist Economics* (Washington, D. C.: U.S. Government Printing Office, 1974), pp. 6-7. pp. 6-7.

73. *Pravda*, April 12, 1975.

74. *Commerce Today*, March 18, 1974, p. 11.

75. Samuel Pisar, *Coexistence and Commerce* (New York: McGraw Hill, 1970), pp. 145-46.

76. Howard M. Holtzmann, "Settlement of Disputes: The Role of Arbitration in East-west Trade," in *East-West Business Transactions,* ed. Robert Starr (New York: Praeger, 1974), p. 540.

77. Robert Starr, "Settlement" op. cit., p. 57.

7

EAST-WEST TRADE IN
COMPUTERS, PETROLEUM AND
NATURAL GAS, AND
CHEMICALS

COMPUTERS

The pluralistic nature of the interests involved in East-West trade is clearly revealed in a study of several of its key components. Computers, petroleum and natural gas, and chemicals represent three of the areas that have aroused greatest interest and concern among policy makers in the United States, Western Europe, and the Soviet Union.

Trade deals in computers and computer technology have been volatile domestic issues in the United States and Western Europe, and they promised to become even more controversial with the disclosure early in 1975 that West Germany had broken a Soviet-directed spy ring which was attempting to extract trade secrets from IBM. The West German prosecutor said that nine persons had been arrested on suspicion of disclosing secrets about Western electronic data-processing equipment to the KGB in the Soviet Union.[1] These illegal actions convinced some policy makers in Western Europe and the United States that the Soviet Union is far more eager for hard technological skills than it is for an elusive ideological and political detente. In a more subtle way, it also reveals the desperation of the Soviet Union as it tries to acquire computer technology skills. It seems that the IBM case in West Germany was marked by an aberration in method, but the incident does reveal the continuing struggle to obtain access to Western technical information at almost any price.

The desperation and the struggle over computers are not unique to the Soviet Union. The United States and Western Europe have often shown themselves to be equally caught up in a great race to provide long-term contracts to the Soviet Union and Eastern Europe for computers and computer projects.

The East Europeans have been determined to develop their own emerging computer technology and are eager to trade and to work out joint ventures with the West to protect their products against the vicissitudes of Soviet interest. Various government agencies and private companies are fighting for the privilege of regulating sales both in the United States and in Western Europe. Research institutes in the East bloc have sought to control the influx of technology acquired from the West so that they can direct its use in the Soviet Union and Eastern Europe. Thus, computers present a good example of the complexity of processes involved in East-West trade and of the usual primacy of institutional interest over long-term policy goals. All parties involved in the computer field have pledged themselves to a continuation of "detente." But what they really want is either profit (in the case of Western technology holders), control (in the case of government agencies), or access (in the case of Eastern technology seekers).

Within the United States, there has been a heated debate over the desirability of providing any kind of computer technology to the USSR. The CIA, the State Department, and the Department of Commerce have all asserted their interest in controlling the issue of licenses for computer products. It took about 18 months before Univac, a division of U.S. Sperry Rand, was finally granted an export license from the U.S. Department of Commerce for the shipment of a $10 million international passenger-booking system to Aeroflot.[2] A similar period elapsed before IBM was able to secure permission from U.S. authorities to export computers to the USSR. Under the approved agreement, IBM will supply a "System 370" computer and related services for production planning and controls in the Kama River truck plant.[3]

While the debate over export of computer technology has raged within the United States, a different kind of debate has been occurring within the Soviet Union. Soviet officials and enterprise managers agree that vast imports of computer technology are essential, but they are in disagreement over the extent of centralization to be exerted over domestic and imported computer systems. During the summer and fall of 1974 an unusually complete public discussion of the computer needs of the USSR took place. Several of the key arguments which emerged from that discussion are the following:

1. Despite the effectiveness of the current Soviet computer systems (based mostly on Soviet "Minsk-32" and COMECON "Ryad" models), there are many shortcomings in their development and operations.

2. There is often a tremendous discrepancy between the tasks a computer is created to solve and those it is asked to perform. Many sophisticated computers are wasted on small jobs, and many large jobs remain unfinished because available computers cannot handle them.[4]

3. There is a lack of standardized programs and of computer replacement parts. The Soviets claim that these problems will be overcome as the "Minsk-32" is gradually adopted as the standard computer for all newly created management systems and as the third-generation "Ryad" computers become standard.

But   progress has been slow, and so far it has been impossible to provide all types of automated management systems with standardized programs and equipment.

4. There are many difficulties connected with computer software. At present, thousands of organizations that have acquired computers are "left alone with them" and are compelled to work out the software for their jobs virtually from scratch. Moreover, information exchanges have not been organized effectively, and work is inevitably duplicated.[5]

5. According to the centralizers, who seemed clearly in the ascendancy by the end of 1974, there was a need for a whole new system of unified and centrally directed state computers. The state network of computers was to be based on a unified system of group time-sharing computers.[6] A time-sharing system would supposedly save money in many ways: It would insure from the start the organizational, technical, and methodological unity of the automated management systems included in it, and it would provide the necessary conditions for a rapid increase in the production of high-capacity computers.[7]

Opinions about potential solutions to Soviet computer problems vary widely. There is agreement only on the basic point that assistance from outside the USSR is absolutely necessary. The Soviet Union has, in fact, turned to the United States, to Western Europe, and to Japan for assistance in the computer field. In addition, it has occasionally sought the assistance of the East Europeans in building a unified computer system for the entire East bloc. Cooperation throughout COMECON in the computer industry has been an important theme in the Soviet and East European press ever since the twenty-eighth COMECON Council session, in June 1963, declared cooperation in the creation and operation of computers to be a matter of high priority.

Active collaboration among socialist countries in the computer industry really began about 1969. Before then, the East-bloc countries produced a total of 27 different types of programmatically incompatible machines. In addition, there was a large variety of peripheral equipment styled to adapt only to particular machines. In December 1969, Bulgaria, Hungary, the GDR, Poland, the Soviet Union, and Czechoslovakia signed a multilateral agreement on cooperation in developing computers.[8] Romania did not participate in the agreement and from that time on has been an especially eager potential partner for Control Data in the United States.

Czechoslovakia was assigned a pivotal role in the development program undertaken after the 1969 agreement. The Czech task was to develop and produce the third-generation, medium-capacity computer code-named "EC 1021," which used integrated circuits, and to produce related software. A committee on electronic computers was set up as an organ of the Federal Ministry of Technical and Investment Development to carry out the entire Czech program. The computer itself was developed by the Mathematical Machine Research Institute in Prague.

The development of third-generation computer technology in the socialist countries was allegedly completed at the end of 1973. The second stage of the cooperation program proved to be more difficult to carry out. It involved the transfer of the "EC 1021" computer (now called the "Ryad" system) into the other East European countries and into the Soviet Union. A number of difficulties appeared, and the introduction of the new computers did not always proceed smoothly. A lengthy article in a Czech publication in May 1974 detailed some of the problems. Because of a shortage of qualified personnel and delays in the installation of computers, the machines were going into operation more slowly than had been planned.[9] At present, the unified computer system seems to be little more than an optimistic dream. The original hope was that in the final stages of the program, the central computing centers of the various East-bloc countries would be tied into the COMECON center in Moscow. The whole network was initially scheduled for completion between 1981 and 1985, but this date is now rarely mentioned.[10]

The most reliable progress information about the whole COMECON computer project came in figures released at the time of the Brno Engineering Fair held in the early fall of 1974 in Czechoslovakia. According to the director of the Czech Mathematical Machine Research Institute, some 20,000 workers from various COMECON countries had made it possible to reduce the types of East-bloc third-generation computers from 27 to 6, and to reduce almost 600 types of peripheral equipment to 150 unified systems.[11] But later in 1974, it was clear that East Europeans and Soviets alike were convinced that in the future, real advances in the computer field could come only from the purchase of Western equipment and licenses.

In fact, the eagerness of all parties to the COMECON agreement to conclude alternative agreements with Western Europe and the United States certainly casts some doubt on the likelihood that the research and development aspects of the COMECON program will be continued. It is more likely that the COMECON system will be used as a managerial device to control the application and use of purchased Western licenses and technology. In the past two years, both the Soviet Union and the East European countries have been aggressive in seeking Western assistance. Whenever possible, the Soviet Union has sought computer technology from the United States rather than from Western Europe.

Among the major agreements which the Soviet Union, working through the State Committee for Science and Technology, managed to conclude are the following:

1. The Bendix Corporation reached a five-year agreement with the State Committee for Science and Technology calling for exchanges of scientific data and information as well as purchase of American exports in the field of electronic products and scientific instruments.[12]

2. The Burroughs Corporation and the State Committee for Science and Technology signed a general protocol on cooperation in the development of

computer technology, including design, programming, manufacture, and application.[13]

3. Sperry Rand received a contract to supply a computerized flight reservation system for Aeroflot. It also signed a long-range agreement with the State Committee for Science and Technology covering some general computer systems, aircraft and marine guidance instruments, and office machines.[14]

4. IBM sold to Metallurgimport an automated control system for a foundry at the Kama River truck plant. IBM is to supply a "System 370" computer with related equipment and services for production planning and controls, as well as ten smaller computers to monitor manufacturing processes.[15]

The Soviet Union clearly prefers to purchase its computer technology from the United States, but in instances where the United States export licensing system has made it difficult for U.S. exporters of computer technology to deal with the USSR, the Soviets have turned to Western Europe, in some cases working through European subsidaries of American corporations. Both IBM and Xerox have sold computer products to the USSR through West European subsidiaries. IBM United Kingdom, Ltd., has attempted to sell air traffic control systems to the USSR, in direct competition with U.S. Sperry Rand. IBM Trade Development SA (France), a new subsidiary of IBM set up to cover the Soviet market, obtained an order from Intourist for a "Model 158" system. The French group also won an order worth several million dollars for a computer for the Kama River truck plant.[16] Rank Xerox (U.K.) won a £ 1 million contract from Technopromimport for the delivery of a wide range of office machinery.[17] IBM and Xerox officials have declined to discuss the possibility that these deals were made to circumvent the more stringent American regulations on exports, but Soviet officials have on several occasions implied that this is the case. International Computers, Ltd. (U.K.), perhaps the most aggressive challenger to the U.S. computer companies, has been negotiating with the USSR on the sale of a complete computer plant plus equipment and hopes to sell its new "2900" large computer series to the USSR.[18] Solartron-Schlumberger (U.K.) completed a large sale of computerized equipment for Soviet oil pipelines,[19] and Accuray International (Belgium) won an important contract from Prommashimport for computerized process control equipment for the Segezba Paper Mill, north of Leningrad.[20]

These agreements indicate that the Soviet Union has been dissatisfied both with the East European assistance it has received in computers and with the long delays often associated with securing export license approval in the United States. East European countries, also unhappy with constraints imposed by the COMECON framework, have successfully signed a number of agreements with Western Europe and with the United States. The East European countries, because of their smaller domestic needs, have been less concerned about complete access to U.S. products than have the Soviets. Still, East European agreements with the United States have been growing in size and importance. Control

Data has been very active in the East European market. It is cooperating in the joint venture Romcontroldata in Bucharest and has completed sales agreements with Bulgaria and Poland. Control Data signed a long-term agreement with Bulgaria for broad cooperation in the computer sector. It delivered a large central computer terminal to Poland, which will connect 11 smaller Polish computer information centers in a circle extending 35 kilometers around Warsaw. Control Data also supplied a computer system to a Polish nuclear research institute and to several Cracow schools and scientific institutes.[21] Data Products, the Techtra Corporation, and Techmation have negotiated smaller sales of computer equipment to be used in industrial settings in Eastern Europe.

The East European countries have been increasingly willing to sponsor independent seminars and exhibitions of computer technology. Especially in the case of the Third International Congress of Cybernetics held in Bucharest in the summer of 1975, these meetings have been attempts to develop computer expertise independently of the Soviet Union. Participation by the United States particularly has been encouraged.

Agreements between West European countries and East European countries have been dominated by International Computers, Ltd., of Great Britain (ICL) and by France's Compagnie Internationale pour l'Informatique (CII). ICL has been successful in its dealings with the Ministry of International Trade in Czechoslovakia and has provided a computerized reservation system for Prague hotels. CII has marketed its "Iris" computer range in Poland and is now exploring joint production possibilities in Poland. CII also has an agreement with Romanian enterprises to produce "Felix C-256" computers for regional computer centers.

As in the case of West European-Soviet trade in computer products, there is evidence that U.S. companies are using West European subsidiaries to complete projects that might be politically sensitive in the United States. Honeywell Bull of France has received orders from the National Bank of Hungary and from the civil service.[22] Other West European companies completing sales in the East European market have included Accuray International (Belgium), Computer Machinery, Ltd. (U.K.), Feedback Data (U.K.), and Siemens of West Germany. Most of these agreements have been in the supply of computerized equipment for industrial processes.

The fact remains that all the East-bloc countries are scrambling for whatever computer technology they can reasonably hope to acquire from the West. At present, congressional and Pentagon opposition to the selling of computer technology enhances possibilities that most East European and Soviet computer technology acquisitions in the near future will come from Western Europe. There are two points of irony in these developments. First, partners in West European-Soviet or West European-East European deals often are not truly European companies at all, but rather are American subsidiaries operating in Western Europe. Second, it is clear that the USSR and East European countries would prefer to do business with companies like IBM and Control Data from their headquarters in the United States rather than through their West European subsidiaries. Yet, the growing tangle of congressional opposition, Department of Defense and Department of Commerce technology transfer regulations, and limited Eximbank credits means that for the foreseeable future Western Europe will be the target of East-bloc computer acquisition hopes. This is true despite the fact that the national computer industries of Great Britain, France, West Germany, and Italy are very weak when compared to the U.S. giants IBM and Control Data.[23]

The most basic flaw of East-West trade in computers remains its unorganized and particularistic nature. There are the export guidelines of COCOM, of the U.S. Departments of Commerce and Defense, and of the various national bodies in West European countries, but there is little agreement among them on standards for permitting exports. The United States has traditionally been fussier than has COCOM. West European national agencies frequently act more like promoters than restricters of technology transfer. EEC and COMECON guidelines have not been very effective in promoting regional agreements. When East European COMECON members are dissatisfied with the kinds of computer equipment they can purchase or buy within Eastern Europe they turn to Western Europe and the United States. The Soviet Union appears to be less eager than it was a few years ago to promote joint Soviet and East European development of the COMECON "Ryad" system as a control device in Eastern Europe. Companies like Control Data, IBM, International Computers, and CII have understandably sought contracts where they could be found most profitably and easily. Banks lending funds to finance exports have worked along pragmatic lines. All this occurs against a background of assumed "detente" and "international cooperation" at national and regional levels. Unfortunately, few have realized that the day-to-day, process-level transactions in computers could someday challenge the hopes for detente now so often voiced at the policy-making or structural level. International guidelines are needed to make certain that a reasonable balancing of competitive interests can be secured at the process level.

PETROLEUM AND NATURAL GAS

One of the boldest recent innovations in East-West trade has been the suggestion that the United States should provide oil and gas development technology to the USSR in return for long-term shipments of oil and gas from the Soviet Union to the United States. While the Soviet Union has the means and the technological know-how to develop its oil and gas resources without American help, a policy of independent development would result in a slower average growth rate of production. The eagerness of the Soviet Union to secure U.S. assistance has not been matched by equal enthusiasm in the United States. Several arguments against the joint development of Soviet oil and gas resources have been raised repeatedly. First the United States requires very substantial funds to aid in the development of complementary and alternative energy sources to those in the Middle East throughout the non-Communist world. It may prove difficult to find capital available for investment projects in Siberia. Second, American investors in Siberia would probably have little influence in how the Siberian oil and natural gas reserves are developed and priced. There are no guarantees that shipments of Siberian natural gas or oil could be counted upon to continue in times of political crisis. Finally, the Soviet Union has strongly hinted all along that cooperation in natural gas and oil projects would be contingent upon a continued flow of Export-Import Bank credits from the United States and government-sponsored credits from West European countries. As a result of the breakdown of the Trade Reform Act of 1973, Eximbank credits cannot be granted to the USSR, and the future of Soviet-U.S. natural gas and oil development projects seems to be in trouble.

Yet, whatever their potential disadvantages may be, many American companies have sought to conclude energy-related agreements with the USSR. In the summer of 1973, several major cooperation agreements were signed. The first multibillion-dollar, U.S.-Soviet natural gas agreement involved Occidental Petroleum, El Paso Natural Gas, and the Bechtel Corporation in a $10 billion, 25-year project. A second multibillion-dollar agreement was signed by Tenneco, Texas Eastern Transmission, and Brown and Root. TASS estimated total proposed U.S. investment at $3.7 billion for pipelines and a liquefaction plant and $2.6 billion for more than 20 tankers to be used in transporting gas to the United States. Exploitation of the gas fields was to start in 1980 and to continue for 25 years. So far, the agreements have not been fully implemented because of problems in securing financing and official approval.

A General Electric sale is probably representative of the most important actual American commitments to date in the development of Siberian energy resources. The General Electric agreement calls for the delivery of 65 gas turbine compressors to be used in the natural gas pipeline system within the USSR.[24] Other agreements involving the sale of equipment to the USSR include the following:

- International Harvester has agreed to sell Mashinoimport 38 gas compressors.[25]
- TRW's REDA Pump Division (U.S.) will deliver 137 electrodynamic submergible pumping units for the secondary exploration of petroleum. TRW has also been awarded a $27 million contract for the planned 1976 delivery of petroleum production systems, accessory equipment, and spare parts.[26]
- Lynes, Inc. (U.S.) sold Mashinoimport testing equipment for oil well heads.[27]

As of July 1975, however, U.S. companies seemed very reluctant to commit further capital to development projects in Siberia. The cancellation of the trade agreement certainly dampened their enthusiasm. Even more significant were some revelations about Soviet "double dealings" during the Arab oil embargo that seemed all too similar to U.S. problems during 1972 and 1973, when wheat was sold to the Soviets. According to some recent figures, the USSR made a handsome profit by selling oil at very high prices to the United States and to Western Europe at the height of the oil embargo. The USSR sold $66 million worth of petroleum to the United States in the winter of 1973-74. Of that amount, $40 million came right at the height of the embargo and represented sales at the new quadrupled world prices. The main European customers for Soviet oil in the last quarter of 1973 were the Netherlands, West Germany, Denmark, and Switzerland. They purchased oil from the Soviets at the new oil-inflated prices.[28] Those U.S. companies still eager to conduct business in the Soviet natural resource development area have begun to turn to licensing projects and to cooperative research and development agreements. Gulf Oil, for example, has signed technical and scientific agreements with five different Soviet ministries.[29] Worthington Pump (U.S.) has signed consultation agreements and joint research and development agreements with the Soviet Ministry for the Chemicals Industry.[30]

There is agreement within the USSR on two crucial points: the need to develop oil and natural gas resources as completely as possible and the need for some outside assistance. There has been disagreement over whether the aid should come from the East Europeans or the West Europeans in the absence of large-scale U.S. participation and investment. Many favor the East Europeans who have long provided a reliable, if less innovative, source of assistance.

Traditionally, the Soviets have divided the entire COMECON area into three regions in terms of energy balance:

Eastern Europe—fundamentally an energy deficit area, covering less than 400,000 square miles, but containing over 100 million inhabitants and having a relatively high level of industrialization.

The USSR in Europe—nearly 2 million square miles, much of it highly industrialized, but with fairly impressive energy resources. However, these supplies have already been extensively developed to provide the foundations for the modern Soviet economy. The 200 million inhabitants of this region are now looking eastward for resources in petroleum and gas.

The USSR in Asia—over 6 million miles with possibly the greatest untapped energy resources in the world, but also one of the most sparsely populated areas of the world.[31]

In theory, COMECON energy planning is unified and takes into consideration the needs of the entire expanse of the Soviet Union and the East

European countries. For years, in fact, the Friendship Oil Pipeline has been discussed enthusiastically by the Soviet press. The official Soviet version of its development is that the USSR, recognizing its own superior oil and gas resources and acknowledging its responsibility to Eastern Europe, suggested at the tenth COMECON Council session in 1958 that a pipeline should be built to transport Soviet oil to Hungary, the GDR, Poland, and Czechoslovakia. The East European countries would help to construct the pipeline and would also assist in the development of Soviet oil and gas resources. The Friendship Oil Pipeline actually opened in 1972. It has been in operation since that time, pumping oil from the Tatar Republic to the East European members of COMECON. The Friendship Pipeline was the first joint construction project undertaken by COMECON member countries. It is a system of main and branch oil pipelines with a total length of about 5,000 kilometers. It begins in the oil fields of the Tatar Republic and extends to the Byelorussian Republic, where it branches out into two lines. The northern branch supplies oil to Poland and to the GDR; the southern branch supplies oil to Czechoslovakia and Hungary.

Until 1972, oil supplies from the Soviet Union enabled Hungary, the GDR, Poland, and Czechoslavakia to cover nearly all of their requirements in oil, diesel fuel, and lubricating oils, and also opened wide possibilities for the development of their petrochemical facilities. Thus, these countries built chemical, oil-refining, and petrochemical works with the expectation of continued shipments of oil from the USSR. Among these East European plants are the ones in Plock (Poland), Schwedt, Buna, and Leuna (GDR), Bratislava and Zaluzi (Czechoslovakia), and Szazhalombatt (Hungary). Poland, especially, seemed to benefit greatly from the Friendship Pipeline. As a result of Soviet oil deliveries, Poland was able to build a big petrochemical industry which manufactured several dozen products, including the initial products for making synthetic rubber, synthetic fibers, paint, varnish, and pharmaceuticals.[32]

Significant changes in the structure and operation of the Friendship Pipeline seem to be underway at present. It is true that long-term trade and cooperation agreements have set up the framework for Soviet-East European oil transactions over a number of years. However, there are also short-term operating agreements which the USSR has been increasingly reluctant to renew. The actual operation of the pipeline is determined by special control boards set up in each country and working through the COMECON structure. As a rule, the representatives to these boards meet every three months to reach agreement on all points connected with the delivery of oil. They negotiate under the heavy influence of Soviet representatives who stipulate what the East Europeans must pay in industrial equipment and consumer goods for the privilege of continued oil deliveries. Until early 1975, oil prices were much less than world average prices, but the USSR doubled the required payments then and is expected to request further substantial increases in the future.

Both East Europeans and Soviets acknowledge the presence of severe strains in the oil supply relationship. The Soviets, aware that the oil can be sold very profitably in the West for hard currency, have repeatedly expressed reluctance to continue supplying the East European countries via the Friendship Pipeline beyond 1975-76. At one point, some Soviet writers were suggesting to the East Europeans that the Middle East might be a more suitable source of supply for their energy needs in the future.[33]

One possible way out for the Soviet Union would be to encourage a much heavier reliance on nuclear power for meeting Eastern Europe's energy needs. The Soviets have provided some support in this direction. The COMECON countries created a new multinational firm called Interatomenergo at the end of 1973 which is to provide technical assistance in the building of nuclear power plants.[34] Some Western observers suggest that the USSR might be willing to continue to supply even oil to the East European countries as long as there is an obvious political gain for the Soviet Union in having the smaller East European countries dependent on it for their supplies of oil. There have been some concrete indications that this is what the Soviet Union intends to do. It has enlisted greatly increased aid from the COMECON countries recently in developing Soviet natural gas resources. In return for East European aid in constructing natural gas pipelines, the USSR has promised to increase its supplies of natural gas to Eastern Europe.

On June 22, 1974, Radio Budapest reported that a four-day COMECON session in Sofia had reached agreement on the exploitation of the Orenburg gas reserves and on the joint construction of a gas pipeline to the western borders of the Soviet Union. Radio Budapest noted that while Romania had signed the agreement, it would not be involved in the actual construction of the pipeline. Four months later, an East Berlin newspaper produced the first details of the participation of various East European countries in the construction of the gas pipeline. Bulgaria, Czechoslovakia, East Germany, Hungary, and Poland were to provide the means and manpower to complete the pipeline by autumn of 1978, while Romania was to contribute only money to buy equipment, and the USSR was to provide only technical help.[35] For the immediate future, Soviet-East European cooperation in the energy field seems to be continuing, though at a reluctant pace.

Both the Soviets and the East Europeans are developing contingency plans for the future. In the Soviet case, cooperation deals with the West European countries have become a possible alternative to U.S. assistance in the exploitation of Soviet oil and gas reserves and to East European assistance as well. The West Europeans have long been eager and successful in concluding cooperation agreements with the Soviets. France and West Germany have been the most prominent players in this particular game. One of the most important developments in 1974 was the holding of a Soviet-French symposium in Moscow in late January to organize bilateral cooperation in the construction of large-diameter oil and gas pipelines as well as new refineries in Siberia.[36]

Important Soviet-French energy deals concluded in 1974 and 1975 include the following:

Black, Sivalls, and Bryson (France), a subsidiary of International Systems and Control (U.S.) won a $25 million contract from Mashinoimport to deliver natural gas processing plants.[37]

Constructions Metalliques de Provence (France) won two contracts totaling $50 million from Techmashimport and Mashinoimport. The Techmashimport contract involved materials to refrigerate and store liquefied gas in the Togliatti-grad region, and the Mashinoimport contract involved filtering equipment for gas cleaning.[38]

In 1974, Vallourec-Export (France) won a $100 million contract to supply steel tubing for natural gas exploration, production, and transport.[39]

In June 1975, Vallourec and Saint-Gobain-Pont-A-Mousson (also of France) reached a basic agreement estimated at about $800 million dollars to supply the USSR with 1 million tons of pipe for the construction of gas pipelines.[40]

West German companies have also been eager to share in the development of Soviet natural resources. Mannesmann AG has been a pioneer in the provision of natural gas transport facilities in exchange for guaranteed future deliveries of natural gas to Germany. In 1975, Mannesmann was negotiating with Soviet authorities for the supply of 1.2 million tons of large-diameter pipe in connection with a previously signed tripartite natural gas contract between Iran, the USSR, and West Germany.[41] Earlier, Ruhrgas AG entered into a tripartite gas supply contract with the FTO Soyuzgazexport and Iran. The complicated agreement provides for the transport of Iranian gas to Soviet-Iranian border areas to be processed. Then, Soyuzgazexport will pump natural gas from the northwest of the USSR to the West German-Czechoslovak border. If plans proceed, the gas supplies are to be delivered initially in 1981, and West Germany has been given the option of routing part of its gas imports to other West European countries, particularly to France, Italy, and Austria.[42]

Italian and British companies have also figured prominently in the natural gas deals. One of the most striking aspects of a number of these West European-Soviet agreements is the fact that many of the West European contractors are subsidiaries of U.S. companies. Walworth Aloyco e Grove International (Italy), two-thirds owned by International Utilities of the United States, is supplying ball valves for the Soviet natural gas pipeline system. Worthington (Italy), a subsidiary of the U.S. Worthington group, has won a contract to provide large pumping units. Cameron Iron Works de France (U.S.-owned) will provide the pipeline fittings.[43] These companies (both subsidiary and parent) are reluctant to discuss the reasons behind the arrangements they have chosen, but one major factor has been the reluctance of commerce and defense department officials to grant export licenses promptly. Another has been the greater difficulty of developing satisfactory arrangements for financing the projects in the United States.

The East Europeans have been doing whatever they can to extricate themselves from heavy reliance on Soviet oil and gas reserves. Poland has been uniquely fortunate because of its own extensive reserves of coal. During and after the 1973-74 energy crisis, Poland stepped up its sales of coal to the West. The energy crisis helped Poland's other deficit-ridden trade with the United States, since east coast states began purchasing large amounts of Polish coal in early 1974.[44] Poland's reserves of hard coal are estimated at about 46 billion tons, and its reserves of brown coal (lignite) are estimated at 15 billion tons. All the other East European countries have solid fuel reserves of lesser significance. The East European countries have greatly stepped up their efforts to find indigenous sources of oil and natural gas. So far, they have not met with much success.

To the East Europeans, it must seem that the Soviet Union holds all the advantages in the energy field. The USSR ranks first in the world in demonstrated deposits of coal, natural gas, peat, and hydroelectric energy. It has more than 50 percent of the world's known reserves in basic fuels and more than 12 percent of the world's hydroelectric potential.[45] The East Europeans are trying their best to develop contacts with the West European countries and with the United States. Such contacts could relieve their heavy dependence on Soviet sources, but to date their successes have been few. Offshore Company (U.S.) has supplied some assistance at Romanian oil drilling sites. CIE Generale d'Automatisme (France) has provided equipment for the oil refinery at Plock.[46] Recognition of the very limited assistance they will probably receive from the West in the near future has encouraged the East Europeans to pursue such independent projects as the Adria Pipeline, which Hungary is building in cooperation with Yugoslavia and Czechoslovakia.

At every stage of East-West trade and cooperation in petroleum and natural gas, there have been potential and actual disagreements. Within the United States, debates have raged between businessmen who want the United States to share in the development of Soviet oil and gas resources and government officials who have been more concerned about the possible future dependence of the United States on unpredictable Soviet oil and gas supplies and who feel that it is inappropriate for the United States to aid the Soviet Union in the Development of militarily essential resources. Within the Soviet Union, there has been debate between those who favor rapid exploitation of oil and gas with the assistance of the United States and those who want a somewhat slower and more independent pace of development. COMECON has provided yet another arena for debate. The Soviets want to use oil and gas supplies to maintain a degree of influence and political control in Eastern Europe, but they have been increasingly unhappy about the relatively low prices received for oil and gas from the East Europeans. The East Europeans have also been eager to secure other sources of oil and gas, but they have had little success.

Patterns of trade and joint undertakings in oil and gas have developed along lines of pragmatic, particularistic interests. COMECON and the EEC have held joint seminars on energy matters, but there has not been any serious discussion of cross-regional energy policies. Companies in the United States have dictated policy initiatives, and government agencies have attempted to stop many of them, so that U.S. policy, too, can hardly be seen as a coherent whole. In the USSR, foreign trade organizations have been more eager than ministerial officials to sign contracts. International financing agencies, insurance companies, and complicated licensing arrangements have added more confusion. The initiators of these agreements want to see their expected profits on small transactions materialize, and they rarely even attempt to view the larger framework within which they are operating. An international framework for managing such trade could be invaluable in preventing future East-West oil and gas deals from resulting in conflict rather than cooperation at the levels of both structure and process.

CHEMICALS

It is in the broad area of chemicals that there has been the most consistent development of trade and cooperation agreements between the United States and the USSR. American corporations have been mostly free to sell their products to the USSR without a real danger that export licenses would be denied. Even financing has been easier to arrange. Soviet foreign trade organizations and various industrial ministries seem more uniformly eager to trade with the United States in chemicals than in other areas.

In 1973, Monsanto became the first American chemical company to sign a cooperation agreement with the Soviet State Committee for Science and Technology. The five-year agreement covered the use of computers in the chemical industry and the development of some synthetic rubber products.[47] A year later, Universal Oil Products signed an agreement with the State Committee for Science and Technology calling for the exchange of information in the areas of chemicals and plastics technology.[48] In May 1975, despite a pronounced decline in many other areas of Soviet-U.S. trade, Rohm and Haas, Inc., signed an agreement with the State Committee for Science and Technology which called for joint research and development in plastics, herbicides, pesticides, and petroleum additives.[49]

Other Soviet-U.S. contracts have called for U.S. construction of chemical processing plants in the USSR, sometimes to be financed by future transfers of products developed in the Soviet Union, and at other times to be financed by private credits and cash. Early in 1974, PPG Industries, Inc., signed one of the largest of these construction agreements with the Soviet Ministry for the Chemicals Industry. PPG is to build a large complex for the production of a variety of chemical products. The plant will be located in one of the USSR's natural gas fields, possibly near Orenburg.[50]

In several instances, European subsidiaries of American firms have built these facilities. Litwin S.A., a French subsidiary of the U.S. firm Amtel, has won a $125 million contract for the construction of a petrochemical plant near Turkestan. France's Norton et Cie and Rapidase, which is a subsidiary of Baxter Laboratories (U.S.), have together been awarded a $20 million contract to build a plant in the Ukraine. KHD-Pritchard of West Germany, which is half-owned by International Systems and Controls Corporation of the United States, has won a large contract from Techmashimport for the construction of a polyvinyl chloride facility in Siberia.[51]

COMECON obligations have imposed some restrictions on the Soviet Union's dealings in chemicals with the United States and Western Europe. The Complex Integration Program of 1971 had focused on chemicals as an area where intra-COMECON coordination was to be emphasized. After an important and well-publicized meeting of the COMECON Standing Committee for the Chemical Industry in late 1973, it seemed that intra-COMECON cooperation might replace East-West contacts for the foreseeable future. According to the Bulgarian representative at the meeting, the COMECON countries had decided to cooperate in building a series of plants to make them more self-sufficient in chemicals. He mentioned specifically plants for fertilizers, insecticides, plastics, synthetic rubber, dyes, paints, and cellulose. In addition, Interchim, an intra-COMECON specialized agency for chemicals, was developing proposals for joint COMECON production of insecticides, paints, and dyes.[52] At an executive committee meeting of COMECON in December 1973, closer cooperation among member countries in the field of chemicals was again stressed.[53] However, the preference of East European COMECON members for their own bilateral and trilateral agreements, the independent development course of Romania, and a growing reluctance of the Soviet Union to supply raw materials for joint COMECON chemical industry ventures have meant that these earlier integration hopes in the chemicals sector have now been partially abandoned. In 1975, not very many influential groups still viewed the joint chemicals program as wise or feasible.

The Soviet Union now prefers to deal with the West Europeans and the Americans. In the West, Soviet raw materials bring in larger amounts of hard currency for the USSR, and the Soviets recognize that Western technical expertise in chemicals far exceeds that of Eastern Europe. Whenever a particular chemicals project does not appear to have overwhelming political significance for continued Soviet control of Eastern Europe, the decision is usually made to seek Western assistance.

The chemicals industry has been an area in which West Europeans have been very successful in challenging U.S. claims to technological superiority and one in which West Europeans have put their longer experience in dealing with the Soviet market to good advantage. In 1973, Montecatini-Edison of Italy reached an agreement with the Soviet Ministry of Foreign Trade on the construction of seven large chemical plants in the USSR to produce ammonia and other basic chemical products. The Soviets, in payment, will supply materials produced by the plant to Montedison.[54] Two months after the initial agreement was signed, the Soviet Ministry of Foreign Trade was conducting negotiations for an additional eight plants. Another significant plant construction agreement was the one between Litwin (France) and Techmashimport. Litwin is to construct a large polystyrene plant near Omsk, Siberia. Litwin is a subsidiary of the U.S. Amtel group and was planning to use the technology of another U.S. company, Cosden Oil and Chemicals, in designing the plant equipment.[55] Two major agreements signed between West European countries and the USSR after Soviet rejection of the Trade Act lend credence to the idea that West European-Soviet cooperation is apt to expand at the expense of the United States. Linde AG (West Germany) won a $100 million contract from the USSR to supply a petrochemical facility to produce ethylene and benzole.[56] Sofregaz (France) was expected to win approval for a 2,000 kilometer ammonia pipeline from Kuibyshev to Odessa.[57] There have also been a very large number of long-term research and development cooperation agreements signed between various West European companies and the Soviet State Committee for Science and Technology.

East Europeans have demonstrated themselves to be no less eager than the Soviets to escape the confines of COMECON in programs concerning the chemical industry. The West Germans have been involved in several important agreements. For example, Farbwerke Hoechst AG (West Germany) has reached an agreement with the Ministry of the Chemical Industry in East Germany to construct three or possibly six turnkey chemical plants.[58] Snia Viscosa (Italy) has been contracted by the Hungarian FTO Chemokomplex to build a plant which will double Hungary's acrylic fiber production.[59] Agreements between the United States and Eastern Europe have been of much less significance. Poland, the only full member of COMECON to possess MFN status before 1975, has been a favorite American partner.

Financing arrangements have become very complex in the chemicals area, and they emphasize the particularistic tendencies of East-West trade. Very often the USSR and East European countries have attempted to pay for turnkey plants with guaranteed shipments of specified amounts of products manufactured by the plant as payment. In other instances, counterpurchase agreements, giving the Western partner East European products in return for Western sales of technology or equipment, have been demanded. In still other cases, credits have been granted through arrangements worked out between private banks in the United States, state banks in Western Europe, and foreign trade banks in the USSR and Eastern Europe. In each case, competitive interests rather than high-level policy declarations have determined the outcome.

NOTES

1. New York *Times,* January 16, 1975.

2. Business International, *Eastern Europe Report*, June 27, 1975, p. 182.

3. Ibid., May 2, 1975, p. 127.

4. D. Zhimerin, "An Automated Management System is an Economic Service," *Pravda*, June 9, 1974, p. 3.

5. V. Seminikhin, "Working Tool of Progress," *Izvestia*, September 18, 1974, p. 3.

6. D. Zhimerin, "Technical Progress and the Improvement of Management," *Ekonomicheskaya gazeta*, no. 27 (July 1974), p. 10.

7. G. Samborsky and D. Simchera, "The Way to Improve the Efficiency of Computer Technology," *Voprosy ekonomiki*, no. 7 (July 1974), pp. 79-89.

8. Radio Free Europe Research, *Czechoslovak Situation Report*, no. 39 (October 23, 1974), pp. 6-9.

9. *Rude pravo*, May 16, 1974, p. 3.

10. Radio Free Europe Research, *Czechoslovak Situation Report,* no. 39 (October 23, 1974): 6-9.

11. Ibid., no. 34 (September 18, 1974), p. 10.

12. Business International, *Eastern Europe Report*, November 1, 1974, p. 342.

13. Ibid., July 26, 1974, p. 226.

14. Ibid., June 27, 1975, p. 182; May 31, 1974, p. 173.

15. Ibid., January 24, 1975, p. 29; May 2, 1975, p. 127.

16. Ibid., December 14, 1973, p. 388; July 26, 1974, p. 236; October 18, 1974, p. 329.

17. Ibid., December 13, 1974, p. 386.

18. Ibid., April 4, 1975, p. 99.

19. Ibid., September 6, 1974, p. 284.

20. Ibid., November 15, 1974, p. 356.

21. Ibid., August 24, 1973, p. 252; June 14, 1974, p. 189.

22. Ibid., June 27, 1975, p. 182; July 13, 1973, p. 196, August 24, 1973, p. 252.

23. For an excellent evaluation of the computer industry in Western Europe, see Nicolas Jequier, "Computers," in *Big Business and the State: Changing Relations in Western Europe*, ed. Raymond Vernon (Cambridge, Mass: Harvard University Press, 1974), pp. 195-228.

24. Business International, *Eastern Europe Report*, August 23, 1974, p. 270.

25. Ibid., February 8, 1974, p. 48.

26. Ibid., April 18, 1975, p. 115; June 27, 1975, p. 185.

27. Ibid., May 16, 1975, p. 143.

28. Marshall I. Goldman, "The Russians and Oil," New York *Times*, January 20, 1975.

29. Business International, *Eastern Europe Report*, March 7, 1975, p. 73.

30. Ibid., December 13, 1974.

31. A. F. G. Scanlon, "The Energy Balance of the COMECON Countries," in *Exploitation of Siberia's Natural Resources,* ed. Yves Laulan (Brussels: NATO, 1974), p. 84.

32. N. Korniyenko, "Friendship Oil Pipeline in Operation,'.' *Foreign Trade* (Moscow), no. 6 (June 1973), pp. 13-14.

33. Robert Campbell, "Siberian Energy Resources and the World Energy Market," in Laulan, ed., op. cit., p. 80.

34. *Ekonomicheskaya gazeta*, no. 52 (1973), p. 19.

35. Radio Free Europe Research, *Romanian Situation Report*, no. 34 (October 24, 1974), p. 13.

36. Business International, *Eastern Europe Report,* February 22, 1974, p. 63.

37. Ibid., September 6, 1974, p. 286.

38. Ibid., August 23, 1974, p. 270.

39. Ibid., November 15, 1974, p. 357.

40. Ibid., June 27, 1975, p. 185.

41. Ibid.

42. Ibid., April 18, 1975, p. 115.

43. Ibid., July 12, 1974, p. 221; November 16, 1973, p. 343; May 3, 1974, p. 143.

44. Radio Free Europe Research, *Polish Situation Report*, no. 29 (September 20, 1974), 4.

45. M. Pervukhin, "The U.S.S.R.'s Energy Resources and Their Rational Utilization," *Planovoye khozyaistvo*, July 1974, pp. 14-21.

46. Business International, *Eastern Europe Report*, April 18, 1975, p. 115; February 7, 1975, p. 45.

47. Ibid., November 2, 1973, p. 328.

48. Ibid., December 13, 1974, p. 386.

49. Ibid., May 16, 1975, p. 140.

50. Ibid., April 15, 1974, p. 110.

51. Ibid., January 11, 1974; March 22, 1974, p. 94; May 2, 1975, p. 127.

52. Ibid., January 12, 1973, p. 15.

53. Ibid., January 25, 1974, p. 23.

54. Ibid., August 10, 1973, p. 225.

55. Ibid., September 6, 1974, p. 284.

56. Ibid., June 13, 1975, p. 169.

57. Ibid., June 27, 1975, p. 182.

58. Ibid., May 30, 1975, p. 155.

59. Ibid., April 5, 1974, p. 110.

8

THE SOVIET-U.S.
GRAIN TRADE

A somewhat different perspective on the plurality of forces engaged in East-West trade may be derived from analysis of the Soviet-U.S. grain trade. The domestic debate in the United States has focused on rivalries among the Department of Agriculture, the Department of State, and congressional committees in the making of agricultural foreign policy. In the Soviet case, the debate over grain purchases has been kept largely within the confines of the Politburo, with only hints of crop failures and farm machinery inadequacies surfacing in the Soviet press. In matters of East-West grain trade, the roles of international organizations and of COMECON and the EEC have been minimal. The large grain companies in the United States and Exportkhleb, the Soviet grain-trading organization, have enjoyed a relatively free hand. With the announcement of the five-year grain agreement in October 1975, the government role in the United States became somewhat more important, but there has been little expectation that the impact of the major players in the grain trade game—U.S. grain companies and Exportkhleb—will be significantly reduced.

THE 1972 GRAIN PURCHASE

The much criticized "Great American Grain Robbery" of 1972 did not represent a radical departure from traditional agricultural policies for either the United States or the Soviet Union. Ever since the early 1960s, the Soviets had purchased grain from Australia, Argentina, Canada, and France, and had come to the United States to purchase grain when these customary suppliers could not fulfill Soviet quotas. In 1964, for example, the Soviet Union purchased 1.8 million tons of grain from the United States.[1] In 1971, the USSR bought 3 million tons of corn and other livestock feed from the United States.

The 1972 situation was different in part because of the magnitude of the Soviet purchase (19 million tons of U.S. grains, worth about $1.2 billion) and in part because 1972 was a year of worldwide grain crop shortages. While the Soviet Union turned first to Canada (which supplied 5 million tons), and then to Australia, France, Sweden, and Romania, it was ultimately forced to rely on American sources because the United States was the only major grain-exporting country with surpluses to sell in the summer of 1972.[2] The 1972 Soviet harvest was small, only 168.2 million tons compared with 195.5 million tons in 1974 and 222.5 million tons in 1973, and crops elsewhere in the world were generally smaller than normal.[3]

The United States erred in not recognizing and exploiting the true situation. As one government report subsequently pointed out, "the 1972-73 situation was probably an ideal one for the extraction of high profits. Instead, U.S. grain exporters provided a [low-priced] surplus to the USSR."[4] Grain exporters and Agriculture Department officials claimed that Soviet buyers were offered low prices because no one knew the extent of Soviet needs.

The 1972 grain purchases quickly became a source of arguments about the management of U.S. foreign agricultural policy. One of the most frequent complaints was that the control system in the U.S. government had been woefully inadequate in dealing with the secret purchasing practices of Exportkhleb. One of the immediate results of the 1972 grain deal was that U.S. grain exporters are now required to report to the Department of Agriculture within 24 hours all export grain sales involving more than 100,000 tons. This is to prevent a recurrence of the 1972 scenario in which Moscow's negotiators worked so discreetly that the competing U.S. grain dealers—Cook, Cargill, etc.—were unaware of the overall dimensions of what was happening. Moreover, key government agencies discovered belatedly and to their embarrassment that federal subsidies were contributing to the bargain purchases by Exportkhleb.

Much of the criticism has been directed at the Department of Agriculture. Correspondence later made public by Congressman John Melcher reveals that both the Australian and the Canadian Wheat Boards had advised the United States Department of Agriculture as early as July 1972 to reduce U.S. export subsidies and to allow world prices to rise in view of shortages expected in most major grain-producing countries. The reduction came only in September 1972, after most of the Soviet orders had been placed.[5] A 1974 General Accounting Office report maintained that information on the scope of the trade by Exportkhleb was available all along to responsible Agriculture Department officials, because the Department's Commodity Exchange Authority received daily and weekly reports on totals of U.S. grain sales.[6]

Agriculture Department officials have claimed that the size and speed of the Soviet purchases came as a complete surprise to them. Testimony in early 1974 before the Senate Permanent Subcommittee on Investigations suggested that at least a few high officials in the Agriculture Department did receive substantial and timely information on the scope of the Soviet buying. A senior vice-president of Continental Grain testified that in July 1972 he had told Carrol G. Brunthaver, assistant secretary of agriculture for trade, of a sale amounting to more than one-third of all the Soviet grain transactions. At the Senate hearings, Brunthaver was unable to recall having received such information.[7] The GAO found that at least six field reports describing the very poor Soviet grain crop outlook had been filed between February 18 and June 26, which again should have alerted the Department of Agriculture to the size of the purchases.[8]

A second major criticism of the 1972 grain agreements concerned the use of U.S. government credits to support Soviet purchases which would have been made for hard currency had credits been less readily obtainable. on July 8, 1972, still oblivious to the magnitude of planned Soviet purchases, the United States announced an agreement to provide $750 million in credits over a three-year period to help the Soviets finance their grain purchases. Thus, the 1972-73 grain shipments were largely financed through the Commodity Credit Corporation (CCC) at subsidized interest rates for two- to three-year periods. This practice was halted by Congress after the 1972 fiasco.

The effects of grain sales on domestic prices also aroused criticism. For almost two years prior to the sale, the Department of Agriculture had pegged the world market price of wheat at $1.63 a bushel. Domestic prices rose in 1972, and the Agriculture Department's world market price should have been placed much higher because of a world shortage of wheat in 1972. Since the United States was the only major grain exporter with surpluses to sell in 1973, the difference between the pegged world market price and higher domestic prices represented a net price advantage for the USSR and a loss for the United States. Subsidy payments to the grain-exporting companies by the Department of Agriculture made up the difference between the price paid by the Soviet Union and the United States domestic price. This amount totaled approximately $300 million between July and September.[9] A related price criticism is that the large and sudden Soviet grain purchase itself resulted in a doubling of the international price of wheat. By August 1973, the price of high-protein wheat had risen to over $5 a bushel, and the average price of wheat had risen to well over $2.49 a bushel.[10] Charges of excess profits were levied against the major U.S. grain companies by many observers because of the Agriculture Department subsidies and because the companies benefited greatly from the sheer volume of the purchases.

Even more serious were charges that the Soviet grain purchase was evidence of the inability of the policy of detente to serve U.S. economic interests as well as it seemed to serve those of the Soviet Union. Secretary of State Kissinger appeared to be especially sensitive to these charges, for he attempted to dissociate the 1972 grain deal from his policy of detente. His testimony before the Senate Finance Committee is revealing:

the Soviet grain deal, whatever criticism may be made of it, had next to nothing to do with detente. To be sure, it followed the Moscow summit by a month. But as it turned out, at the Moscow summit there was next to no discussion of the grain deal because the assumption at that time was that the amount of purchases would be so low as to not justify the attention of the two national leaders.

There was some very subsidiary conversation at the fringes of the summit and the issue elapsed. It was then decided that the Soviet Union would send a technical mission, and the negotiations were handled primarily in the Department of Agriculture, and by then Secretary of Commerce Peterson. So whatever one may say about the grain deal, it was not a part of the detente policy, and whatever difficulties arose with the wheat deal—and I believe there were several—were due first to an intelligence failure in a sense that there was not an adequate awareness at the high levels of our government as to the shortages that existed in the Soviet Union; and second, to an inadequate exchange of information between the companies and the government so that there was no understanding of the scale of the purchases that were actually being conducted.[11]

Still other critics claimed that the huge grain sales to the Soviet Union made the United States unable to respond to very real food needs elsewhere, particularly in West Africa and Bangladesh.[12]

THE 1975 GRAIN PURCHASE

By the time Exportkhleb representatives appeared in the United States to negotiate wheat and feed grain sales once again, it appeared that U.S. grain companies and the Washington bureaucracy alike would give their requests more careful scrutiny than had been the case with the sales of 1972. In retrospect, it appears that many of the 1972 errors were simply repeated. In 1975, as in 1972, it was many weeks after the Soviets made their initial purchases before grain companies or the Department of Agriculture became aware of the severity of the crop failure in the USSR or of the huge amounts of wheat the Soviets actually intended to purchase. Only belatedly did the Ford administration take advantage of the Soviet need for grain by concluding a long-term grain purchase agreement.

The first 1975 Soviet grain purchase was announced on July 16 when Cook Industries, Inc., reported a sale of 73 million bushels.[13] On July 19, the Cargill Company reported a sale of 44 million bushels.[14] Two days later, the Department of Agriculture announced a further sale by the Continental Grain Company of 177 million bushels of corn and 51 million bushels of barley.[15] The sales occurred in quick succession, and the only hint of impending Soviet plans had been a report in the *Times* of London on July 8, which said that the Soviets were trying to get up to 3 million tons of wheat from Canada and 7 million tons from the United States. Before the July buying spree was over, the Soviets had purchased 9.8 million tons of grain. Shortly thereafter, an International Long-shoremen's Association refusal to load ships with grain bound for the USSR forced President Ford to announce a moratorium on further grain sales. It was only after the signing of the five-year agreement toward the end of October that sales were resumed and an additional 3 million tons of grain were sold to the Soviet Union.

Inaccurate Soviet crop estimates by U.S. experts apparently misled the Department of Agriculture into thinking that Soviet purchases in July and August would be minimal. In June, agricultural forecasters were predicting a total Soviet grain production of 200 million tons (down from the original esti-mate of 210 million tons). The July estimate was 195 million tons, but by September U.S. experts estimated that the Soviet harvest would fall 40 million tons short of the target of 215.7 tons. In early December, figures released in veiled form at a meeting of the Politburo led to a revised estimate of 137.2 million tons. On December 13, a still lower figure of 133 million tons was given.[16] On January 31, 1976, the final figure was placed at 140 million tons.[17] At any rate, it was only after the five-year agreement on grain had been signed that the United States was fully aware of the disaster of the 1975 harvest in the USSR. The agreement is generally viewed as a practical move for the United States, and Soviet willingness to commit the USSR to fixed purchases over a five-year period underscores the seriousness of the shortfall in this year's crop.

The five-year agreement was negotiated by Under Secretary of State for Economic Affairs Charles W. Robinson, thus representing a victory of sorts for the Department of State in its efforts to secure control of agricultural foreign policy and to reduce the influence on that policy-making process of Secretary of Agriculture Earl Butz. Under the agreement, the Soviet Union is obligated to purchase a minimum total of 6 million metric tons of corn and wheat (at market prices) in about equal amounts in the five years between October 1, 1976, and October 1, 1981. The Soviets retain the option of buying an additional two million tons each year, but any purchase exceeding 8 million tons would require further negotiations between the two governments and the specific permission of the president. The agreement includes an escape clause for the United States, because sales can be halted at the minimum 6 million-ton level if the United States corn and wheat crop in any given year falls below 225 million tons. It is not expected that this would happen very often, since even the very poor 1974 U.S. grain crop was 226 million tons. As a response to criticism of the 1972 CCC credits, these sales will be on a cash-only basis with government subsidies excluded. All sales are to be worked out with private U.S. grain export-ers, but the Department of Agriculture will have review powers.[18]

The negotiating teams working on the grain agreement also attempted to obtain a petroleum link-up clause. It now appears that this petroleum agreement will remain in abeyance because of sharp disagreements over price and because Secretary of State Kissinger and other officials have been less willing to make long-range commitments to development projects within the USSR in view of Soviet involvement in Angola. At the time of the grain agreement, the United States was given an option to buy over 200,000 barrels of oil a day at a price that would "assure the interests of both countries." There was also some discussion of a second-stage petroleum agreement, involving perhaps an additional 700, 000 barrels a day, under which the United States would have provided advanced oil recovery technology to enable the Soviets to get more oil out of existing wells.[19] Some viewed the potential oil agreement (at prices below those charged by OPEC) as a way of convincing Moscow that commodity cartels are unacceptable. The idea was that Moscow could be persuaded that it has an interest in discouraging raw-materials cartels in the Third World if it wishes to benefit from free-market prices when it buys American grain. Actually, an oil agreement with the USSR would be a reversal of the U.S. position at the height of the oil crisis in early 1974, when the United States was urging France and other West European governments not to make special bilateral deals with the Arabs. If completed, the oil deal would add another strand to the economic ties that are growing alongside broad political efforts at detente. For the United States, the oil from the USSR would amount to only about 3 percent of total imports. The agreement would seem to be more useful to the Soviet Union, for oil sales would probably help to offset the hard-currency costs of grain imports from the United States in addition to paying for oil recovery equipment from the United States. American oil companies like Gulf, Standard Oil of Indiana, and Phillips have all signed technical cooperation agreements with the Soviets in 1975 and would almost certainly be eager to participate in any new agreements as well.[20]

A recently signed maritime shipping agreement is commonly regarded as the third prong of the grain agreement. Early in December, the United States and the USSR agreed to extend their maritime grain-shipping pact for another six years. The agreement carries a minimum merchant-shipping rate of $16 a ton for grain carried by U.S.-flag vessels from the United States to the USSR and guarantees such vessels one-third of all American grain carried to the USSR.[21]

Many U.S. observers have been happy about the new five-year grain agreement even without a petroleum link-up provision. The most important effect of the agreement will probably be an end to the sporadic buying of U.S. grain by the Soviets which caused such disruption both in 1972 and in July 1975. Some also see it as representing a beginning in a new, calculated use of U.S. food power to achieve specific goals. A few analysts have even suggested that as a condition for the grain agreement, the Soviets were persuaded to abstain during Secretary of State Kissinger's summer 1975 efforts to reach an Egyptian-Israeli accord.[22]

The 1975 grain negotiations resulted in a vociferous debate among various governmental and nongovernmental actors closely involved in agricultural exports.

One of the most interesting conflicts was that between the Department of State and the Department of Agriculture. The State Department clearly blamed the Agriculture Department for the problems of 1972. In 1974, the State Department managed to block a $500 million shipment of corn and wheat to the USSR. The Agriculture Department cited the Soviet Union for failure to keep a "gentlemen's agreement" not to attempt such large purchases, but the State Department maintained that the Soviet Union had been led to believe by the Department of Agriculture and by private dealers that it would be able to purchase just about the amount of grain in the later suspended shipment.[23] The result of the distrust inherited from 1972 and 1974 was that negotiation of the 1975 long-term agreement was taken out of the hands of Earl Butz and the Department of Agriculture.

The Agriculture Department has also acquired few friends in the Department of the Treasury or on the Federal Reserve Board. Treasury Secretary William Simon, in remarks which clearly opposed the position of Secretary of Agriculture Butz, stressed restraint in sales of grain to the USSR in the summer of 1975.[24] Similarly, after the first July 1975 wheat sales, Arthur Burns warned a Senate committee that he expected a sizable increase in U.S. bread prices as a result, and more generally that the grain sales would have a serious inflationary impact. Butz responded by noting that "Mr. Burns should stick to his business and I'll stick to agriculture."[25]

While he was not a part of the negotiating team which drew up the long-term grain agreement, Butz has long been one of its firmest public supporters, defending it as a measure to stabilize the international grain market and to secure the Soviet Union as a regular rather than occasional grain customer. In defending the measure, he has received severe criticism even from some of the usually loyal constituents of the Department of Agriculture, since farm organizations and the grain companies have argued for a "free-market" in grain export policy.[26]

Farm groups in general have supported greatly increased exports to the USSR and Eastern Europe, along with government credits to help East-bloc countries pay for those exports.[27] They have been generally unhappy with the new long-term agreement. They welcome its introduction of stability into the export market, but they dislike the relatively low minimum target for grain shipments and are opposed to government intervention to decide on policies for exports of over 6 million tons a year. The liberal Farmers' Union and its president, Tony Dechant, have expressed "outrage at the continuing political interference of the Ford Administration with agricultural commodity markets." The Farmers' Union blames the government for moving in July 1975 to push prices down "just when farmers had a chance to sell their crops at record-breaking prices."[28] Orren Lee Staley, president of the National Farmers' Organization, also had uncomplimentary words for the long-term agreement: "It's outrageous and illegal interference with farm exports, not just for this year, but for five."[29] William J. Kuhfuss, president of the 2.4 million-member American Farm Bureau, called the five-year agreement "a dangerous precedent for future political international commodity agreements," and warned of "the apparent trend toward government domination of international trade in agricultural commodities."[30]

The farm organization leaders had harsh words not only for the five-year agreement and for Secretary Butz, but also for the International Longshoremen's Association, whose dock workers had refused to load grain on ships bound for the Soviet Union in August and September 1975 to protest the potential effect that huge sales might have on U.S. prices. Their actions led initially to President Ford's continuing an embargo on further grain sales and also to the lengthy negotiations on the agreement. On several occasions, Kuhfuss of the American Farm Bureau accused the Ford administration of "selling out to labor." Kuhfuss denounced the position of the ILA as unwarranted interference in U.S. foreign policy and repeated his organization's contention that grain exports were not the prime cause of rising food prices.[31]

At a rather late stage in 1975 developments, several congressional committees became active proponents of the long-term agreement. The Senate Agriculture Committee held meetings in September which were billed as a new attempt by Congress to shape U.S. grain export policy. Republican Senator Robert Dole of Kansas accused the Ford administration of having no policy on grain exports and said he would urge Congress to require a bilateral sales agreement between the United States and the Soviet Union for at least a three-year period. The Senate Foreign Relations Committee held hearings on the grain agreement of 1975 in October. Earlier, just a day before Cook Industries, Inc., announced the first big wheat sale, the House Ways and Means Committee announced that it planned an investigation into reports that the USSR was planning another grain deal.[32] At best, all of these efforts amounted to a retrospective look at the 1975 grain sales. They played almost no role in actual formulation of grain policy.

Though their actual policy-making activities are sometimes hard to document, the major U.S. grain companies were active participants in the political process of 1975. By the time the five-year agreement had been reached, they had incurred the displeasure of a host of would-be government investigatory agencies. In early November, the *Wall Street Journal* enumerated a number of anti-grain company activities then underway: A House committee was debating a bill to take all grain transactions with foreigners out of the hands of the grain companies and put them under the control of a government agency. A Senate panel was investigating the grain companies' role in East-West trade. Grand juries had indicted several companies in grain inspection scandals. The ICC was investigating charges of rail car black-marketing by exporters. The FTC was looking into possible antitrust aspects of the grain trade.[33]

In recent years, the grain companies have become deeply involved in attempts to influence public opinion and to help formulate public policy in matters of grain exports. The grain companies at first remained silent when charges of "profiteering" were levied against them in 1972. Then, when the GAO ultimately verified their claims that initial sales to the USSR had resulted in small monetary losses, they began to defend themselves more vigorously.[34]

A few comments about the role of the grain companies in East-West trade are in order. Continental Grain, Cook Industries, and Cargill are the major exporters of grain to the USSR and Eastern Europe. Other major exporters which have been somewhat less active in East-bloc markets include the Bunge Corporation, Louis Dreyfus Corporation, and Garnac Corporation. The merchandising of grain exports is a highly risky business. Private companies must buy, store, sell, and transport huge quantities of grains. Because the grain is bought in a short period but moved into commercial channels the year round, assessing supply and demand is difficult, and large sales can be won or lost on differences of as little as a few cents a ton. For this reason, exporters carefully guard information about quantities involved in their dealings, the prices at which they buy or sell, the amounts they have already bought or sold or have left to buy, and the techniques they use in negotiating with a buyer. Any disclosure of this information would put a grain exporter operating in a highly competitive industry on extremely small margins at a competitive disadvantage. Secrecy is an inevitable outcome of the competitive nature of the export business and is not, industry spokesmen assert, an attempt to conceal facts from the public.[35]

Controversy about the role of grain companies and their possible receipt of excess profits in 1975 really goes back to 1972, when it was felt that some Department of Agriculture officials may have had inside information about impending Soviet grain purchases and might have passed this information on to favored companies.

THE SOVIET UNION AND THE 1975 GRAIN AGREEMENT

There are many who feel that the only party who really succeeded in making unequivocal gains from the grain purchases in 1972 and in 1975 was the Soviet Union. Whenever huge purchases are made by a monopsonist, the private market system, with its large numbers of sellers and policy makers, is at a disadvantage. The monopsonist has the advantage of secrecy; he is also capable of exerting a considerable impact on the market. It was largely to counterbalance this effect that the United States government sought the 1975 grain agreement. That the Soviet Union accepted its terms is more a factor of the weak position of Soviet agriculture than of Soviet eagerness to promote the economic aspects of detente.

The Soviet press has remained completely silent on the matter of grain purchases from the United States. However, it has indicated that farm troubles exist. On September 4, 1975, *Izvestia* admitted that the past summer did not justify certain hopes of the grain growers, because the harvest "was not bountiful everywhere" and "did not fully repay the labor put into the ground." In a series of articles in August and September, *Pravda* avoided an overall assessment of the Soviet harvest, but it did report that there were not enough good mowers in Western Siberia, that there were too few trucks to move grain, and that there were problems with combines that left a good deal of cut grain in the field.[36]

Some of these were recurring problems. Leonid Brezhnev had disclosed, at the December 1973 meeting of the CPSU Central Committee, that huge losses of grain had occurred even during 1973's record harvest because of inadequate storage and transport facilities. The 1974 harvest brought problems, too. The New York *Times* surveyed Soviet press comments on the ongoing harvest on July 14, 1974. It noted that in the Kursk area, more than a third of the 6,288 grain harvesters were not ready for deployment. Many lay idle for lack of spare parts, according to *Sovetskaya Rossiya.* *Sel'skaya zhizn* noted that Kazakhstan had only 216,000 of the 364,000 machine operators it required for the harvest. At one farm in Western Siberia, the harvesting equipment worked so poorly that 1,000 workers were sent into the field to collect the crops by hand. Troops were used to transport crops in Siberia and Kazakhstan.

Press reports discussing the 1975 harvest concentrated on difficulties caused by lack of machinery and by inadequate research. Mr. Runchev of the All-Union Academy of Agricultural Sciences, in a lengthy *Pravda* article, wrote of the acute shortage of transportation on the collective and state farms. Requirements for trucks had not been met, and even during the harvest period, tens of thousands of extra trucks were sent from cities to farms in the RSFSR alone. The cost of this was said to run into millions of rubles. Runchev blamed the planning agencies for inadequacies and said that decisive steps should be taken to furnish collective and state farms with more adequate equipment.[37] Others have blamed research institutions and their inability to apply theoretical knowledge to practical agricultural measures for the problems that culminated in this year's disastrous harvest. An *Izvestia* survey late in 1975 counted seven regional branches of the All-Union Academy of Agricultural Sciences and 28 specialized centers but noted that these agencies had inadequate ties to the basic production needs of state and collective farms.

The 1975 harvest was such a sensitive topic that even articles about inadequacies in machinery and in research efforts have been carefully balanced with optimistic general reports. It seems likely that some high government leaders, particularly agricultural officials, have been reluctant to let any of the bad news filter down officially to the Soviet public. When *Pravda* and *Izvestia* published a report by the Central Statistical Administration on plan fulfillment for the first half of 1975, there was no mention of problems in harvesting grains, though by this time the first round of Exportkhleb purchases in the United States had already been completed. The report had an optimistic tone and noted that collective and state farms had overfulfilled the plan for spring sowing (with no mention of severe problems in the ongoing harvest!). The report simply concluded that "in this year's conditions, agricultural toilers conducted hay making and fodder procurement work earlier than usual and the large-scale harvesting of grain crops has begun." Soviet readers were also informed that the collective farms and state farms had increased the numbers of livestock and poultry (with no hint of the decision already made to slaughter many of the cattle because of inadequate feed grain supplies).[38]

One of the few comprehensive and less optimistic reports was given by P. M. Masherov, candidate member of the Politburo of the CPSU Central Committee and first secretary of the Central Committee of the Belorussian Communist party. His speech to a Belorussian party meeting was published in *Sovetskaya Belorussia* on July 6. His message was not repeated in *Pravda* or *Izvestia*, but similar ideas were finally expressed publicly at high-level Communist party meetings in Moscow in December. Masherov's picture of the results of a massive agricultural effort was grim. During the current five-year plan, the state had invested over 5.8 billion rubles in Soviet agriculture, or 79 percent more than in the preceding five-year plan. The capital-to-labor ratio had risen by 78 percent during this five-year plan, and what he called the power-to-worker ratio had risen by 49 percent. Deliveries of commercial fertilizers had increased by 40 percent. The results of these massive efforts are astonishing. The gross output of collective and state farms had increased only 29 percent during the 1971-75 period and labor productivity had risen by only 37 percent. The output-to-capital ratio had actually dropped. Masherov did not hesitate to assign blame for these failures. He said that "the glaring discrepancy between the growth rate of agricultural production and that of material and technical resources is the fault of our cadres, the farm's managers and specialists, who in many cases do not follow the best practices." Between 1971 and 1974 in the Belorussian Republic, "under actual conditions," the potential yield of grain crops had been realized by slightly over 80 percent, that of potatoes by 60 percent, of flax by 75 percent, and of sugar beets by 70 percent.[39]

It was not until December, well after the signing of the long-term grain agreement, that party and government officials gave public recognition to the disastrous harvest, and even then they did so only in cryptic terms. Western observers derived the 137 million-ton crop estimate (now regarded as accurate despite newer figures claiming a harvest of 140 million tons) from the remarks of Grigory I. Vashchenko, chairman of the Budget and Planning Commission of the Council of the Union, one of the Supreme Soviet's two chambers. Vashchenko, also a member of the Communist party's Central Committee, said that the total grain harvest for 1971-75 exceeded by 8 percent the total achieved during the previous five-year plan. In his annual report to the Supreme Soviet at the same time, Deputy Premier Nikolai Baibakov omitted all mention of the harvest, though he did indirectly disclose that the crop failure was partially responsible for a cutback in Soviet economic goals to the lowest projected growth rates since World War II.[40]

One reason for the Soviet embarrassment is undoubtedly the fact that agriculture has been one of Brezhnev's areas of special concern and emphasis. Beginning in March 1965, Brezhnev had embarked on a large-scale program to improve agricultural output through larger expenditures for farm machinery, storage facilities, and fertilizers. Western observers state that more than 131 billion rubles ($175 billion) has been spent during the 1971-75 plan period. This investment amounts to the highest-level agricultural subsidy in the world, and it was of course intended in part to expand meat production and to improve the carbohydrate-rich diet of the Soviet people.[41] While considerable progress was made in increasing food output during 1966-70 (especially in the good harvest years of 1968 and 1970), agricultural production has actually stagnated in the years since 1970, despite huge new state investments.[42]

To Western observers, there was an even more startling side to the disastrous 1975 Soviet harvest. It represented a continuation of the downward slide in the overall quality of Soviet crops, which has occurred despite the Soviet emphasis on better seeds, better fertilizers, and improved technology. This trend was first admitted publicly in 1973 in Soviet agricultural journals, when it was noted that Soviet production of high-protein wheat was only 3.5 million tons, compared with 3.8 million tons in 1970. In 1975, articles in the Soviet press indicated that the quality of fodder was below standard, the sugar content of sugar beets had been declining, the textile industry was complaining about the low quality of cotton, and there had been a decline in the fat content of milk.[43]

Also of great concern to Soviet agricultural planners is the fact that Soviet crop yields have been significantly lower than yields in Eastern Europe. Yields of most crops in Eastern Europe are two to three times those achieved in the USSR. For example, in 1971-72, the Soviet Union harvested 15 quintals of wheat per hectare (one quintal equals about 220 pounds; one hectare equals 2.5 acres). Poland harvested 25.8 quintals, Czechoslovakia harvested 34.4 quintals, Hungary harvested 30.8 quintals, and East Germany harvested 39.5 quintals per hectare.[44]

One of the most immediate results of the poor 1975 harvest has been a reevaluation of the 1976-80 Five-Year Plan. The plans for 1976 are especially cautious. National income is scheduled to rise by only 5.4 percent in 1976 compared to a 1975 target of 6.5 percent, with an unimpressive 4 percent actually achieved. The industrial growth rate (4.3 percent) set for 1976 is the lowest since 1946, and projected growth in the consumer-goods sector is a very low 2.7 percent.[45] Agricultural failures, of course, are not the only causes of reduced plan goals, but in an economy where agriculture employs more than one-quarter of the total Soviet labor force and utilizes about one-fifth of the country's assets, harvest failures drag down the rest of the economy to a greater extent than they would be in other industrialized nations. N. Baibakov, head of Gosplan, has conceded that the comparatively low growth rates of production planned for 1976 (and beyond) are because of shortages in agricultural output from the 1975 crop, as well as a lag in putting new production units into production.[46]

A side effect of the poor harvest that is certainly influencing planning decisions is a decline in the Soviet Union's hard-currency reserves. Western experts now believe that the USSR will have a record $5 billion hard-currency trade deficit for 1975, based on imports of agricultural goods and machinery of $13 billion and exports of $8 billion. This would be triple the record deficit of 1973. Since only about $1 billion of grain purchases were actually paid for in 1975, some $3 billion will have to be paid in 1976. In 1975, the Soviets relied on higher than usual sales of gold and on relatively generous credits from Western governments and banking institutions to pay their bills. The USSR's current long-term foreign debt is over $7 billion, up from $4.5 billion in 1974.[47]

The high-level debate on causes and implications of the 1975 harvest has been carefully concealed from the Soviet masses, but the debate has apparently centered on several key issues: Who is to blame for the agricultural failure? Can the USSR continue to buy both agricultural goods and high-technology products? Should there be reliance on credits or on gold sales when purchasing grain abroad? Should oil shipments be used to pay for grain purchases? It is likely that the questions will not receive any definitive answers within the forseeable future. And it is certain that the details of the high-level Soviet debate will not be revealed.

SOVIET-U.S. GRAIN TRADE AND EASTERN EUROPE

Agricultural problems in the USSR provide unprecedented opportunities for the United States to forge somewhat stronger economic ties with East European countries. Eastern Europe, which usually gets about half its 10 million metric ton annual grain import needs from the USSR, was forced to look to the United States for most of its import needs in 1975.[48] The Soviet Union had reportedly notified several East European countries that it would send credits instead of grain in 1975.[49] For example, Poland would normally have gotten 2 million tons of grain from the USSR, but it received no grain in 1975. In December, Secretary of Agriculture Earl Butz announced that a new five-year agreement with Poland calls for shipments of at least 2.5 million tons of U.S. grain annually for five years.[50] Similar agreements with other East European countries would enhance U.S. bargaining power in both Eastern Europe and the Soviet Union.

American sales to East European countries (Poland, Romania, and East Germany) totaled about 4.5 million tons by September, includng both wheat and corn to be supplied in 1975-76. In contrast, in recent years, U.S. grain sales to Eastern Europe have averaged less than 2 million tons a year. By September, Agriculture Department officials were predicting that total sales to Eastern Europe could jump to as much as 7 or 8 million tons by early 1976.[51] Fitting these sales into long-term agreements would create additional stable markets for U.S. farm products and would perhaps facilitate somewhat greater economic independence of Eastern Europe in relation to the Soviet Union.

As in the case of the Soviet Union, East European agricultural problems are of a long-term nature. Even in years when harvest conditions are generally better than they were in 1975, the East European countries have suffered from a deficiency of grain, meat, and butter products. Part of the basic East European agricultural problem stems from changes which occurred in the 1960s as a result of economic reforms designed to increase economic incentives and efficiency, particularly in industrial sectors. The result of the reform programs was that domestic food supply did not keep pace with growing demand for more and better-quality food products. The disparity between supply and demand became especially apparent in the late 1960s after the socialization of agriculture reached completion in Bulgaria, Czechoslovakia, East Germany, Hungary, and Romania. In Poland, where private agriculture has remained dominant, the problems have been somewhat different in that machinery problems seem more serious than structural imbalances in the economy.[52]

Press reports have documented several problem areas in 1975 East European crops which were especially troublesome in the context of the crop shortfall in the USSR. In most East European countries, and particularly in Bulgaria, Poland, and Hungary, there was more concern over the 1975 crop than usual, perhaps because of anticipated Soviet problems. In Bulgaria, the press criticized the poor organization of volunteer school brigades in bringing in the harvest and complained of "ill-intentioned pickers [who] leave rows and trees unpicked on purpose, so that they can pick them at night for their own profit and with personal enthusiasm."[53] Actually, most Western observers felt that the wheat and barley harvest in Bulgaria turned out to be better than expected after reports of bad weather early in the summer.[54]

In Hungary and Poland, most of the harvest problems came from poor management and problems with farm equipment. The Polish harvest was helped by favorable weather conditions and by some improvements in mechanization. However, Zycie gospodarcze (August 17) reported that only 20,000 combines were available instead of the 40,000 needed; and only 330,000 tractors were in the fields, as opposed to 800,000 needed. There were severe shortages of spare parts for machinery, particularly for foreign-manufactured units. As a result, 5,000 C-355 tractors imported from Czechoslovakia and 700 Dutras from Hungary were left inoperative.[55]

The Hungarian press mentioned a "considerable shortage" of wheat but stressed that the country's domestic supply and reserves would be guaranteed. Agrotroszt (the state enterprise that supplies agricultural machinery and other agricultural needs) complained of delivery shortfalls to be blamed on its foreign suppliers in the USSR, GDR, and Czechoslovakia. The Soviet Union had not delivered the promised T-150K tractors in time for the harvest, and Czechoslovakia and East Germany were millions of forints behind schedule in promised deliveries of spare parts. Hungary's own factories were also behind schedule and failed to deliver badly needed plows and high-powered sowing machines in time for use in 1975.[56] There were also shortages in the supply of combines coming from COMECON countries, particularly the Soviet Union and East Germany, and disruptions in making arrangements for transporting grain to the granaries.[57]

In addition to these problems in organizing the 1975 growing and harvesting season, East European countries have been engaged in severe disagreements within the forum of COMECON. The Romanians have been particularly critical of efforts to step up coordination of agricultural machine building with COMECON, seemingly with good reason in view of the domestic spare parts and delivery problems plaguing most East European countries. The Romanian press has ridiculed the idea that an all COMECON agricultural-industrial complex should gradually result from the merging of those sectors of their economies where national agricultural planning complexes have already been developed. The Romanian view is that each East European country represents a complete unit which is best managed on the basis of a national plan for socioeconomic development.[58]

The East Europeans have also had a difficult time in agricultural relations with Western Europe. In recent years, the Common Market countries have imposed duties on agricultural products such as beef from outside countries. This has been particularly hard on Hungarian exports of beef, which have traditionally fetched good prices in Western Europe. The drop in beef exports has meant that Hungary is losing significant amounts of projected hard-currency earnings.[59] The fact that the Soviet Skotoimport company has purchased fattened cattle which Terimpex (the Hungarian foreign trade company) had originally planned to export to Italy and is reportedly paying in dollars should ease a small part of the burden.[60] But the larger problem of EEC restrictions on agricultural imports from Eastern Europe remains.

These problems have led in turn to unprecedented East European borrowing (to pay for grains they must import and for farm machinery) on West European money markets. A $150 million Eurocurrency loan to Hungary early in December 1975 is reported to have met with a lukewarm reception. Borrowing problems were even spreading to the United States. The Manufacturers Hanover Trust Company recently completed a $50 million loan syndication for Poland for three-year grain credits. It had to be placed among smaller banks, many of whom were first-time lenders to Eastern Europe.[61]

The United States remains one of the best sources of potential and actual agricultural assistance to the East European countries. Unfortunately, many top U.S. policy decisions have failed to differentiate between the very dissimilar

situations of the East European countries and the USSR and have failed to exploit an opportunity to diversify East European economic linkages. For example,
in September 1975, U.S. grain sales to Poland and other East European countries
were suspended until a long-term agreement could be worked out with the
Soviet Union.

It does appear, however, that the United States is beginning to emphasize
foreign agricultural policies more suited to the particular situations of the
East European countries. A long-term grain pact was signed between the United
States and Poland in Warsaw on November 27, 1975. Under the terms of the
agreement, Poland promised to buy 2.5 million tons of grain annually (with a
margin of 20 percent either way) for five years. The Agriculture Department's
Commodity Credit Corporation will extend some credit facilities but has not
guaranteed to finance the whole deal, since congressional authorization would be
required.[62]

East Germany is also buying more grain from the United States than ever
before to make up for shortages caused by the Soviet harvest. West German
grain dealers report that orders for a record 3 million tons of grain have been
placed in the West this year, nearly all of them in the United States. With a
stronger hard-currency position than Poland, East Germany has been less concerned about receiving U.S. credits for the purchases. To finance the 1975
purchases, East Germany borrowed Eurodollars for two-year terms from the
European offices of U.S. banks.[63]

In 1974, Hungary purchased soybeans and other agricultural products worth
a total of about $3.5 million and exported in return bottled wines and canned
hams. The Hungarians were less interested in purchasing agricultural products
in 1975 than they were in securing advanced U.S. farm machinery. In October,
U.S. Secretary of Commerce Rogers Morton visited Hungary to discuss improved
trade relations with the United States.[64] This was followed by the visit of
Secretary of Agriculture Butz in November. Butz discussed with the Hungarian
minister of agriculture and food the possibility of expanding economic and
scientific cooperation between the two countries.[65] Both Morton and Butz
reportedly encouraged the Hungarians to hope for MFN treatment within the
near future.

The Hungarians have developed some highly successful agreements with the
Steiger Company and with the John Deere Company and apparently hope for
many similar arrangements if MFN can be obtained. Official publications of a
specialized nature, such as *Vilaggazdasag* (World Economy), have presented a
clear analysis of the Soviet-U.S. grain transactions, and Hungarian officials seem
keenly aware that U.S. technology could contribute a great deal to Hungarian
agricultural production.[66] Sophisticated farm machinery is particularly sought by
the Hungarians, and they know that such equipment is not to be purchased from
the USSR or other East European countries. Beginning in 1973, the first batch
of U.S.-manufactured Steiger tractors was sent to Hungary. Workers began

referring to the air-conditioned cabins of the Steiger as a kind of "sanatorium on wheels," and the reception was so enthusiastic that the Gyor Wagon and Machine Works purchased the license for the Steiger tractor at the end of 1974. Production started in 1975, and the first Hungarian-made Raba-Steiger tractors went into operation in May. In addition to tractors, sophisticated cultivators from the American John Deere Company have been licensed for production in Hungary.[67]

SOVIET-U.S. GRAIN TRADE AND THE POLICY OF DETENTE

> Russian dependence on American wheat to meet its own food needs has doubtlessly contributed to the recent mood of detente and may help encourage the Russians to share their untapped Siberian energy resources with the United States.[68]

Hopes like these were fuel for beliefs that U.S. grain sales could be turned into political currency within the general framework of detente. But they fail to reflect a fundamental difference in Soviet and U.S. perspectives on grain sales and on detente. For many U.S. supporters of grain sales, the shipments presented an opportunity to use the weapon of "food politics." Some saw in the Middle East negotiations underway at about the same time a willingness to negotiate which was attributed to severe grain shortages in the USSR.[69] Others felt that the five-year grain agreement and its hoped-for second-stage petroleum agreement could be used to solidify support for political detente with the Soviet Union in the United States. For the Soviets, the grain purchases most likely represented nothing more than an immediate solution to some very pressing economic problems.

There are few U.S. observers who have been completely opposed to the grain sales, but many have pointed to some serious potential problems. The grain export companies concede that the five-year agreement with the Soviets is probably in the public interest because of the impact Soviet purchases have had on domestic markets. But they are afraid that the Soviets, over the next five or ten years, will build up extensive storage facilities which would enable them to disrupt world markets by selling at low prices should they ever acquire a storage surplus.[70] Others have begun to realize that one of the potentially most attractive aspects of the sales—the possible oil link-up—will most likely never materialize; and even if it does, it will not be arranged at price levels that would undermine the price structure of OPEC.[71] Finally, critics foresee that the large U.S. commitments under the agreement with the Soviet Union may make it much more difficult for the United States to be flexible in serving the food needs of the famine-plagued developing nations.[72]

NOTES

1. For details of the 1963-64 grain sales, see Leon M. Herman, *The 1963-1964 Wheat Sales to Russia: A Summary of Major Developments* (Washington: Library of Congress, Legislative Reference Service, April 7, 1964).

2. Marshall I. Goldman, *Detente and Dollars* (New York: Basic Books, 1975), pp. 193-94.

3. New York *Times*, July 11, 1975.

4. John P. Hardt and George D. Holliday, *U.S.-Soviet Commercial Relations: The Interplay of Economics, Technology Transfer, and Diplomacy* (Washington; D.C.: Government Printing Office, June 10, 1973), p. 67.

5. *Congressional Record*, April 9, 1973, H2501-2502.

6. New York *Times*, February 13, 1974.

7. Ibid.

8. Comptroller General of the U.S., Report to Congress, *Russian Wheat Sales and Weaknesses of the Export Subsidy Program* (Washington: General Accounting Office, July 9, 1973), p. 18.

9. Hardt and Holliday, op. cit., p. 67.

10. Goldman, op. cit., p. 194.

11. Statement of Henry Kissinger, *The Trade Reform Act of 1973*, vol. II, p. 467

12. Stephen S. Rosenfeld, "The Politics of Food," *Foreign Policy*, no. 14 (Spring 1974), p. 28.

13. New York *Times*, July 17, 1975.

14. Ibid., July 20, 1975.

15. Ibid., July 22, 1975.

16. Ibid., July 10, 1975; September 18, 1975; December 4, 1975; December 14, 1975.

17. Ibid., February 1, 1976.

18. *Wall Street Journal*, October 21, 1975.

19. New York *Times*, October 25, 1975.

20. *Business Week*, November 3, 1975, pp. 30-31.

21. *Wall Street Journal*, December 19, 1975.

22. *Business Week*, December 15, 1975, pp. 54-56.

23. New York *Times*, October 6, 1974; *Wall Street Journal*, October 9, 1974.

24. New York *Times*, August 1, 1975.

25. *Wall Street Journal*, September 5, 1975.

26. Ibid., October 22, 1975.

27. See especially statements of the National Grain and Feed Association and of the American Soybean Association, *The Trade Reform Act of 1973*, op. cit., vol. 6, pp. 2408-12.

28. New York *Times*, October 16, 1975.

29. *Wall Street Journal*, October 22, 1975.

30. Ibid.

31. New York *Times*, August 1, 1975; September 16, 1975; *Wall Street Journal*, October 22, 1975.

32. New York *Times*, July 10, 1975.

33. *Wall Street Journal*, November 5, 1975.

34. Ibid., November 7, 1975.

35. "Cargill Grain Company," case no. 4-373-161, mimeographed, Harvard Business School, Cambridge, Mass., 1973, pp. 4-5.

36. *Pravda*, September 16, 1975.

37. Ibid., September 23, 1975, p. 2.

38. *Pravda* and *Izvestia*, July 20, 1975, pp. 1-2.

39. P.M. Masherov, "Fittingly Greet the 25th C.P.S.U. Congress," *Sovetskaya Belorussia*, July 6, 1975, pp. 1-2.

40. New York *Times*, December 4, 1975.

41. Ibid., December 10, 1975.

42. Douglas B. Diamond and Constance P. Krueger, "Recent Developments in Output and Productivity in Soviet Agriculture," in U.S. Congress, Joint Economic Committee, *Soviet Economic Prospects for the Seventies*, 93rd Cong., 2d Sess., April 12, 1974, p. 316.

43. Radio Free Europe Research, *USSR Background Report*, no. 154 (November 6, 1975), pp. 1-5; a review of "Quality is an Extremely Important Indicator in Competition," *Ekonomika sel'skogo khozyaistva*, no. 6 (June 19, 1975).

44. Alec Nove, "Will Russia Ever Feed Itself?" New York *Times Magazine*, February 1, 1976, p. 48.

45. Business International, *Eastern Europe Report*, December 12, 1975, p. 343.

46. *Wall Street Journal*, December 3, 1975.

47. Ibid., December 19, 1975.

48. Ibid., August 22, 1975.

49. Ibid., September 17, 1975.

50. *Business Week*, December 15, 1975, p. 56.

51. *Wall Street Journal*, September 23, 1975.

52. Gregor Lazarcik, "Agricultural Output and Productivity in Eastern Europe and Some Comparisons with the USSR and U.S.A.," in U.S. Congress, Joint Economic Committee, *Reorientation and Commercial Relations of the Economies of Eastern Europe,*, 93rd Cong., 2d Sess., August 16, 1974, pp. 329-31.

53. Radio Free Europe Research, *Bulgarian Situation Report*, no. 26 (September 26, 1975): 1-4.

54. Ibid., no. 24 (August 27, 1975), pp. 3-4.

55. Radio Free Europe Research, *Polish Situation Report,* no. 26 (August 28, 1975), pp. 2-5.

56. Radio Free Europe Research, *Hungarian Situation Report*, no. 49 (November 28, 1975), p. 11.

57. Ibid., no. 28 (June 24, 1975), p. 15.

58. Radio Free Europe Research, *Romanian Press Survey*, no. 997 (November 24, 1975), pp. 1-2, translation of G. Grigorescu, "The Development of Agriculture in Light of the Increasing Interdependence of other Branches of the National Economy," *Revista Economica*, no. 44 (October 31, 1975).

59. Radio Free Europe Research, *Hungarian Situation Report,* no. 42 (October 7, 1975), p. 4.

60. Ibid., no. 32 (July 30, 1975), p. 8

61. New York *Times*, December 15, 1975.

62. Radio Free Europe Research, *Polish Situation Report,* no. 38 (December 8, 1975), p. 9.

63. New York *Times*, January 20, 1976.

64. Radio Free Europe Research, *Hungarian Situation Report*, no. 43 (October 14, 1975), p. 7.

65. Ibid., no. 50 (December 3, 1975), p. 11.

66. Tamas Zala, *Vilaggazdasag,* August 23, 1975; translated in Radio Free Europe Research, *Hungarian Press Survey,* no. 2360 (September 2, 1975), p. 1.

67. Radio Free Europe Research, *Hungarian Situation Report*, no. 27 (June 16, 1975), p. 6.

68. Lester R. Brown, "The Next Crisis? Food," *Foreign Policy*, no. 13 (Winter 1973-74), p. 22.

69. *Business Week*, December 15, 1975, p. 56.

70. *Wall Street Journal*, November 5, 1975.

71. New York *Times*, October 12, 1975.

72. Emma Rothschild, "Food Politics," *Foreign Affairs* 54, no. 2 (January 1976): 291.

CHAPTER
9
CONCLUSIONS

The challenge to the policy of detente is to provide a restructuring of relationships through which the Soviet Union and Eastern Europe can gradually become full members of the international community in areas of politics, ideology, military style, and economics. This analysis has been concerned only with the political and economic aspects of that process in the issue area of trade. It has attempted to demonstrate that at present there is not an adequate distinction between the levels of international economic process and international economic structure in the arena of East-West trade and that issues of economic policy have become overpoliticized. Governments, corporations, and regional groupings wage high-pitched battles over sometimes minor transfers of technology, but very often the process of trade simply continues, even if it does so through more convoluted channels.

If we are to reap lasting benefits from detente, we must provide a new framework for the management of trade relationships. This should be a framework in which minor issues are resolved smoothly on a day-to-day basis and major issues are dealt with properly at the higher levels of decision making. It should be a framework capable of separating the elements of politics from those of economics in specific cases. The components of that framework are to be found in the actors we have considered here: the EEC, COMECON, the national governments of the United States and the Soviet Union, corporations, bureaucracies, international organizations, special agreements, banks, and intergovernmental commissions. An analysis of the framework shaped by the interaction of these components suggests that detente's goals, contents, and limits in the area of trade will differ from policies currently pursued by the U.S. government.

174

THE GOALS OF DETENTE IN EAST-WEST TRADE

The Soviet Union and the countries of Eastern Europe should be able to conduct business transactions with the West on a pragmatic rather than ideological basis. If projects that will serve the economic interests of all parties involved can be identified, then they should be pursued. If projects have little or no economic merit but are undertaken primarily because they are believed to be capable of enhancing "the spirit of detente," they should be abandoned. Economic issues devoid of major political content should be dealt with separately from those issues which affect the political interrelationships of major decision makers.

In the highly politicized economic arena of East-West trade, this separation will not be easy to achieve. The key may well be to strengthen government controls over broad guidelines for trade but to enhance as well the ability of corporations to make their own decisions about what to sell, what to license, and when to engage in joint ventures. Government prohibitions on transfers of technology deemed politically sensitive should be spelled out clearly in advance of actual transactions. Government decisions on the general availability of credit to finance sales and joint ventures should be determined in advance of company negotiations with the East bloc for specific projects.

The separation will be even more difficult because, as the preceding chapters have indicated, economic power is so frequently translated into political power that it becomes difficult to keep the relationship from becoming tautological. Political power can be used to improve one's position in the economic arena, and economic power is frequently used to influence political policies. But we must separate them if we are not to become increasingly disappointed when grain sales do not result in political concessions in Angola or when progress at the SALT talks or at the European Security Conference cannot be transformed into petroleum sales agreements between the United States and the Soviet Union. It may be useful to think of political issues in East-West trade as those which mold and challenge the fundamental structure of interdependence, and economic issues as those which control the transfer of goods, money, and technology within that structure.

Closely related to the need for pragmatic conduct of business is the need for a clear distinction between the structural levels of economic detente and the process levels. Minor day-to-day economic issues should be resolved according to standardized procedures. Major structural economic issues should be resolved by high-level consultations between governments. In effect, this would mean a depoliticization of most sales, licensing, and cooperation agreements. If Western companies can deal with them in pragmatic ways, they should be allowed to do so. This would also mean that joint ventures, major product sales, licensing agreements, and research and development cooperation agreements should be based on equal access to economic information about all countries involved. No special considerations should be given to Soviet or East European demands for secrecy if these demands are not matched on the Western side.

The Soviet Union should be accepted as fully as possible into the international financial community. Since so many of the most troublesome problems of East-West trade result from the inability of the Soviet Union and the East European states to convert their currencies on the free market, as much as possible should be done to ease them into somewhat greater convertibility. This will not be easy, for it demands some basic changes in Soviet and East European behavior. It would force the East-bloc countries to develop a more realistic price structure and to implement more fully the aspects of their economic reform programs which long ago called for a greater emphasis on profits. While the acceptance of the East-bloc countries into the international financial community is to be encouraged, that acceptance must be accomplished on the basis of solid Soviet and East European contributions to currency convertibility. The East-bloc countries should be required to provide the financial services they now demand and expect from the West.

The maneuverability of the East European countries should be preserved and enhanced. Flexibility of their economic position is in the best interests of all parties to detente. Even the USSR does not benefit as much as it once did from close economic integration with Eastern Europe. By supporting East European economic flexibility as an integral goal of detente, the United States would be acting to preserve a broader negotiating framework at the structural level of East-West trade. It seems advantageous to prevent a return to bipolar Cold War confrontations, and action to insure a moderate amount of separation in Soviet and East European economic interests would assist in achieving that end.

National and regional policies should reflect a balancing of the separate and particular interests which they comprise. Since East-West trade rests ultimately on the desires of corporations and subnational bureaucracies, these groups must be assured adequate access to the national and regional policy-making centers. Regional and national policies and actors should set firm guidelines, but enterprises, foreign trade organizations, and trade-related bureaucracies must be allowed reasonable scope to pursue their own interests. This, of course, involves a delicate balancing of national and regional governmental and intergovernmental interests against corporate interests. In an era of mutual distrust between governments and companies, this may prove to be an especially difficult task.

THE CONTENT OF DETENTE IN EAST-WEST TRADE

International organizations like the International Monetary Fund, the GATT, and the UN's Economic Commission for Europe should play a primary rather than a secondary role in making policy decisions affecting the structure of East-West trade. There has traditionally been more mutual respect for organizations like the ECE than there has been for regional structures like the EEC or COMECON. This mutual trust should be exploited now by assigning each of the three organizations specific policy functions. The International Monetary Fund could be assigned rule-making and rule-enforcing functions in determining the amounts, interest rates, and terms of credits, and in setting the value and convertibility of currencies. The GATT could be assigned the task of adjusting tariffs and import quotas and of regulating pricing and antidumping measures. The Economic Commission for Europe might be assigned tasks in the areas of economic information gathering and joint economic planning. It should be expanded in such a way that its membership includes the United States when East-West trade issues are discussed.

The United States should work with the EEC in developing broad guidelines for dealing with COMECON. The kinds of triangular struggles between the United States and the EEC and the USSR or Eastern Europe which have emerged during the past 10 to 12 years are destructive of the interests both of the United States and of Western Europe and should be avoided in the future. An Atlantic structure should be expected to function only at the level of developing a general outline for East-West trade. But it should insure that the credit policies of American and West European governments will be relatively uniform and that government establishment of credit limits and interest rates will not distort even further the vigorous economic competition between U.S. and West European firms. A new commission on trade relations between the United States and the EEC might be the answer.

Correlatively, the United States should not push too hard for formal EEC-COMECON relations because a strengthening of those links would almost certainly result in a diminished policy-making role for the United States. The Soviets have already become more eager to deal with West European companies and governments because of what they see as heavy congressional interference in foreign policy making in the United States. The Soviets are beginning to buy more and more goods from West European countries (even when they perceive U.S. products to be superior) simply because it is easier to deal with the West Europeans. Especially since the end of the European Security Conference, the Soviet press has been emphasizing the potential market unity of the whole of the European continent. The United States retains first place in the hopes of Soviet traders at present, but to hold this position it must be more eager to standardize policies with those of Western Europe and more careful not to impose excessive restrictions on corporate activity.

Within the United States, national bureaucratic actors, like the Bureau of East-West Trade, the Council on International Economic Policy, and the East-West Trade Policy Committee, should be reorganized into more coherent groups with definite lines of responsibility. The East-West Trade Policy Committee now reviews all major transfers of technology, considers all government credits in excess of $5 million, and submits quarterly reports on East-West trade to Congress. Currently viewed as a major vehicle for implementing Kissinger's views on East-West trade, the committee could be reorganized so as to equalize the input of government agencies directly involved in East-West trade.

Corporate strategy should operate with a view toward national policies as well as profit making. While corporations should respect the difference between process and structure and should remember that their own functions come primarily at the process level, they should attempt to align their pursuit of corporate goals with broader national economic goals. American corporations have a special responsibility to maintain open lines of communication with government agencies like the Bureau of East-West Trade and the Department of Commerce. The recent focus on grain scandals and business bribes abroad should provide the stimulus needed to promote mutual responsiveness. In the past, businessmen have at times been justifiably angered by the erratic and irrational policies of the Department of Agriculture, Eximbank, and Congress. Government policy making should systematize policy expectations for corporations but should not make it impossible for corporations to conduct business with the East.

National control policies on East-West trade should respect national security needs, but they should be modest in content and goals. National control systems should be efficient and predictable. This caution applies particularly to the United States, where an inefficient and unpredictable control system has caused unnecessary hardship and uncertainty for businessmen. Erratic decisions on the acceptability of computer sales have been especially troublesome, and a consistent program by an expanded and more representative Committee on East-West Trade Policy would help.

Incidental actors should be incorporated into the international framework of the International Monetary Fund, the GATT, and the ECE. At the very least, guidelines for their operation should be formulated. These actors should be made aware of the responsibility to align their particular interests with the whole structure of East-West trade. Included here would be such agencies as the US-USSR Trade and Economic Council and other bilateral trade organizations. While their authority cannot be given up to international organizations, their activities could be more effectively coordinated.

In summary, what is envisioned is a more balanced and comprehensive structuring of the whole of East-West trade. To enhance the capabilities of the currently underutilized forums of the ECE, IMF, and GATT does not mean that COMECON, the EEC, or national decision-making centers could or should fade from the scene. The hope is that internationalizing some of the basic issues of trade will make it possible more often to resolve the tensions of the structural level with less difficulty at the process level of ordinary transactions.

THE LIMITS OF DETENTE IN EAST-WEST TRADE

The end result of a regularized and structured policy of detente would be a more stable and ordered relationship between East and West, but the result would not be a convergence or sharing of the policy objectives of East and West. This is precisely why a new set of rules for East-West trade is so badly needed. Since we cannot assume that all players have the same goals or even congruent goals, we must at least make certain that they are playing the game according to one set of rules and possible punishments.

Detente on the economic plane will not necessarily spill over to the other planes of ideological or military or political relationships. The Soviets have made it very clear for years that the various aspects of detente or peaceful coexistence are separable. They are pursuing a course of economic reconciliation because they feel it is in their interest to do so and because they seem to believe that the balance of economic power is shifting in favor of socialist countries. What is perceived by the United States as a desperate need for Western products and technology by the Soviets is sometimes viewed by the Soviets as merely a prelude to an eventual reverse Western dependence on Soviet technology and raw materials. While we can hope and even expect that there will be some spill-over from East-West economic cooperation into the political arena, we cannot be certain that this will occur. We should pursue detente for the simple reasons that regular trade relations with the USSR would bring greater stability into the world financial system and that this would benefit the United States as well as the Soviet Union.

While a policy of economic detente may assure that the growing inter-dependence of East and West will be accompanied more often by cooperation than by conflict, it certainly does not foreshadow an end to conflict between East and West. For the Soviets, detente means that the United States rather than the Soviet Union will be expected to accommodate itself to a changing balance of forces in the world. Soviets have separated the various components of detente and have concentrated on the economic ones. The United States has been less inclined to separate the factors and more inclined to generalize about hopes for cooperation. In the end, the efforts may put an unequal burden on the United States. American "achievements" may be manifested primarily in an expanded "influence" effect in the USSR and Eastern Europe. Yet the policy of economic detente remains a pragmatic one, not only because the alternatives are undesirable, but also because the modest goal of restructuring East-West trade relationships makes sense in a world filled with troubling new realities in all areas of U.S. foreign policy.

THE REALITY OF DETENTE IN EAST-WEST TRADE

Where, then, do we stand at present? Has there been progress toward the regularized structure that seems desirable, or have the recent setbacks in U.S.-

Soviet trade because of a lack of MFN and government credits destroyed hopes for economic detente in the foreseeable future? The answer is far from certain, but the present outlook seems to be one of very modest progress toward a meaningful framework for East-West trade.

In many ways, domestic policy in the United States remains the biggest stumbling block. As noted in Chapter 2, the policy-making process has been chaotic rather than coherent, and one can expect U.S. attempts to deal unilaterally with the USSR on trade to be marked by failure and hesitation until a firmer national policy emerges. While it is to be hoped that the East-West Trade Policy Committee can assume a larger role in formalizing and implementing guidelines, it seems less likely that the committee can serve as a comprehensive backdrop for the debates of competing domestic pro- and antitrade groups. This is partly because special interests are accustomed to fighting for their programs through other channels and partly because the domestic debate has become more confused and all-encompassing.

One source of that domestic confusion is the lingering uncertainty as to whether detente applies to Soviet-U.S. relations per se or to Soviet-U.S. relations in other world areas as well. In 1972, Nixon and Brezhnev appeared to entertain a relatively limited conception of detente which applied only to relations between the two superpowers. The Nixonian idea was that the United States had to secure bilateral agreements that Moscow would be afraid to jeopardize by adventures in remote areas. Such ideas have worked almost in reverse, with the grain shipments continuing to the USSR in 1976 despite Soviet expeditions in Angola and the foot dragging at the SALT talks apparently having little impact on U.S. grain sales to the Soviet Union. Actually, as early as October 1973, after the outbreak of the war in the Middle East, Kissinger began to enlarge the Nixon-Brezhnev conception of detente by noting that "the Soviet Union cannot disregard the principles of detente anywhere in the world without imperiling its entire relationship with the United States." There has still been no clear-cut or consistent definition of detente, and matters have been made worse rather than better by the active congressional participation in debates over emigration of Soviet Jews and the linkage of grain and petroleum deals. Likewise, the debate that resulted in the dismissal of Defense Secretary James Schlesinger lingers on. Schlesinger was an adherent of the view that detente had to encompass military as well as economic relations.

Within the USSR, continuing debates between Brezhnev and Kosygin on the needs for foreign technology versus domestic reforms and between centralizers and decentralizers over management techniques have prevented the development of a completely uniform position. Still, the prevailing feeling is that extended economic contacts with the United States and Western Europe are desirable and that economic detente is the proper policy vehicle to secure those contacts. In contrast to the United States, there is little doubt that the political and economic components of detente are separable. Economic detente for the Soviets means the expansion of foreign economic ties with the United States, or with Western Europe if U.S. companies prove unable or unwilling to assume the burdens of East-West sales partnership. The Draft Program of the CPSU Central Committee for the twenty-fifth congress stressed the Soviet desire "to provide for the further development of trade and mutually advantageous economic, scientific, and technical cooperation with the industrially developed capitalist countries on a long-term basis."[1] The permanence of such links with the West was emphasized by G. Rozanov in a December 1975 article in *International Affairs* where he noted with satisfaction that "the Soviet Union's economic relations with the advanced capitalist countries are becoming increasingly comprehensive in character."[2]

Political detente is viewed differently, as the growing victory of socialist forces everywhere and the supposed realization by Western countries that international political changes are in keeping with an "inherent law" which makes diplomats in the West revise their views and adapt to ongoing changes.[3] For the Soviets, there is no necessary correlation between the "broad Soviet peace offensive" and the pragmatic measures that accompany economic detente. Political detente does not entail a "commitment to guarantee the social status quo in the world and to halt the process of class and national liberation struggles engendered by the objective laws of historical development."[4] This may be read as a clear sign to U.S. policy makers that they are very wrong if they expect the economic and political components of detente to march in unison, but it should not discourage the United States from action to strengthen economic detente.

One of the most encouraging aspects of Soviet policy from the U.S. point of view should be the newly emerging willingness of the USSR to rely more heavily on the United Nations. Spurred by the new strength of the Third World countries in the UN, the Soviet Union now claims that it has "always regarded the U.N. as an exceptionally important instrument for achieving the noble aims and implementing the principles set down in its Charter."[5] The United States would do well to take advantage of this mood by urging the UN's Economic Commission for Europe to take on heavier responsibilities in East-West trade. The Soviet Union has not always been a friend of the United Nations, and while the United States may find the reasons for current Soviet enthusiasm distasteful, it should seize the opportunity to formalize a relatively neutral and stable vehicle for enlarging ties between East and West.

COMECON is in a state of change at the present time, and its internal debates and search for contacts with the West could well be used advantageously by the United States. For perhaps the first time, the USSR is finding the economic burden of supplying raw materials to COMECON to be very heavy. For this reason, COMECON has been allowed to follow a more adventurous policy of economic contacts with the West than would have been possible in the past.

The biggest problem for the East European members of COMECON in the near future will be a lack of hard currency and credits. In fact, there has been an emerging contrast between buoyant Western sales to the USSR and stagnating exports to other East European countries. In the first seven months of 1975 (and therefore before the effects of the big grain shipments could be felt), U.S. exports to the USSR were 81 percent above the same seven-month period in 1974. In contrast, sales to the smaller East European markets revealed only a 7 percent increase.[6] The present situation indicates that economic ties between Eastern Europe and the West are already so close that an economic downturn in the West affects economic conditions in the East. Because East European countries have generally chosen to purchase as much as possible from the West despite the recession, they have incurred rapidly mounting trade deficits. Unlike the USSR, they cannot count on gold sales or raw materials supplies to the West to brighten the economic picture. The amount of credits raised by East European countries in the West in 1975 is estimated at between $6.5 billion and $9 billion, including some $2 billion of publicized Eurocurrency loans. This borrowing has raised Eastern Europe's total Western debt to a record level, estimated at about $23-28 billion and sometimes placed as high as $32 billion.[7]

The United States would be wise to receive East European demands for credits as generously as is pragmatically possible. It should be particularly careful not to equate the needs of the Soviet Union with those of Eastern Europe. An independent U.S. policy for the East European countries is especially important in view of Soviet pressures for continued integration in COMECON and for continued investment by East European countries in Soviet development projects. The Romanians and Hungarians have been expressing fears that these heavier investment demands will make it more difficult for them to develop ties with Western countries.

On the one hand, we may expect to see efforts to continue the step-by-step economic integration now taking place within COMECON, a process which tends to remove decision making from strictly national institutions and to place greater authority in the hands of newly created COMECON agencies. Alternatively, we may expect to see simultaneous opposition to this process by several East European countries which are struggling to maintain and expand their bilateral ties with the United States, the EEC, and with individual West European countries. Because an Eastern Europe less dependent on the USSR is in the interest of the United States, Americans would be well advised to look sympathetically on East European requests for credits and for participation in joint ventures. When these projects give firm evidence of profitability and of a solid return on investment, the United States should encourage them.

A major problem between the United States and Western Europe has been a competition over the terms of government credits offered to East-bloc countries. Because of restrictive credit policies dictated by Congress and imposed by the Export-Import Bank, U.S. firms have been at a disadvantage in supplying favorable credit terms to both the USSR and Eastern Europe. Some recent efforts, particularly those by the United States and West Germany, to curb competition among Western countries on export credits have resulted in a new agreement on prior disclosure of interest rates. At a meeting sponsored by the OECD in Paris, representatives of Eximbank and West European export credit agencies agreed to reveal the interest rates on specific transactions still in the negotiation stage if they are requested to do so by another Western government.[8] One can hope that future agreements of a similar nature will produce enhanced cooperation between the United States and Common Market countries as they attempt to develop trade arrangements with the East.

The banks, corporations, and other independent agencies which compose the infrastructure of East-West trade have also been integrated somewhat more effectively into the slowly emerging framework. We have seen the importance of these independent actors in facilitating sales in chemicals, computers, petroleum, and grain. They can act directly by making or implementing decisions on East-West trade policy. They can perform indirect roles by speeding up or blocking decisions of nations or regions, and they can set agendas for policy decisions by creating issues which must be resolved by national governments or regions. An expanded role for agencies such as the IMF, GATT, or the ECE could probably facilitate more regularized participation by these groups in the East-West trade process.

Soviet journalists have been emphasizing that "the main feature of the international economic detente is that it is a stable process." These days, even Lenin is interpreted as advocating continuing business cooperation among states with differing social systems.[9] The United States should encourage that pragmatic process of economic accommodation wherever possible. It can best begin by reassessing its own domestic policy-making process in East-West trade.

NOTES

1. *Pravda*, December 14, 1975; *Izvestia*, December 14, 1975.
2. G. Rozanov, "Promoting Links with the West," *International Affairs* (Moscow), no. 12 (December 1975), p. 49.
3. A. Stepanov, "Detente Must Be Made an Irreversible Process," *International Affairs* (Moscow), no. 12 (December 1975), p. 45.
4. G. Arbatov, "Maneuvers of the Opponents of Detente," *Izvestia*, September 4, 1975, pp. 3-4.
5. N. Kapchenko, "The United Nations and International Detente," *International Affairs* (Moscow), no. 12 (December 1975), p. 69.
6. Business International, *Eastern Europe Report*, October 17, 1975, p. 291.
7. Ibid., February 6, 1976, p. 33.
8. Ibid., November 14, 1975, p. 319.
9. Stepanov, op. cit., p. 44.

SELECTED BIBLIOGRAPHY

BOOKS

Arbatov, Georgi A. *The USA: The Scientific and Technological Revolution and Foreign Policy Trends.* Moscow, 1974.

———. *The War of Ideas in Contemporary International Relations.* Moscow, 1973.

Belyaev, Y. N., and L. S. Semenova. *Sotsialisticheskaya integratisiia i mirovoe khozjaistvo.* Moscow, 1972.

Bergsten, Fred C. ed. *The Future of the International Economic Order: An Agenda for Research.* Lexington, Mass.: Lexington Books, 1973.

van Brabant, Jozef M. *Bilateralism and Structural Bilateralism in Intra-CMEA Trade.* Rotterdam: Rotterdam University Press, 1973.

Brown, Seyom. *New Forces in World Politics.* Washington: Brookings Institutions, 1974.

Business International. *Doing Business with Eastern Europe.* Geneva, 1972.

———. *Doing Business with Romania.* Geneva, 1973.

———. *Doing Business with the USSR.* Geneva, 1971.

Camps, Miriam. *The Management of Interdependence.* New York: Council on Foreign Relations, 1974.

Feonova, L. A., M. L. Postolenko, S. P. Nikitin. *Organizatsiia i tekhnika vneshnei torgovlii v SSSR.* Moscow, 1974.

Giffen, James Henry. *The Legal and Practical Aspects of Trade with the Soviet Union.* Revised Edition. New York: Praeger, 1971.

Goldman, Marshall I. *Detente and Dollars.* New York: Basic Books, 1975.

Holzman, Franklyn D. *Foreign Trade Under Central Planning.* Cambridge, Mass.: Harvard University Press, 1974.

Johnson, Chalmers, ed. *Change in Communist Systems.* Stanford: Stanford University Press, 1970.

Kaser, Michael. *COMECON: Integration Problems of the Planned Economics.* 2nd edition. London: Oxford University Press, 1967.

Keohane, Robert O., and Joseph S. Nye, Jr. eds. *Transnational Relations and World Politics.* Cambridge, Mass.: Harvard University Press, 1972.

Kindleberger, Charles P., ed. *The International Corporation*. Cambridge, Mass.: MIT Press, 1970.

Kretschmar, Robert S., and Robin Foor. *The Potential for Joint Ventures in Eastern Europe*. New York: Praeger, 1972.

Laulan, Yves, ed. *Round Table: Exploitation of Siberia's Natural Resources*. Brussels: NATO Economic Directorate, February 1974.

Lukaszekski, Jerzy, ed. *The People's Democracies After Prague: Soviet Hegemony, Nationalism, Regional Integration?* Brussels: Tempelhof, 1970.

Marer, Paul. *Soviet and East European Foreign Trade, 1946-1969: Statistical Compendium and Guide*. Bloomington: Indiana University Press, 1973.

McMillan, Carl H. ed. *Changing Perspectives in East-West Commerce*. Lexington, Mass.: Lexington Books, 1974.

McMillan, Carl H., and D. P. St. Charles. *Joint Ventures in Eastern Europe: A Three Country Comparison*. Montreal: C. D. Howe Research Institute, 1974.

Meznerics, Ivan. *Law of Banking in East-West Trade*. Dobbs Ferry, N. Y.: Oceana, 1973.

Owen, Henry, ed. *The Next Phase in Foreign Policy*, Washington, D.C.: Brookings Institution, 1973.

Pisar, Samuel. *Coexistence and Commerce*. New York: McGraw-Hill, 1972.

Pozdniakov, V. S. *Gosudarstvennaia monopoliia vneshnei torgovli v SSSR*. Moscow, 1969.

Ransom, Charles. *The European Community and Eastern Europe*. Totawa, N. J.: Rowman and Littlefield, 1973.

Schaefer, Henry Wilcox. *COMECON and the Politics of Integration*. New York: Praeger, 1972.

Smith, Glen Alden. *Soviet Foreign Trade: Organization, Operations, and Policy, 1918-1971*. New York: Praeger, 1973.

Starr, Robert, ed. *East-West Business Transactions*. New York: Praeger, 1974.

Tokavera, P. A. ed. *Mnogostoronnee ekonomicheskie sotrudnichestvo sotsialisticheskikh gosudarstv: sbornik dokumentov*. Moscow, 1972.

Vaganov, V. S. *Vneshnyaya torgovlya sotsialisticheskikh stran*. Moscow, 1966.

Vernon, Raymond. *Big Business and the State: Changing Relations in Western Europe*. Cambridge, Mass.: Harvard University Press, 1974.

Wasowski, Stanislaw, ed. *East-West Trade and the Technology Gap: A Political and Economic Approach*. New York: Praeger, 1970.

Wilczynski, Josef. *The Economics and Politics of East-West Trade.* New York: Praeger, 1969.

ARTICLES AND PERIODICALS

Andreyev, D., and M. Makov. "The Common Market After Eleven Years." *International Affairs* (Moscow), no. 1 (January 1969), pp. 43-49.

Aroche, Charles. "Western Europe: Crises and Prospects." *International Affairs* (Moscow), no. 1 (January 1975), pp. 23-32.

Bergson, Abram. "Toward a New Growth Model." *Problems of Communism* 22, no. 2 (March-April 1973): 1-9.

Bergsten, C. Fred; Robert O. Keohane; and Joseph S. Nye. "International Economics and International Politics: A Framework for Analysis." *International Organization* 29, no. 1 (Winter 1975): 3-36.

Berliner, Joseph S.   "Some International Aspects of Soviet Technological Progress." *South Atlantic Quarterly* 72, no 3 (1973): 340-50.

Berman, Harold, J. "The U.S.-USSR Trade Agreement from a Soviet Perspective," *American Journal of International Law* 67, no. 3 (July 1973): 516-22.

————, ed. "Soviet-American Trade in a Legal Perspective: Proceedings of a Conference of Soviet and American Legal Scholars." *Denver Journal of International Law* 5 (Special Issue, 1975): 217-367.

Brown, J. F. "Detente and Soviet Policy in Eastern Europe." *Survey* 20, no. 213 (Spring-Summer 1974): 46-58.

Business International. *Eastern Europe Report.* Bi-weekly to January 1976, weekly thereafter.

Casey, William J., et al. "Technology Exchange with the USSR." *Research Management* 17 (July 1974): 7-20.

Chenery, Hollis B. "Restructuring the World Economy." *Foreign Affairs* 53, no. 2 (January 1975): 242-63.

Commerce International. Monthly. Publication of the London Chamber of Commerce.

Cooper, Richard N. "Economic Interdependence and Foreign Policy in the Seventies." *World Politics* 24, no. 2 (January 1972): 159-81.

DeHaven, James C. "Technology Exchange: Import Possibilities from the USSR." Rand Corporation, Santa Monica, April 1974. R-1414-ARPA.

Diebold, William, Jr. "U. S. Trade Policy: The New Political Dimension." *Foreign Affairs* 52 (April 1974): 472-96.

Doernberg, Stefan. "Socialist Foreign Policy and the World Situation." *International Affairs* (Moscow), no. 3 (March 1975), pp. 57-61.

Dufey, Gunter. "Financing East-West Business." *The Columbia Journal of World Business* 9, no. 1 (Spring 1974): 37-41.

Einzig, Paul. "Soviet Eurodollar Transactions." *International Currency Review* 4, no. 2 (March-April 1972): 9-13.

Fallenbuchl, Z. M. "COMECON Integration." *Problems of Communism* 22, no. 2 (March-April 1973): 25-39.

Financial Times.

Gamarnikow, Michael. "Industrial Cooperation: East Europe Looks West." *Problems of Communism* 20, no. 3 (May-June 1971): 41-48.

Ginsbergs, George. "The Implications of the 20-Year Comprehensive Programme of Economic Integration." *American Journal of International Law* 67, no. 5 (November 1973): 48-55.

Goldman, Marshall I. "Who Profits More from U.S.-Soviet Trade?" *Harvard Business Review* 51, no. 6 (November-December 1973): 79-87.

Golosov, V. "Restructuring of International Economic Relations." *International Affairs* (Moscow), no. 1 (January 1975), pp. 41-50.

Grebennikov, B. , and L. Nikolayev. "Economic Competition of the Two World Systems." *International Affairs* (Moscow), no. 8 (August 1971), pp. 108-10.

Grigoryev, A. "USSR—FRG Economic Relations." *International Affairs* (Moscow), no. 10 (October 1974), pp. 47-53.

Grigoryev, I. "The Important Features of the International Detente." *International Affairs* (Moscow), no. 3 (March 1975), pp. 61-62.

Grossman, Gregory. "Prospects and Policy for U.S.-Soviet Trade." *American Economic Review* 64, no. 2 (May 1974): 289-93.

Harrison, John W. "The Unknown Competitor—Soviet International Banking." *The Banker's Magazine* 158, no. 3 (Summer 1975): 83-85.

Hoffman, Stanley. "Notes on the Elusiveness of Modern Power." *International Journal* 30, no. 2 (Spring 1975): 183-206.

Holzman, Franklyn, and Robert Legvold. "The Economics and Politics of East-West Relations." *International Organization* 29, no. 1 (Winter 1975): 275-320.

Houser, Robert C., Jr., and Steven I. Frahm. "Technology, Trade, and the Law: A Preliminary Exploration." *Law and Policy in International Business* 6, no. 1 (1974): 85-149.

Hoya, Thomas W. "The Changing U.S. Regulation of U.S. Trade." *Columbia Journal of Transnational Law* 12 (1973): 1-38.

Huhs, John I. "Developing Trade with the Soviet Union." *The Columbia Journal of World Business* 8, no. 3 (Fall 1973): 116-30.

Ilyin, A. "Soviet-French Cooperation Gains Strength." *International Affairs* (Moscow), no. 9 (September 1973), pp. 74-78.

Izvestia.

Jamgotch, Nish, Jr. "Alliance Management in Eastern Europe." *World Politics* 27, no. 3 (April 1975): 405-29.

Kaser, Michael. "COMECON's Commerce." *Problems of Communism* 22, no. 4 (July-August 1973): 1-15.

––––. "COMECON's Objectives in the EEC." *International Currency Review* 7, no. 1 (January-February 1975): 37-39.

––––. "The EEC and Eastern Europe: Prospects for Trade and Finance." *International Affairs* (London) 49, no. 3 (July 1973): 402-12.

––––. "The Soviet Balance of Payments." *International Currency Review* 5, no. 4 (July-August 1973): 88-93.

––––. "The Soviet Balance of Payments." *International Currency Review* 6, no. 3 (May-June 1974): 60-62.

––––. "Soviet Trade Turns to Europe." *Foreign Policy*, no. 19 (Summer 1975), pp. 123-35.

Kennedy, Edward M. "Beyond Detente." *Foreign Policy*, no. 16 (Fall 1974): pp. 3-29.

Kintner, William R. "The U.S. and the USSR: Conflict and Cooperation." *Orbis* 17, no. 3 (Fall 1973): 691-719.

Korbonski, Andrzej. "The Political Economy of COMECON." *Problems of Communism* 23, no. 2 (March-April 1974): 74-77.

Krause, Walter, and F. John Mathis. "The U.S. Policy Shift on East-West Trade." *Journal of International Affairs* 28, no. 1 (1974): 25-37.

Kudrin, M. "Objective Factors of Detente." *International Affairs* (Moscow), no. 3 (March 1975), pp. 53-57.

Ladygin, B. "The Motive Forces of Socialist Integration." *International Affairs* (Moscow), no. 10 (October 1974), pp. 22-29.

Lebedinskas, A. "Joint Investment Activity of CMEA Countries." *International Affairs* (Moscow), no. 1 (January 1975), pp. 15-22.

London *Times.*

Manfred, A. "USSR-France: Traditions of Friendship and Cooperation." *International Affairs* (Moscow), no. 11 (November 1974), pp. 51-61.

Mondale, Walter F. "Beyond Detente: Toward International Economic Security." *Foreign Affairs* 53, no. 1 (October 1974): 1-23.

Le Monde.

Morgan, John P. "The Financial Aspects of East-West Trade." *Columbia Journal of World Business* 8, no. 4 (December 1973): 51-56.

Morgan, Roger. "West-East Relations in Europe: Political Perspectives," *International Affairs* (London) 49, no. 2 (April 1973): 177-89.

Morozov, V. "CMEA Countries: Wide International Cooperation." *International Affairs* (Moscow), no. 4 (April 1974), pp. 9-15.

Nemchinov, Sergey V. "Science-Industry Systems in USSR Bridge Gap Between Research and Application." *Research Management* 18 (January 1975): 25-28.

New York *Times.*

Nikitin, V. "Peaceful Co-existence and Soviet-U.S. Relations." *International Affairs* (Moscow), no. 6 (June 1974), pp. 3-9, 114.

Nikl, Miroslav. "International Aspects of a New Stage in the Development of the CMEA." *International Relations* (Prague), no. 1 (Annual Issue, 1972), pp. 22-30.

Nikolayev, Y. "A New Milestone in Soviet-American Relations." *International Affairs* (Moscow), no. 9 (September 1974), pp. 3-15.

Nye, Joseph S., Jr. "Multinational Corporations in World Politics." *Foreign Affairs* 53, no. 1 (October 1974): 153-75.

Padolski, T. M. "Socialist International Banking Under the Microscope." *The Banker* (London) 123, no. 574 (December 1973): 1465-70.

Parsons, A. Peter. "Recent Developments in East-West Trade: The U.S. Perspective." *Law and Contemporary Problems* 32, no. 2 (Summer-Autumn 1972): 548-56.

Pinder, John. "A Community Policy Towards Eastern Europe." *The World Today* 30 (March 1974): 119-28.

Planovoye khoziaistvo.

Pravda.

Predescu, Alexander. "New Developments in East-West Economic Relations." *Intereconomics*, no. 8 (August 1975), pp. 249-52.

Pryor, Frederic L. "Barriers to Market Socialism in Eastern Europe in the Mid-1960's." *Studies in Comparative Communism* 3, no. 2 (April 1970): 31-64.

Pubantz, Jerry. "Marxism-Leninism and Soviet-American Economic Relations Since Stalin." *Law and Contemporary Problems* 37, no. 2 (Summer-Autumn 1972): 535-47.

Radio Free Europe Research. Munich. *Background Reports*. Frequent issues.

Ransom, C. F. G. "Obstacles to the Liberalization of Relations Between the EEC and COMECON." *Studies in Comparative Communism* 2, nos. 3-4 (July-October 1969): 61-78.

———. "The Future of EEC-COMECON Relations." *The World Today* 27 (October 1971): 438-48.

Rosecrance, Richard, and Arthur Stein. "Interdependence: Myth or Reality?" *World Politics* 26, no. 1 (October 1973): 1-27.

Rosenfeld, Stephen S. "Pluralism and Policy." *Foreign Affairs* 52, no. 2 (January 1974): 263-72.

Rymalov, V. "Some Aspects of the General Crisis of Capitalism." *International Affairs* (Moscow), no. 7 (July 1974), pp. 98-109.

Schukin, Geroge S. "The Soviet Position on Trade with the United States." *The Columbia Journal of World Business* 8, no. 4 (December 1973): 47-50.

Sheidina, I. "Soviet-American Scientific and Technical Ties." *International Affairs* (Moscow), no. 12 (December 1974), pp. 46-51.

Shiryayev, Y., and A. Ivanov. "Detente: Economic Implementation." *International Affairs* (Moscow), no. 11 (November 1975), pp. 23-32.

Smolinski, Leon. "Towards a Socialist Corporation: Soviet Industrial Reorganization of 1973." *Survey* 20, no. 1 (Winter 1974): 24-35.

Starr, Robert. "A New Legal Framework for Trade Between the United States and the Soviet Union: The 1972 U.S.-USSR Trade Agreement." *American Journal of International Law* 67, no. 1 (January 1973): 63-83.

Stein, John Picard. "Estimating the Market for Computers in the Soviet Union and Eastern Europe." Rand Corporation, Santa Monica, May 1974. R-1406-CIEP/ARPA.

Stojic-Imamovich, Edita. "New Elements in the Conceptions of Socialist Countries of Eastern Europe on East-West Economic Relations." *International Problems* (Belgrade), no. 1 (Annual Issue, 1972), pp. 81-99.

Strange, Susan. "What is Economic Power and Who Has It?" *International Journal* 30, no. 2 (Spring 1975): 207-24.

Sutina, E., and Y. Rilov, "USSR-USA Cultural Cooperation." *International Affairs* (Moscow), no. 7 (July 1974), pp. 150-51.

Touscoz, Jean. "Les diverses formes de la cooperation est-ouest en Europe." *Etudes internationales* 4, no. 9 (September 1973): 235-52.

Trend, Harry. "COMECON's Organizational Structure." Part 1, RAD Background Report/ 114 (Eastern Europe). RFE Research, July 3, 1975, pp. 1-12.

――――. "COMECON's Organizational Structure." Part 2, RAD Background Report/138 (Eastern Europe). RFE Research, October 7, 1975, pp. 1-37.

Trybuna ludu.

Vernon, Raymond. "Apparatchiks and Entrepreneurs: U.S.-Soviet Economic Relations." *Foreign Affairs* 52, no. 2 (January 1974): 249-62.

Vetrov, A. "Strengthening of All-European Business Contacts." *International Affairs* (Moscow), no. 8 (August 1973), pp. 67-74.

Vneshnyaya torgovlya.

Voprosy ekonomiki.

Wall Street Journal.

Wasowski, Stanislaw. "Economic Integration in the COMECON." *Orbis* 16, no. 3 (Fall 1972): 760-79.

Wolf, Thomas A. "New Frontiers in East-West Trade," *European Business,* no. 39 (Autumn 1973), pp. 26-35.

Zakhmatov, M. "USSR-U.S.A.: Prospects for Economic Cooperation." *International Affairs* (Moscow), no. 11 (November 1973), pp. 41-46.

Zhurkin, V. "Detente and International Conflicts." *International Affairs* (Moscow), no. 7 (July 1974), pp. 89-97.

PUBLIC DOCUMENTS

Baibakov, N. K. *Gosudarstvennyi piatiletnyi plan razvitiia narodnogo khoziaistva SSSR na 1971-1975 gody.* Moscow: Gosplan, 1972.

Council for Mutual Economic Assistance, Secretariat. *A Survey of Twenty Years of the Council for Mutual Economic Assistance.* Moscow, 1969.

Council for Mutual Economic Assistance. *Statisticheskii ezhegodnik.* Moscow, 1970, 1971, 1972.

European Economic Community, Executive Secretariat of the Commission. *Bulletin of the European Communities.* Monthly. Frequent supplementary issues.

European Economic Community. *Journal officiel des Communautes europeennes.*

Herman, Leon M. *East-West Trade: An Overview of Legislation, Policy Trends, and Issues Involved.* Washington: Library of Congress, Legislative Reference Service, June 17, 1968. Report No. GGR-118.

————. *The 1963-1964 Wheat Sales to Russia: A Summary of Major Developments.* Washington: Library of Congress, Legislative Reference Service, April 7, 1964.

U.S. Congress, Joint Economic Committee. *New Directions in the Soviet Economy.* 89th Cong., 2d Sess., 1966.

————. *Reorientation and Commercial Relations of the Economies of Eastern Europe.* 93rd Cong., 2d Sess., August 16, 1974.

————. *Soviet Economic Prospects for the Seventies.* 93rd Cong., 1st Sess., June 27, 1973.

U.S. Congress, Joint Economic Committee, Subcommittee on Priorities and Economy in Government. *Allocation of Resources in the Soviet Union and China.* 93rd Cong., 2d Sess., April 12, 1974.

U.S. Department of Commerce, Bureau of East-West Trade. *U.S.-Soviet Commercial Agreements, 1972: Texts, Summaries, and Supporting Papers.* Washington: Government Printing Office, January 1973.

U.S. House of Representatives, Committee on Banking and Currency, Subcommittee on International Trade. *The Fiat-Soviet Automobile Plant and Soviet Economic Reforms.* 89th Cong., 2d Sess., March 1967.

U.S. House of Representatives, Committee on Foreign Affairs, Subcommittee on National Security Policy and Scientific Developments. *U.S.-Soviet Commercial Relations: The Interplay of Economics, Technology Transfer, and Diplomacy.* 93rd Cong., 1st Sess., June 10, 1973. (Prepared by John P. Hardt and George D. Holliday).

U.S. Senate, Committee on Finance. *Background Materials Relating to the United States-Soviet Union Commercial Agreements.* 93rd Cong., 2d Sess., April 2, 1974.

U.S. Senate, Committee on Finance. *Hearings on the Trade Reform Act of 1973.* 93rd Cong., 2d Sess., 1974. Pts. 1-6.

U.S. Senate, Committee on Foreign Relations. *Hearings on Detente.* 93rd Cong., 2d Sess., 1974.

U.S. Senate, Committee on Foreign Relations, Subcommittee on Multinational Corporations. *Western Investment in Communist Economies.* 93rd Cong., 2d Sess., August 5, 1974. (Prepared by John P. Hardt, George D. Holliday, and Young C. Kim).

U.S. Senate, Committee on Government Operations, Permanent Subcommittee on Investigations. *Russian Grain Transactions.* 93rd Cong., 1st Sess., October 9, 1973.

CONNIE M. FRIESEN received her Ph.D. in Government from Harvard University in 1972. She graduated from Concordia College (Moorhead, Minnesota) in 1967. Dr. Friesen has taught at the University of Massachusetts in Amherst and has been a research affiliate at the Center for International Affairs and the Russian Research Center, both at Harvard.

THE CHEMICAL AND PETRO-CHEMICAL INDUSTRIES IN RUSSIA AND EASTERN EUROPE, 1960-1980

Cecil Rajana

EAST-WEST BUSINESS TRANSACTIONS

edited by Robert Starr

FROM THE COLD WAR TO DETENTE

edited by Peter J. Potichnyj
Jane P. Shapiro

THE FUTURE OF INTER-BLOC RELATIONS IN EUROPE

edited by Louis J. Mensonides
James A. Kuhlman

THE POLITICS OF MODERNIZATION IN EASTERN EUROPE:
Testing the Soviet Model

edited by Charles Gati

MULTINATIONAL CORPORATIONS AND EAST EUROPEAN SOCIALIST ECONOMIES

Geza P. Lauter
Paul M. Dickie

NATURAL GAS IMPORTS FROM THE SOVIET UNION:
Financing the North Star Joint Venture Project

Joseph T. Kosnik

SOVIET INDUSTRIAL IMPORT PRIORITIES:
With Marketing Considerations for Exporting to the USSR

Christopher E. Stowell